# STUDENT'S GUIDE
## TO
# THE
# LONG
# SEARCH

## A STUDY OF RELIGIONS

Miami-Dade Community College
*Miami, Florida*

**KENDALL/HUNT PUBLISHING COMPANY**
2460 Kerper Boulevard,
Dubuque, Iowa 52001

Originators of this curriculum have sought balance in an area where
complete objectivity is unattainable. Advocacy should not be inferred
from inclusion, placement, or treatment of materials in this Student's
Guide. Selection of major denominations for analysis implies neither
editorial preference over other denominations nor disregard for persons
who embrace no religion or find denominationalism divisive and prefer
a noninstitutional faith.

*For additional information contact:*
  Auxiliary Services
  Miami-Dade Community College
  11011 S.W. 104 Street
  Miami, Florida   33176

   (Phones 305/596-1361 or 1364)

401845   01

# ACKNOWLEDGMENTS

Project Co-Directors Franklin G. Bouwsma
Virginia Gentle
 Miami-Dade Community College
 Miami, Florida

Project Assistant Karen E. Young
 Miami-Dade Community College

Coordinating Editor C. Edward Cavert
 Director of Learning Systems
 Northern Virginia Community College
 Annandale, Virginia

Content Editor Grace E. Cairns
 Professor Emeritus of Philosophy
 Florida State University
 Tallahassee, Florida

Associate Editor Ervin Lewis
 Miami-Dade Community College


## Contributors

James L. Ash, Jr. Assistant Professor of Religion
University of Miami; Miami, Florida

Eric Crystal Assistant Professor of Anthropology
University of California; Berkeley, California

Paul R. Dekar Assistant Professor of Christian History
McMaster Divinity College; Hamilton, Ontario

Seymour Fersh

Professor of Education
Fairleigh Dickinson University; Rutherford, N.J.

Yosef ben-Jochannan

Associate Professor of History
Cornell University; Ithaca, New York

William E. May

Associate Professor of Moral Theology
Catholic University of America;
Washington, D.C.

Muhammad Abdul-Rauf

Director, The Islamic Center;
Washington, D.C.

Stanley Spector

Professor of Chinese Studies
Washington University; St. Louis, Missouri

Barry Tabachnikoff

Rabbi, Congregation Bet Breira;
Miami, Florida

Joshua Zim

Information Officer, The Nalanda Foundation; Boulder, Colorado

A Personal Epilogue by Dr. Ninian Smart, primary consultant for the BBC's film series "The Long Search."

# CONTENTS

# INTRODUCTION

The most important preparation for learning about and understanding other peoples and cultures is a proper "mind set." Your study should start with an awareness of how we perceive others—and ourselves. From the moment of birth, infants in all cultures are encouraged to be ethnocentric—to believe that their homeland, their language, and every other aspect of their culture are not only different from, but superior to, those of other people. This cultural conditioning limits our ability to benefit from what has been created by other people. Today we have increasing opportunities to enrich ourselves because we can travel—in person or through the media—to cultures different from our own. But the value of such experience depends on our respect for and appreciation of the differences among people. If we fail to keep an open mind, we will succeed only in turning "windows on the world" into magic mirrors which tell us that our culture is "fairest of them all."

Perhaps in starting out we should reflect on what Aldous Huxley wrote in 1926, following his first trip around the world:

> So the journey is over and I am back again . . . richer by much experience and poorer by many exploited convictions, many perished certainties . . . I set out on my travels knowing, or thinking I knew, how men should live, how governed, how educated, what they should believe. . . . Now, on my return I find myself without any of these pleasing certainties. . . . The better you understand the significance of any question, the more difficult it becomes to answer it. Those who like to feel that they are always right and who attach a high importance to their own opinions should stay at home.

***The Television Series.*** "The Long Search" is a series of 13 programs about man's religious experience. The series is not a study of history or theology but a series of encounters with men and women of four continents who are living their faiths. What insights, what truths have the organized religions of the world to offer in this age of overpopulation, materialism, inflation, Marx, H-bombs, and black holes?

The programs chart the experiences of one man, Ronald Eyre, whose journey takes him from London (where he lives) on a voyage of more than 150,000 miles to India, Japan, Israel, Romania, Sri Lanka, Indonesia, Taiwan, the United States, Egypt, South Africa, Spain, and Italy. From the Protestant churches of Indianapolis to the Zen monasteries of Japan, from the Vatican to the tribe of the Torajas in the Celebes, the programs look beyond the splendid and the exotic toward the meaning of religion for individual people.

*The Student's Guide.*  The Student's Guide gives a frame of reference from which you can begin your study of each of the world's major religions. The guide helps to focus on specific, basic concepts during initial study so that you can organize your thoughts and plan your strategy for the continued study which will be a part of your personal "Long Search" for meaning in your own life and in the lives of others.

Each chapter in the guide relates to a specific program in the television series, although the chapters may not be in the same sequence in which you see the programs broadcast. At the beginning of each chapter, you are given a list of the important concepts you should master in your initial study. It is your task to apply these concepts to your personal goals and objectives. You must decide how the knowledge you gain from the course relates to your own needs and background.

Each lesson also contains a capsule view of the religion on which the lesson focuses. Written by eminent scholars in the field, these brief overviews will make the programs and text more meaningful to you.

Study questions will assist in assessing your understanding of the reading for each lesson. Finally, a short synopsis of the corresponding television program's contents and objectives is given for you to study before viewing so you can become a more active participant in the viewing experience.

## How to Study

That wonderful computer called your brain can handle the necessary information for your understanding of the world's religions provided you program it sensibly. Television, textbooks, and study guides can provide as much or as little information as you need to form an accurate and useful picture of any aspect of the religion being studied. But this information will be more valuable if you mentally arrange it in some systematic framework or scheme. Naturally there are many possible schemes, and, indeed, one major purpose of providing a suggested scheme in this Student's Guide is to help you construct additional and better ones for yourself. Our method is to offer you a series of concepts, based on our previous experience with the subject, and a certain amount of preliminary knowledge. As you seek evidence to support these concepts, you will select and reject data, and an astonishing amount will remain with you. But it will be even more gratifying when you start asking new questions and formulating additional concepts of your own. Eventually, you may find, as we have, that answers to *small* questions about other peoples, societies, religions, and philosophies begin to add up to some *big* conclusions about mankind's behavior. Of course, you will want to test these conclusions further, which means you will have to ask some more small questions and you will need more data to answer them. So the process begins again, but now at a higher yet deeper level, since you will already know quite a lot. At this point, you will probably not only start reviewing the materials you already have but begin looking for additional material in books, magazines, film, television, and newspapers. Discussions with friends and family members will help sharpen your observations. Suddenly you may discover that what you are seeking is something that people in every time and place have been interested in, and that you are communicating with some of the great minds of all time. Inevitably this will lead to reflection on the problems, patterns, and fruits of your own life. Thus, step by step, you will travel from the great thinkers of the past to yourself and the present. Handling data, or "facts," will seem natural to you. You will be able to interpret and order these data and also change your interpretation as you continually grow in knowledge and perception.

## The People Who Contributed to This Student's Guide

Your appreciation of the basic information in this Student's Guide will be increased if you know something about the people who wrote for or contributed material to it. Each of these people was chosen to help with your study because of a specific area of expertise in subject matter or methodology. Here, then, are your individual guides in this educational "long search."

*James L. Ash, Jr.,* wrote the capsule view of Primal Religions in Chapter 1 and the capsule views of Catholic Monasticism, Orthodox Christianity, and Protestant Fundamentalism in Chapter 9 of this Student's Guide. Dr. Ash has degrees from Abilene Christian College, Southern Methodist University, and the Divinity School of the University of Chicago. He is an assistant professor of religion at the University of Miami, in Florida. His principal field of interest has been American religious history. His competence for teaching includes more than a dozen undergraduate, graduate, or specialized courses dealing with characteristics of major or minor denominations and sects.

*Grace E. Cairns* wrote the capsule view of Religion in the Ancient Near East, Chapter 7, and is coauthor of this Student's Guide. She is also coauthor, with S. Vernon McCasland and David Yu, of the book *Religions of the World.* Dr. Cairns is professor emeritus of philosophy and religion at Florida State University, a position she has held since 1970. During her 30-year association with Florida State she served a year in India as a Fellow with the American Institute of Indian Studies. Her publications also include *Philosophies of History,* which she wrote in 1962, and *Contemporary Indian Philosophies of History,* in 1977. In addition, she has contributed numerous articles to scholarly journals. Among the most recent of these was "Holism and Social Progress in T.M.P. Mahadevan's Philosophy of History." Grace Cairns received a Ph.D. from the University of Chicago, after degrees from Oberlin and Goucher Colleges.

*C. Edward Cavert* is coauthor of this Student's Guide for "The Long Search." Dr. Cavert is Director of Learning Systems for the Extended Learning Institute of Northern Virginia Community College, in Annandale. He was one of the founding staff members of the University of Mid-America. Over the past 20 years he has contributed to media and education in Schenectady, N.Y., the Nebraska

Department of Education, the Nebraska Educational Television Network, the University of Nebraska, and the Lincoln, Nebraska, Public Schools. He has consulted widely on educational technology in the learning process, and his publications on the design of instruction for media were pioneer efforts in the field. He received a doctorate from the University of Nebraska, after degrees from Syracuse University and from North Central College, Naperville, Illinois.

*Eric Crystal* contributed the paper on the Toraja of Indonesia, in Chapter 1 of this Student's Guide. Dr. Crystal is a research associate at the University of California, Berkeley. He was a consultant to the BBC in the filming of the Toraja segment in the series "The Long Search." During that time he was also a consultant for Canadian International Development Agency in Indonesia. He has done extensive field work and study at Sulawesi, Indonesia, and is the recipient of film grants from the National Geographic Society and the California Academy of Sciences. His most recent publications include a record "Music of Sulawesi" and a 16 mm color-sound film "Ma'bugi: Trance of the Toraja." His graduate studies were in anthropology and Indonesia language at the University of California, Berkeley, where he received a Ph.D. in 1971.

*Paul Dekar* contributed the capsule view of Zulu Zion, a study of Christianity in Africa, for Chapter 2 of this Student's Guide. Dr. Dekar is an assistant professor of Christian history at McMaster Divinity College in Hamilton, Ontario, Canada. His instructional areas have been in Christian history, history of religions, African history, American religious studies, social sciences, and religion and psychological studies. Special interests have been modern African and American religious studies, social thought, myth-ritual-symbol systems, primitive religion, and international relations. Dr. Dekar, an ordained minister of the Baptist Convention of Ontario and Quebec, was pastor of an English-language parish and a U.S. Department of State foreign service officer in the United Republic of Cameroon during the 1960s. Among his publications is an African Bibliography titled *Dag Hammarskjold Collection on Nations.*

*Seymour Fersh* contributed the capsule view of Hinduism (Chapter 3) and the paper on Jains, Parsees, and Sikhs, also in Chapter 3. Dr. Fersh is professor of education at Fairleigh Dickinson University, Rutherford, New Jersey. Previously he was for 13 years education director of the Asia Society, and for six summers served as associate director of the Asia Institute at Rutgers University. He was a Fulbright professor in India, 1958-1959, and has visited most parts of Asia. Dr. Fersh is the author of school textbooks *The Story of India, India and South Asia,* and *Learning About Peoples and Cultures.* His book for teachers will be published in early 1978 by Teachers College Press of Columbia University, titled *Asia: Teaching About/Learning From.* Dr. Fersh has also served as a consultant to the Office of Education, UNESCO, and many school systems and universities. He did graduate work at Columbia and Yale Universities on a Ford Fellowship and received a Ph.D. from New York University in 1955.

*Yosef ben-Jochannan* contributed the paper on Zulu Christianity as another dimension of religions in Africa for Chapter 2. He is a visiting professor of history at the African Studies and Research Center, Cornell University, and also a visiting associate professor of history at Malcolm-King College in New York City. For 22 years, Dr. ben-Jochannan was an east African specialist in physical anthropology for the United Nations Economic, Scientific, and Cultural Organization. He is the author of many books about African religions, anthropology, and life-styles including *We the Black Jews, The Black Man of the Nile, Cultural Genocide in the Black and African Studies Curriculum,* and *African Origins of the Major "Western Religions."* He has taught on the college level since 1942 and has lectured in eight countries in South America, Central America, Canada, Mexico, Europe, Asia, Africa, and the Caribbean Islands. After receiving an LL.B. from LaSalle Extension University in Chicago, Dr. ben-Jochannan was awarded a Ph.D. in cultural anthropology from the Universidad de la Habana, in Havana, Cuba.

*William E. May* contributed the capsule view of Judaism for Chapter 8 and of Christianity for Chapter 9 of this Student's Guide. He is associate professor of moral theology in the Department of Theology at the Catholic University of America, Washington, D.C., where he has been teaching since 1971. Previously, Dr. May was for many years an editor in the field of religious publishing, serving as associate editor for Newman Press from 1954-1955, associate editor and later trade book editor-in-chief of Corpus Instrumentorum, a division of Times-Mirror-World Corp., 1969-1970. Dr. May received a doctorate in philosophy from Marquette University in 1968. He is the author of four books, the most recent of which is

*Human Existence, Medicine, and Ethics.* He has also written more than 30 articles in scholarly journals.

*Muhammad Abdul-Rauf* contributed the capsule view of Islam in Chapter 10 of this Student's Guide. Since 1971 Dr. Rauf has served as director of the Islamic Center at Washington, D.C. He was also director of the Islamic Cultural Center of New York, director of the Department of Islamic Missions, and founder of the Islamic Institute in Kuwait. Since 1944 he has taught at Al-Azhar, where he is still a staff member on loan to the Islamic Center in Washington. He has also taught at various universities, including Georgetown University, where he is a part-time professor. He has published many books in Arabic and English, the most recent of which were *Bilal, A Leading Companion of the Prophet* and *Islam: Faith and Devotion.* He was awarded the honor Johan Mangky Negera in 1963 by the King of Malaysia for exceptional service in the area of education and social welfare. He has been honorary director of the World Muslim Congress Office of the United Nations Non-Government Organization Conference since 1969 and is also Chairman of the Council of Imams of North America. Dr. Rauf received his advanced degrees from Cambridge University and London University.

*Stanley Spector* contributed the capsule views of Buddhism (in Chapter 4), the Chinese Religions (Chapter 5), and the study of Japanese Buddhism (Chapter 6). Dr. Spector is currently professor of Chinese Studies and director of the Office of International Studies at Washington University, St. Louis. He received a doctorate in Chinese History from the University of Washington, Seattle, in 1954. Over the past 25 years he has taught widely in the United States, Asia, and Europe, covering such fields as Chinese history and culture, Asian civilization, and people and cultures of Southeast Asia. He is a former consultant to the U.S. Office of Education in the field of international education, and has worked broadly in the field of internationalizing the humanities. Among his published works are *Li-Hung-chang and the Huai Army,* a study of the works of Mao Tse-Tung, and numerous articles on China and foreign policy in Asia. A former Ford Foundation Fellow, he has twice been a recipient of overseas research grants from the Social Science Research Council, and in 1975-1976 was a Fulbright Senior Research Scholar in Nagoya, Japan; Hong Kong; the People's Republic of China; and Singapore. He is former Chairman of the Midwest Conference on Asian Affairs, and former President of the Chinese Language Teacher's Association of America.

*Barry Tabachnikoff* contributed to Chapter 8 of this Student's Guide with the paper "Who Are the Chosen People?" Rabbi Tabachnikoff is Rabbi of Congregation Bet Breira in Miami, Florida. He was ordained at the Hebrew Union College in 1963 and received a Master of Hebrew Letters at the University of Pennsylvania. He has continued his graduate studies at the St. Louis University Divinity School and at the Hebrew Union College. He is coauthor of the book *Time to Rhyme Jewish Holiday Book* and the article "House of Choice," which appeared in the Polydoxy Journal. He serves as adjunct instructor for the Department of Philosophy and Religion at Florida International University, in Miami, and was an adjunct instructor at Miami-Dade Community College, in Miami.

*Joshua Zim* provided the capsule view for the study of the East and West religions in contemporary America which is part of Chapter 11 of this Student's Guide. Dr. Zim is information officer for the Nalanda Foundation, in Boulder, Colorado, a nonprofit educational foundation which brings the inspiration of Buddhist teachings into secular American life. Dr. Zim was graduated with honors from Harvard University. He traveled overland to India and studied with various Hindu teachers and yogis. Upon his return to the United States, he resided at the Lama Foundation, where he served as coordinator. Subsequently he met and became a student of the Ven. Chogyam Trungpa, Rinpoche, a Tibetan Buddhist meditation master. Dr. Zim recently published a collection of short fiction pieces titled *Empty Heart*.

# Chapter 1
# WAY OF THE ANCESTORS

## A STUDY OF PRIMAL RELIGIONS

We often think of our "world" as homogeneously modern, scientific, and literate; yet there is a substantial segment of groups on our planet which does not participate in our vision of what the "world" is like. Central Africa, the Amazon Basin in South America, the extreme northern part of Asia, and some areas of the South Pacific are home to millions of local tribesmen who might fight brush fires by shouts and drums, wear amulets to repel the spirits that cause disease, or leap high into the air in a newly planted field to insure the tall growth of grain. If we asked a man from one of these tribal cultures why it rains, he might reply that it rains whenever a spirit in the sky takes a bath. Similarly, he might assert that a tree grows because the demon in it is getting more powerful, or that people get sick because a foul spirit has entered them. Is it possible for us to understand a world view so completely different from that of our own culture?

In this chapter you will study how primal man views himself and the world, what religious concepts and practices he uses, how they differ from the religious concepts and practices of our culture. The first section of the chapter contains the material about the general characteristics of all primal religions. In another dimension on these primal religions, an anthropologist focuses on the religious practices of a specific tribe, the Toraja of Indonesia. The Toraja have a religion that has been influenced by contact with modern practices, but many of the ancient customs remain.

1

# A PREFACE TO YOUR STUDY

The major concepts listed first will help focus your study and identify the main ideas in this chapter about primal religions. A capsule view of the cultural and geographic setting for primal religions is provided by Dr. James L. Ash, Jr., Assistant Professor of Religion at the University of Miami. Another dimension of primal religions in Southeast Asia and the specific study of the Toraja religion in Indonesia is provided by Dr. Eric Crystal, research associate at the Center for South and Southeast Asia Studies at the University of California, Berkeley.

The study questions in the section "As You Read" will help assess your understanding of the material provided in this Student's Guide.

Another perspective on this topic will be revealed in the program *Way of the Ancestors* from the television series "The Long Search." In "The Toraja of Indonesia: Another Dimension of Primal Religions," Dr. Crystal, who advised the BBC in the filming of this episode in Indonesia, gives a personal insight to the material the program contains.

The "Questions for Thought" section in this chapter leaves you with some issues and concerns which you will want to consider in applying these ideas to your life and beliefs.

# IMPORTANT CONCEPTS

The major ideas in this chapter focus on world views of primal man and on ritual techniques in primal religions. Look for the following ideas in organizing your thoughts on the main concepts as you read and view.

*Primal Religions Are Local or Insular.* They are tied closely to the land and area where they thrive. They are not transplanted by missionaries and taken to other cultures. They are not transcultural or universal. They reflect an isolation from other cultures in other locations and times. They display a firm grounding in the social values of the tribe which practices them.

*Primal Religions Embrace a World View That Is Prescientific.* Their view of cause and effect is very different from ours. Their world is governed not by mechanistic and predictable natural laws but by the activity of unseen, mysterious, and sometimes capricious spiritual forces which affect physical things in many ways.

*Primal Religions Deal with Practical Matters of Survival.* They do not deal with abstract and theoretical concepts, but with how to obtain a successful hunt, a good crop, or a healthy child.

*Primal Religions Emphasize Magical Techniques.* They tend to coerce the spirit powers rather than to petition them, using special techniques passed down from previous generations. Often the major religious official is the shaman, a powerful medium who is master of the spirit world.

## A CAPSULE VIEW OF PRIMAL RELIGIONS

### The World View of Primal Man

It is certain that if we view members of primal societies simply as backward savages, we will never be able to understand them. Thus we are using the word "primal" to denote the common characteristics of these local and insular cultures, rather than the ordinarily used term "primitive," simply because the latter has negative connotations in popular usage. If we are to understand such cultures, we must not begin by implying that they are crude, backward, or even unsophisticated; to the contrary, their way of dealing with the world, given its assumptions, is quite logical and in some cases even brilliant.

Since members of primal societies are, after all, human beings like ourselves, we ought to be able to find some common experiences to which we can constructively relate. Perhaps our closest experience analogous to that of primal man is early childhood, before the presuppositions of the scientific world view became a part of our mental universe. (This does not mean that the primal world view is childish or immature, but only that our closest experiential link to it is in those earliest experiences before we had time fully to learn the world view of our culture.) Can you remember the first time you experienced a severe thunderstorm? Can you imagine how you might interpret the experience if others around you believed that all such phenomena were directly controlled by spirits who might well destroy your life? Can you remember being awakened by an especially vivid nightmare, certain that someone or something was in your immediate presence and was threatening you? Remembering such experiences makes it easier to understand the response of primal man to his world, a world of spirits, of strange and awesome powers, and of the proper techniques with which to make this threatening world friendly. The primal world of our Halloween celebration made a way of life, including the appeasing of ghosts and goblins with offerings of food and obtaining the help of mediums, witches, and sorcerers.

Modern anthropologists are hesitant to claim that our contemporary examples of primal societies are identical in every respect to the prescientific and preliterate societies of prehistoric times. Yet the vast majority of archeological findings confirms a general similarity. Thus we are dealing with contemporary examples of practices whose roots may well reach back before the dawn of civilization.

There are serious limitations to our knowledge of the earliest forms of primal religion. According to anthropologists, our species, *Homo sapiens,* has been present on Earth for about one million years, but man has been literate for only 5,000 years. The vast bulk of our existence as a species occurred before the time when written records could provide detailed information for future generations. The exact origin of man's religious experience, like the exact origin of his linguistic and racial characteristics, is therefore virtually impossible to know. There are, however, some commonly accepted religious features of the world view of primal societies, both contemporary and ancient.

*Mana: An Awesome, Silent Power.* Many primal societies believe that an unseen supernatural force is present everywhere, a force which can help or hurt humans. It is much like electricity, which, given the proper channels and controls, can cook one's dinner, but without controls can cause instant death. The name anthropologists have given this force is *mana,* a Melanesian term popularized by R.H. Codrington in the 1890s. Codrington influenced anthropologist R.R. Marrett, who constructed an influential, evolutionary theory of religion in which a belief in mana was the first stage, preceding a belief in personal spirits.

Mana is impersonal but can attach itself to persons or things. A sacred stone or tree, for example, may be considered permeated with a special concentration of mana, in which case one would have to be very careful how he conducted himself while nearby. Often chieftains or other special persons are regarded as filled with extraordinary mana. One primal society has its monarchs fed by attendants because the monarchs' hands are so full of mana that they cannot touch their own bodies.

The concept of mana has contributed to our understanding of religion in general by exposing a dimension of experience common to all religions. The German theologian Rudolph Otto, influenced by the concept of mana in the works of Marrett, asserted that all religions are grounded in the nonrational experience of an awesome and mysterious force. Otto's famous work *The Idea of the Holy* exemplifies the fact that elements of so-called primitive religion are present in the so-called advanced religions as well. In this setting, the term "primal religion" is especially appropriate because "primal" literally means "elementary," "basic," or "primary."

*Animism: The Belief in Spirits.* A distinctive characteristic of primal man's world view is its concept of nature. Unlike our idea of a passive natural world of regularized and predictable phenomena, primal man's surroundings are pervaded by spiritual beings of all kinds, making his life threatened and precarious. This belief is termed animism, after the Latin word *anima* (life). Primal societies assume that spirits can inhabit inanimate objects as well as living things. Much of the religious life of primal societies is occupied with the task of rendering these spirits helpful or at least harmless. Animism is distinguished from the belief in mana by the fact that spirits are personal beings, whereas mana is an impersonal force.

The prominent English anthropologist Edward Tylor brought animism to the attention of Westerners in his *Primitive Culture* (1866). He claimed that religion itself began when the dead appeared in dreams to primitives, leading to a belief in ghosts or spirits, and later to ancestor worship, and finally to the worship of gods. Although there are too many contradictory data for Tylor's scheme to enjoy popularity today, he did point out a plausible psychological explanation for the belief in spirits, namely, the vivid dream-life of primal man. If primal man's dead grandmother appeared in a dream, it was not illogical for him to conclude that her spirit had visited him during the night.

*Totemism: A Tribal Covenant with an Animal Species.* The tribe or clan is a basic reality to primal cultures. Persons are dependent on the clan for everything needed to sustain life—protection from nature, therapy for disease, acquisition of hunting and agricultural skills, and the learning of the proper ritual techniques to deal successfully with the all-important spirit world. For these reasons, a life of individual independence from one's social unit is practically impossible. Man is part of a tribe in the same way that he is part of the universe or part of the mana-filled world of nature.

The crucial importance of the tribe is often symbolized in the religious practice of totemism, through which a group asserts its own solidarity by affirming a spiritual kinship with an animal or plant species. A tribe might consider, for example, the bear as its totem animal. It would regard all bears as brothers, and would look to a bear spirit as its special guardian, a kind of patron deity. It would ordinarily refrain from killing bears or eating bear meat, certain that the totem species possesses great mana. It would perform rituals to ensure the prolific reproduction of the bear species, and view any threat to the bears as a threat to its own existence. This feature of many primal religions is further evidence of the close bond between man and nature noted before.

*High Gods: Creators of the Universe.* Many primal societies have a mythology based on an account of creation by a single supreme deity. Usually this deity withdraws after pushing the sky back from the earth or separating the water from the land, living afterward far away. From this remote vantage point, usually in the sky, the deity can watch the acts of men and punish them, if necessary. Ordinarily, however, the high gods have little to do with the ordinary religious life of people. The spirits that are most frequently venerated and dealt with are part of the immediate environment and do not possess the status or power of a high god. Often these less powerful spirits are ancestor-heroes, elevated to a semidivine status.

*The Absence of Historical Perspective.*   Most truly primal cultures have nothing analogous to our linear view of history. We think of ourselves as living in a unique period of history, a time unlike any that has been before. We see our Century as different from the 19th, for example, although we recognize that we are influenced by certain 19th Century events. Most of us think of our culture as more advanced than the previous cultures from which our culture grew. Perhaps, without knowing it, we have embraced a linear view of history, a view that primal man would never understand.

His view of history hardly goes beyond his own immediate environment. The myths of the culture heroes of long ago are the closest thing to a knowledge of the past that he possesses. He does not think of his own era as unique; in fact, he is probably not even aware of his life span as occurring in a discrete "era." If he has a view of history, it is probably cyclical rather than linear. Time consists of the regular repetition of events such as birth, death, the spring rains, or the autumn harvests. This aspect of the world view of primal man enhances the mystery and perhaps the precariousness of his existence. The world of his own culture is, so far as he knows, the only world that exists and the only world that has ever existed.

## The Ritual Techniques of Primal Man

Primal societies are intensely occupied with obtaining the basic necessities for survival. There is little time for the luxury of abstract reflection about the nature of man or the gods. Thus the majority of primal rituals have very down-to-earth and practical goals, such as insuring a successful hunt or a bountiful harvest, recovering from an illness, eliminating one's enemies, or initiating a boy into the responsibilities of manhood. Although the tremendous variety of ritual practices belies a general description, there are some ritual techniques common to many primal societies.

*Magic: Coercion of the Spiritual Powers.*   An early historian of religions, James G. Frazer, brought the importance of magic in primal societies to the attention of the Western world in the 19th

Century. Frazer conceived of magic as man's purposive coercion of nature to his own ends, and claimed that magic was the origin of religion. Frazer's classifications for different types of magic have become famous. "Imitative" magic is founded on the assumption that if humans mimic an act of nature, they can cause the act itself to occur. Imitating the sounds of a thunderstorm, for example, might cause a cloud to produce rain. "Contagious" magic is founded on the assumption that things once in contact can influence each other even after they have been separated. Damage to your cut hair or fingernails, for example, could do damage to the rest of your body. Haitian voodoo cults illustrate both imitative and contagious magic with a practice that most of us have heard of. They fashion an image of an enemy out of wax (imitative) and embed it with the fingernails or hair of the enemy (contagious). They then stick pins in the image and expect the enemy to die.

Magical practices occur in great variety, but their common feature is *coercion* of the natural or spiritual powers. If the deity, spirit, or object has no "choice" but to do the bidding of the person who performs the ritual, the practice can be called magical. Magic thus contrasts with prayer because prayer is usually defined as petitionary and noncoercive. Prayer can be offered with no assurance as to the result. The deity or spirit may or may not respond favorably. One who resorts to magic, however, feels certain that, if given acts are performed properly, a definite goal will be achieved.

***Shamanism: Dependence on a Spirit-possessed Medium.*** In most primal societies there is a spiritual specialist who knows all the spiritual lore and magical techniques of the tribe. He is called on to perform cures, to tell the future, and to conduct all sacred tribal ceremonies. This person is called the shaman, a Siberian word for what most of us would call a "witch doctor." The shaman is first and foremost a medium. He is regarded as possessed by a very powerful and wise spirit, or sometimes a whole family of spirits. These patron spirits enable him to conduct what we would call seances, in which tribal members can learn the future, talk with lost relatives or gods, and find answers to all sorts of everyday questions. Most shamans are ecstatics, that is, they perform their sacred duties in a state of supernormal consciousness during which visions, glossolalia (unintelligible "spirit" speech), and other psychic phenomena occur.

8

Sometimes they enter trancelike states after consuming hallucinogenic plants or after bodily deprivations such as fasts.

The shaman functions as a window to the spiritual world, through which a tribe member can gain access to useful information. He also uses magical techniques of coercion to control spirits for the tribe members' benefit. He can, for example, when in an ecstatic state, direct the spirits of death and disease, driving them into people ("sorcery") or out of people ("exorcism"). Often the shaman also dispenses what we would call "natural" cures and medicines, sometimes with surprising expertise and sophistication.

*Fetishism: Protection by the Power of Special Objects.* A fetish in primal societies is an object with extraordinary mana. We would call it an inanimate object, but primal man would not understand our concept since everything that exists is in some sense living, to him. The fetish is like our good luck charm; from the moment it is possessed, it seems to bring good fortune, health, and prosperity. A fetish can be virtually any kind of object, but most frequently it is a stone, an unusual piece of wood, or a bone. Sometimes an object possessed by an important person can later become a fetish—for example, the hunting spear of the chieftain or the antelope's horns used in sacred ceremonies by the shaman.

Fetishes can be "natural" (taken from the environment as it is) or "manufactured." Manufactured fetishes are common among African tribes and are produced by the tribal magician. He calls up certain powerful spirits and forces them to enter the object and remain there. The owner of the fetish can then summon the powerful assistance of these spirits whenever it is needed. Occasionally the manufactured fetish is worshiped with sacrifices and prayers. The power of a fetish can be thwarted by the presence of other, more powerful fetishes in the neighborhood, in which case the tribal magician might "recharge" the weak fetish by forcing more powerful spirits into it.

*Taboo: Prohibition of Dangerous Contact.* In order to survive in the precarious, mana-filled world, where touching the wrong thing might bring fatal pollution or even instant death, certain rules are established by tribal consensus and handed down from generation to generation. These "hands off" rules are called taboos. They can apply to persons, things, places, or acts. Some examples of typical taboos would include touching the body of the chief, coming near a woman in childbirth, killing the totem animal of one's tribe (see "Totemism," p. 6), touching a murderer before he has undergone ritual purification (see "Purification," below), drinking from the shaman's sacred spring, or engaging in sexual intercourse before battle.

*Purification: The Ritual Removal of Pollution.* There are techniques by which the taboo breaker can counteract his contact with dangerous mana, as well as techniques by which polluted persons can become cleansed. A woman in childbirth, a warrior who has murdered in battle, a person possessed by a disease-causing spirit, or a child who has just completed initiation rites are all candidates for purification. Often they are regarded by other members of the tribe as taboo until they have performed the prescribed cleansing acts. Such acts might include bathing at a sacred pool, fasting, shaving the head, offering special sacrifices, or jumping through fire.

*Sacrifice: Gifts to the Spirit Powers.* In all cultures, gifts serve the purpose of relating the donor and the recipient. It is thus not unnatural that in primal societies gifts are offered to those spiritual powers which affect daily life so markedly. When primal man finds his coercive magic unsuccessful, he might resort to sacrifices, which are usually petitionary. If he has offended one of the spirits, he might try to placate its wrath by a gift of a slain animal, a sweet potato, or a drink of cool water. If the ancestor spirits are worshiped, he might take them a portion of their favorite dish. Often communal sacrifices are held at important sacred celebrations. Usually an animal is slain and cooked, offered to the spirits, and then consumed in a sacred meal by all members of the tribe.

*Funeral Rites: Ushering the Dead to the Other World.* Virtually all primal cultures assume that the human personality continues its existence after death. Ordinarily it lives in some other world, and elaborate rites have been developed to insure its happy passage to that world. When these rites are properly performed, the departed personality is often able to benefit those friends who performed them. Sometimes the spirit of the dead person is seen as a threat to the normal life of the tribe. In such a case, the funeral ritual might include a long twisting trek from the village to the burial ground in order to confuse the spirit, still lingering about or in the body, and keep it from finding its way back to the village to haunt the living. In other primal cultures, the newly dead are viewed as unadjusted to their new environment and needful of reassuring expressions of love and honor from the living. These attitudes result in funeral offerings to the departed, including food and drink, weapons, clothing, or precious objects, often buried with the body if burial is practiced, or burned on the pyre if cremation is the custom. Sometimes the dead are honored at elaborate and expensive celebrations, as in the case of the Toraja tribes, discussed below.

## The Contemporary Relevance of Primal Religions

If primal religions can be viewed as basic or primary rather than backward, we will be able to see much in our own culture that is analogous to the practices which we have been discussing. Have you ever tried to find the 13th floor in a hotel or office building? Have you wondered why rabbits' feet are sold? Have you noticed the prevalence of astrology today? All these popular practices are modern examples of the prescientific world view of primal man, coming to the surface. Perhaps this fact tells us that the nature of popular religion is not altogether compatible with the scientific world view of our age. The fact that there are indisputable elements of magic in all the major, contemporary religions *as popularly practiced* shows very clearly that aspects of primal religion will continue to be with us for a long time.

## STUDY QUESTIONS

The following study questions will help organize your thoughts after you have read the Capsule View of Primal Religions by James

L. Ash, Jr. Think through each question completely before checking your answer against the material in the Capsule View.

1. In what ways are our experiences in early childhood similar to that of primal man?

2. While the forms of an unseen, supernatural force may vary, what are some of the common features of belief in this kind of force among primal societies?

3. What is primal man's concept of nature and how does this belief manifest itself in religious ritual?

4. Why, in a primal society, is a life of individual independence from one's social unit virtually impossible?

5. Explain the concept of totemism as it is found in primal religions.

6. How do the high gods differ from those spirits of a semidivine status in primal religions?

7. How does primal man's perspective of history differ from ours? What effect does that perspective have on primal religious beliefs and rituals?

8. Contrast magic in the rituals of primal religions with prayer in organized religions.

9. Why would primal man need a shaman, or spiritual specialist, in his religious rituals? How does the shaman function?

10. Of what importance are fetishes to primal man in religious rituals?

11. What are taboos? Why are they important in primal religions? How can the bad effects of a taboo be removed or cleansed away?

12. Why are sacrifices common to most primal religions?

13. Why are the funeral rites important in most primal religions?

14. How does your viewpoint change when you look on primal religions as basic or primary rather than backward?

## AS YOU VIEW

Another perspective on primitive religions is provided by the television episode *Religion in Indonesia: The Way of the Ancestors.* To organize your thoughts in advance, study the program description below, and review the guiding questions based on it in "Viewing with a Purpose" at the end of this Guide. This will help you to participate more actively in the viewing experience.

There are almost 200 million people scattered across the world who belong to tribal religions which are local, exclusive, and frequently animist. Although no single group can be chosen as typical, one program in "The Long Search" is devoted to primal religion—that of the Torajas, who live in a mountain fortress on the island of Sulawesi in Indonesia. Many primal religions appear to be dying out as a result of contact with the outside world, yet the Toraja religion shows remarkable survivability. There are 300,000 Torajas, of whom 100,000 still worship in the old ways. They live in a world in which every act has religious significance, a world in which there is little distinction between the profane and the sacred. As viewers, we set off for Torajaland expecting to find idyllic simplicity and lost innocence. What we find is a religious system of great complexity and the self-awareness of the teenager rather than the innocence of the child. Our search for the primal experience takes us to the funeral of the last Toraja queen; only to find it tourist-ridden and exploited. But we go on to encounter a priest of the old religion and a native healer, a missionary from Holland, and a volunteer agronomist from Belgium. We attend the funeral of the High Priest of the Torajas and the coronation of his son.

## QUESTIONS FOR THOUGHT

The following questions cover concerns or points of interest related to primal religions. They are intended to help extend your thinking about what you have learned.

1. Why do you think that primal faiths are today the targets of monotheistic missionary fervor?

2. What will mankind gain and what will be lost if primal religions are assimilated into the modern world of advanced cultures and technology?

3. The geography of Southeast Asia is particularly suited to the proliferation of primal religions. In what other regions of the world would you expect to find primal religions and what form would you expect them to take because of their specific geographical influences?

4. What features do primal religions and world religions share in common? What are some of the unique features of a primal religion not found in a world religion?

5. A primal religion is primarily associated with the ecological and cultural region in which it is found. World religions, on the other hand, transcend local environment and culture to achieve the broadest possible universal appeal. With this assumption in mind, describe the characteristics of a primal religion as it would develop in your own community or neighborhood.

## TO EXTEND YOUR STUDY

The following resources will provide you with material for a more in-depth study of primal religions. Use these as a reference point and starting place to continue your study.

Robbins Burling, *Hill Farms and Padi Fields* (Prentice-Hall, 1965)
An excellent introduction to the cultural area which defines and explores differences between highland and lowland peoples on mainland Southeast Asia.

Lucien Hanks, *Rice and Man* (Aldine Atherton, 1972)
More detailed yet entirely readable discussion of rice agriculture in Southeast Asia with emphasis on Thailand.

Eric Crystal, "Ceremonies of the Ancestors" (Pacific Discover, Jan.-Feb., 1976)
An illustrated article detailing the essence of Toraja religious belief.

Eric and Catherine Crystal and Lee Rhoads, "Mabugi: Trance of the Toraja" (21-minute color/sound film, distributed by Extension Media Center, University of California, Berkeley)
> A film on Toraja trance ritual.

"Music of Sulawesi," recorded by Eric and Catherine Crystal (Folkways Records, Inc., New York)
> Details the integration of Toraja musical performance with religious ritual.

W. Richard Comstock, *Religion and Man: The Study of Religion and Primitive Religion* (New York: Harper & Row, 1972)
> The best introductory survey of the data.

Mircea Eliade, *Shamanism: Archaic Techniques of Ecstasy.* Translated by Willard R. Trask (Princeton: Princeton University Press, 1964)
> Excellent and interesting as a scholarly study by the world's most famous historian of religion.

Annemarie de Waal Malefijt, *Religion and Culture* (New York: Macmillan, 1968)
> A good introduction to the anthropological study of religion, emphasizing data from many primal cultures.

Rudolph Otto, *The Idea of the Holy.* Translated by John W. Harvey. Second edition (New York: Oxford University Press, 1950)
> The classic exposition of primal religious experience, showing how it occurs in all religions.

# THE TORAJA OF INDONESIA
## Another Dimension on Primal Religions

*by*

Eric Crystal
*Center for South and Southeast Asia Studies*
*University of California, Berkeley*

Southeast Asia is most diverse geographically as well as in adaptive ecological and essential ethnographic terms. Lowland peoples have long been subject to influence emanating from afar and it is today the lowland where the bustling capital cities such as Jakarata, Bangkok, and Hanoi are situated. Foreign influence continues to pervade if not prevail and national elites interface directly with the world at large. In the mountain hinterlands, local ecology and hoary cultural traditions are markedly distinct from the lowlands. Primal religion persists in isolated highland or dispersed island locales. Traditions, which lay great stress on ceremonies of death, recall in myth and ritual practice ancient migrations in prehistoric times, and support an unusually sophisticated array of crafts and folk art.

The concerns of primal faith are particular rather than universal. The ancient tales of the ancestors, the ageless landmarks of the familiar environment, the specific deities of the traditional faiths are of little meaning in distant rural locales or in teeming capital cities. Proselytization and primal religion are not at all complementary. Beyond the familiar confines of village or ethnic group, and apart from sacred language and hoary legends recounting the emergence of The People as a unique and distinct group, ancestral religion soon loses its efficacy. Primal religion rarely, if ever, takes an evangelical bent. Yet, conversely, primal faiths in today's world are most often the target of monotheistic missionary fervor; the expansion of Christian and Muslim faiths is very often at the expense of primal religions, which become divested of their potency by the advance of technological and social change in the 20th Century.

Man has always referred to the supernatural in attempting to cope with life crises and natural catastrophes beyond the pale of available scientific understanding or technological capability. A century of anthropological field work suggests that religious belief and

16

ritual practice characterize all traditional cultures, irrespective of their level of technological sophistication. Still, in noting the universality of human religious belief and practice, some distinctions must be made with regard to the classification of religions around the globe today. One of the most useful distinctions is that of world religion versus primal religion.

*World Religions.* The term "world religion" implies a faith with many millions of geographically dispersed adherents, supported by sacred texts and a crop of trained specialists dedicated exclusively to religious pursuits. World religions such as Christianity, Islam, Buddhism, and Hinduism have extended far beyond the cultures in which they first originated. Despite local nuances, such world religions maintain a core of belief and practice which clearly differentiate them individually from competing world faiths or collectively from diverse primal faiths.

*Primal Religions.* Primal religions are directly associated with the ecological and cultural regions in which they arise. They are relevant exclusively to specific and unique ethnolinguistic groups which subsist by means of simple farming or foraging adaptations. Primal faiths correlate with preliterate cultures where concern for preserving ancient life-styles takes precedence over advancing the cause of technological and social progress.

## The Characteristics of Primal Religions

Why are primal religions so fascinating to anthropologists, philosophers, and laymen alike? First, because they are geographically discrete, culturally unique, and ecologically based. They are faiths which are inextricably tied to the traditional life-style of small scale subsistence societies. Village cultures in sub-Saharan Africa, tropical Asia, or equatorial America are certain to have had no direct links with each other. And yet, in examining the structure of primal religion cross-culturally, striking similarities very often appear over vast geographic expanses.

Belief in life after death, recourse to altered states of consciousness, and the utilization of binary opposition (coming to understand the whole of the universe through matched pairs of opposites such as male and female, hot and cold, and left and right) occur widely around the world. Therefore, studies and comparisons of small scale societies and their unique primal religions may allow us to come to a deeper understanding of the functioning of the human mind. The field of study of primal religion can be expected to enhance our appreciation of the rules by which culture everywhere tends to be organized, as well as to stimulate the elicitation of the deep social structures which pervade human communities worldwide.

Primal religions are ecologically rooted as well as transcendentally oriented. Such faiths place great stress upon the integration of man within the natural world. Whether interest is focused upon crops or game, man in the primal world view is an integral part of the ecosystem rather than of a divinely inspired super-being to whom animals, fields, and lakes have been given for exclusive exploitation. In contrast to the Western world, primal religions recognize a host of gods and supernaturals. Deities must be constantly attended to by means of offerings and sacrifices to ensure their continued benevolence toward the human community. Primal religions are deeply embedded in the soil of the regions in which they are practiced. Myths of origin incorporate prominent landmarks such as mountains, lakes, and valleys in a sacred oral tradition which is passed on from generation to generation.

## Modern Influences on Primal Religions

In the next 25 years primal religions will undoubtedly come under increasing pressure from without. The characteristic geographic isolation, which has allowed for the survival of primal faiths across much of the tropical world, is in most cases being compromised with each passing year. All peoples today reside in regions encompassed by great nation-states interested in advancing agricultural growth and forest product exploitation, intent upon stimulating tourism to generate foreign exchange, and dedicated to conforming the oftentimes embarrassingly simple dress and life-style of their least developed peoples to the routine standards of modesty of the contemporary world.

In the 20th Century the spread of great empires, advance of technology, cataclysmic eruption of world wars, emergence to power of nationalist movements, and inexorable drive toward economic development in regions formerly regarded beyond the pale of civilization have taken an immense toll in the submergence of traditional societies and the obliteration of primal religions. What is more, the vitality and resilience of surviving primal religions have in many cases been severely compromised by the advance of social change in recent years. Yet the view toward the future need not be hopelessly pessimistic. On Indian reservations in the United States, in villages in Papua-New Guinea, and in highland areas of eastern Indonesia, there are movements afoot to revitalize primal religions with a view to assuring survival in a changing but not altogether hostile world.

From the anthropological perspective, maintaining mankind's cultural diversity is a moral imperative as well as an intellectual necessity. Primal religions offer students of man an opportunity to glimpse the essence of human social order, a chance to observe directly the unique genius of people in one place as they have evolved culturally over time. The opportunity to examine and compare disparate primal faiths offers some hope for achieving a deeper and more comprehensive understanding of what it is in the human psyche that demands supernatural reinforcement and the means by which cultures regulate belief and ritual practice.

## Culture of Southeast Asia

Perhaps no geographical region of the world offers so arresting an array of cultures and high civilizations as does Southeast Asia. Bounded on the west by India and on the north by China, the peoples of monsoon Asia have been exposed to world religions and civilizations for many centuries. Yet the unique genius of indigenous Southeast Asian culture has survived and flourished, despite contact with powerful civilizations from afar since long before the time of Christ. The countries of Burma, Thailand, Laos, Vietnam, Cambodia, Malaysia, Singapore, the Philippines, and Indonesia which comprise the Southeast Asian region are distinct from each other and at the same time highly diverse internally.

Despite a wide range of language families, farming technologies, and adaptive strategies to be found within any one Southeast Asian country, certain themes are common throughout the region. "Unity in Diversity," the Indonesian national motto, encapsulates the essence of Southeast Asian cultural complexity.

19

As a general rule, the peoples of the plains and those of the mountains are culturally distinct.

*The Culture of the Peoples of the Plains.*  On the flatlands, vast populations have for centuries been supported by the intense farming of fertile alluvial rice plains. With abundant grain crops and flourishing trade, the peoples of the plains developed elaborate state systems, with ruling monarchs, attentive administrative officers, and dutifully obeisant peasants (in time of plenty) long before contact with India occasioned the diffusion of Hindu-Buddhist principles of state and religion to lowland population centers throughout Southeast Asia.

On the plains, then, great civilizations were influenced from afar, replete with monumental temples and graceful palaces staffed by well-versed scribes, warriors, priests, and nobles. These civilizations flourished for many centuries before the first Portuguese sailors ventured into the region in the late 15th Century.

*The Culture of the Peoples of the Mountains.*  In the mountainous hinterlands of all the Southeast Asian states, however, religious activity and economic pursuits continued unaffected by new currents of thought from abroad. Indeed, many remote areas came under effective colonial control only in the early 20th Century.

Geographical and cultural isolation tended to allow primal religious traditions to flourish in the mountain regions despite the advance of civilization on the adjacent plains. Trade in forest products, such as resins, hardwoods, bird nests, precious metals, tusks, antlers, etc., linked the mountain peoples in direct trade relationships with the peoples of the plains. And yet, so different were their levels of technology and means of subsistence that perfunctory economic and political contacts did not affect the fundamental, cultural cleavage between Southeast Asian hill and lowland zones.

## The Life-style of the Primal Peoples

Highlanders often farm rice by means of slash and burn cultivation. Lowlanders, or mountain dwellers with high population densities, use irrigation techniques on carefully worked level fields which may be planted year after year.

The slash and burn method of "nomadic" agriculture involves the cutting of the highland forest in the latter part of the dry season and the burning of cuttings on hillside fields just before the coming of the seasonal monsoon rains. Ash and rainwater fertilize the sloping hillside plots, thus enhancing the yield. Slash and burn fields must be abandoned after a few years in favor of new land, as the fertility of the soil is quickly exhausted. Low density peoples using slash and burn technology (such as the Hanunoo of the Philippines) allow their fields to lie dormant for several years before returning to cut the second growth, burn, and plant again.

Slash and burn techniques do not produce yields adequate for high density populations or for peoples with large houses and other permanent structures who do not wish to abandon village sites every three to five years. A number of large mountain cultures in Southeast Asia farm as do the lowlanders by flooding fields with water and transplanting rice shoots from carefully tended seedbeds to level rice paddies in which the inflow and outflow of water are carefully controlled. In the highlands, irrigated rice farming may be practiced only in narrow valley floors or in elaborately constructed hillside terraces; the latter duplicate on a miniature scale the vast flooded paddies of the lowland plains. The most renowned terraces in all of Southeast Asia are those of the Ifugao in the Mountain Province of Luzon in the Philippines. Other highland groups of considerable size which employ terracing extensively are the Batak of northern Sumatra and the Toraja of south Sulawesi, Indonesia.

## Characteristics of Southeast Asian Culture

Mountain cultures of Southeast Asia are representative of much that is indigenous to Southeast Asia as a whole. Artistic motifs, architectural styles, ritual concerns, and ecological preoccupations, which have been masked by subsequent Muslim, Hindu, or Buddhist intrusions in lowland states, oftentimes may yet be observed in highland regions which have tenaciously retained ancient Southeast Asian cultural patterns.

Some aspects of Southeast Asian culture about which we may generalize are: dependence upon rice as a staple grain; use of water buffalo as draft animals and as a measure of prestige; care of pigs, in non-Muslim regions; skill in the use of wood, especially bamboo; the

21

chewing of betel nut; and a pervasive belief in agriculturally oriented spirits and deities.

Certain motifs prevail in isolated regions throughout Southeast Asia which recall prehistoric migrations of Malayo-Polynesian speaking peoples from the mainland to islands of Southeast Asia about 7,500 years ago. Houses are boat-shaped in a number of cultural areas. Religious rituals, especially burial ceremonies, often make reference to the journey of the deceased to the place of origin of the ancestors. Several Dayak groups in the interior of Borneo traditionally place their dead on boats and send them on their way downstream toward the supposed land of the ancestors. Coffins are often crafted in the shape of ocean-going vessels. Rituals sometimes involve the unfurling of sails atop large clan houses reminiscent of the first coming of pioneer settlers from distant shores.

The ceremonial traditions of mountainous Southeast Asia lay great stress upon rituals of death. Exactly why this should be is unclear (so, also, we do not really understand why some cultures lay inordinate stress upon marriage, others upon birth, and yet others on puberty). Death rituals in native Southeast Asian cultures are occasions not only for the dispatch of the soul to the nether world but also for the reaffirmation of the status of the deceased and his family in the community and for the display of the full panoply of vocal, dance, and plastic arts of the cultural area.

The stress upon death ceremonies is not to deny the importance of rituals having to do with subsistence activities and the healing arts. Rice as the staple grain of Southeast Asia is the focus of much ritual activity. At every point in the agricultural cycle, commencing with the extraction of seed grain and the symbolic sowing of the first handfuls of rice into well-prepared seedbeds iridescent with still irrigation water, the spirits which guard the rice must be cajoled and plied with sacrificial offerings. In many Southeast Asia cultures the spirit of rice is thought to be female, and palm leaf or rice straw effigies in the image of the "mother of the rice fields" are often fabricated. At harvest time voices are subdued as deft female hands wield the small bamboo and steel-cutting tool with which the grain is reaped by hand. In many cultures only women are allowed to cut the rice stalks; men, it is feared, might ritually pollute the domain of the controlling rice spirit.

## The Symbolic Expressions of Southeast Asia

The symbolic elements of indigenous Southeast Asian religions are unusually rich. Representational arts such as ikat weaving, wood sculpture, bamboo, etching, beadwork, and gold and silvercraft are often totally integrated with primal religious belief and ritual. Textiles from particularly rich areas (central Borneo, Sumba Island, central Sulawesi) may impart not only the greatest feats of the dyer's art but also convey considerable information about the symbols of the universe which are of central importance to the world view of the people producing them.

There is little that is haphazard in traditional Southeast Asian village communities. The orientation of houses, colors employed in plaiting, house painting and dying, the form of sacrificial animals, and calendrical systems computed in accord with lunar cycles correlate closely with tenets of local primal religions. An incident as small as the manner in which a reed sleeping mat is laid upon the floor may cause great consternation if the direction of the plaiting is incorrect. Among the Toraja of Sulawesi Island in Indonesia, the direction south connotes death, misfortune, and all that is to be avoided. Youngsters entrusted with the task of laying out mats for guests quickly learn that it is taboo for the plaiting to run towards the south. Only a mat unfurled to receive a corpse would be so placed.

## The Primal Faiths of Indonesia

Indonesia is the largest, most diverse, most populous nation in Southeast Asia. With its population of 130 million it is also the largest Muslim country in the world, with 90 percent of the population adhering to the tenets of Islam. Yet in remote island and mountain locales primal faiths persist. In the mountains of north Sumatra, in the Lesser Sunda Islands, and in the mountains of south Sulawesi in Tana Toraja, thousands of adherents of ancestral ways maintain ceremonial traditions that may be as old as the practice of agriculture itself in tropical Asia.

## The Tana Toraja of Indonesia

The 300,000 people of Tana Toraja constitute one of the numerically less significant ethnic groups of Indonesia. Yet the vigor of traditional Toraja culture is such that this small group manifests in microcosm a host of prototypical Southeast Asian cultural patterns.

The Toraja were first brought under colonial control in 1905 after a long resistance against invading Dutch colonial forces. Prior to the 20th Century the region had been almost completely isolated from outside contact, except for economic relations based on the sale of local coffee and the appearance of itinerant traders at weekly markets. Effective colonial government lasted only 35 years, until the Japanese displaced the Dutch in 1941 as the governing authority.

Christian missionaries made an early impact in Tana Toraja, and their extensive school system attracted students from the most remote districts. Nevertheless, resistance to a new faith was pronounced; the first Dutch evangelist to be permanently stationed in Tana Toraja was assassinated during the first decade of Dutch colonial rule.

Up until the present decade, government statistics reported that slightly over half of the population remained loyal to the ancestral faith—*Aluk To Dolo* (ceremonies of the ancestors). The national census taken in 1971 revealed, however, that traditional religion in Tana Toraja had declined, in the 15 years since the previous survey, to about one-third of the populace. About 5 percent of the Toraja have embraced Islam; the vast majority of converts to monotheism have opted for the Protestant faith. The traditional, primal religion of the Tana Toraja is now followed by about 120,000 people.

Many Christians and Muslims within the region are syncretists, who selectively participate in *Aluk To Dolo* rituals with varying degrees of economic and devotional commitment. The ancestral faith has been legitimized by the government although it has never been taught in the schools as are Islam and Christianity. This is a point of some contention within the Toraja region; conversions seem prompted by peer group pressure and teacher proselyting within the educational system.

### The Toraja Religious System

*Aluk To Dolo* is a primal religion which recalls the fundamental characteristics of Southeast Asian culture. Death ceremonies are most prominent within the Toraja religious system. In the funeral arena scores of water buffalo and pigs are slaughtered with the purpose of providing the soul of the deceased with familiar domestic animals at his new abode in the land of the souls. The scale and munificence of a Toraja funeral confirm the status of the deceased and his surviving family in the village community. The Toraja often remark that "the greatness of a person is only manifest at the time of death." Clothes, jewelry, even diet are of secondary importance in the traditional Toraja world view. What is most valued is the ability to stage a large funeral for one's closest relatives, the capacity to respond with generosity when a funeral ends. A debt of a water buffalo incurred generations earlier must be repaid in kind. Funerals which occur with great regularity after the rice harvest are the most commonly observed Toraja religious ceremonies, but they are by no means the only such rites.

The regularity and grand scale of Toraja funerals tend to obscure the symmetry to life and death rites which underlie the Toraja ceremonial system. The neatly divided Toraja ritual world entails rituals of life and rituals of death which ultimately complement each other. Funerals are elaborate in accordance with the status of the deceased. Life rites, which relate to the fertility of the fields and fecundity of animals and man, are similarly ranked. Paramount death and life rituals to a great extent mirror images (i.e., reversed images), of each other. Large processions in funerals proceed from right to left (the side rites celebrating the harvest, the ascendancy of a ritual specialist, or the prosperity of an individual move from left to right, the direction of life). Compass points are crucial in Tana Toraja. South is associated with death, as is the west, the direction of the setting sun. North and east are associated with fertility and crop production, with the life-giving warmth of the rising sun. Toraja houses and rice granaries face to the north. As one stands at the face of a stately Toraja family house, facing north to the headwaters of the Sa'dan River, the west is on the left, the east on the right. The association of left with the undesirable and the right with all that is propitious is characteristic of not only the Toraja but apparently primal religions everywhere.

## The Toraja Death Ritual

As with all death rites, the Toraja death ritual is essentially oriented toward the problems of removing the corpse and potentially malevolent ghost soul to a proper place of interment. The Toraja believe that within each person resides a soul or *bombo* which tends to wander during serious illness and must return to the body if death is not to result. Seers gifted with supernatural powers are said to be able to observe wandering souls leaving the bodies of critically ill persons. Sometimes such souls are encountered along the roadway or in the marketplace—an ominous sign that death may be at hand even though the individual may seem outwardly hearty.

The Toraja do not dispose of the body immediately after death. Instead, the deceased is normally kept for long weeks, months, and even years in the residence until elaborate funeral preparations are complete. So great is the expenditure of material resources in the form of domestic animals, rice, coffee, bamboo, and other things that a period of months is normally required to amass requisite resources for a large five-night or seven-night Toraja funeral.

Normally interment may not take place while the growing rice is still in the fields. This is because ceremonies of death and life (rice-related rituals) are seen to be mutually contradictory and must take place at separate times. Only after the rice is stored behind the elaborately etched doors of the rice granaries may the preparations for a funeral legitimately begin.

Large funerals demand the construction of special ceremonial fields, apart from those preparations in the home of the deceased. A hardwood statue in the likeness of the departed is carved from the wood of the jackfruit tree. When a *tau tau* statue is used, it is moved along with the body and the invisible but omnipresent *bombo* ghost soul, in procession from house to rice granary and then on to the ceremonial field. From there it will be taken to the *liang* cave burial site situated high above the fields in a limestone cliff face.

The entire ceremony takes seven nights, although legitimate pauses for ritual reasons sometimes extend actual burial to as long as three weeks after the arrival of the body at the ceremonial ground. The body is ultimately sealed behind a carved wooden door, with the burial vault and the statue emplaced nearby on a rock ledge. From there the soul is thought to continue its journey. Ultimately the *bombo* reaches Puya, the Land of the Souls, believed to be situated to the south of the Tana Toraja region.

## The Toraja Life Rituals

Life rituals are mainly rice-related and are much less frequently observed, but are of equal importance for the balanced Toraja ceremonial system. Many such rituals are carried out by the individual household or by small village units, and attract little attention beyond the confines of the specific area concerned.

The BBC film crew for "The Long Search" documented the extraction of seed rice from granaries at Pemanukan Village. The ritual involved preparing the grain to be symbolically sown in the first seedbed of the new agricultural year. Chickens were sacrificed by each village household, just as at funerals pigs and water buffalo are dramatically slaughtered. All Toraja rituals are accompanied by animal sacrifice. The more valuable the domesticated animal slaughtered, the more people attend and the more elaborate the cultural displays which are presented. At funerals the chant for the deceased and *badong* dance may be performed only if several water buffalo are slaughtered. The sacrifice of a single chicken to the *deata* spirits which control the fertility of the fields need not be accompanied by more than a perfunctory, spoken prayer. Night-long chants and dramatic performances, on the other hand, are performed at the paramount harvest festival, which sees the sacrifice of scores of pigs.

The Toraja live closely with their domesticated animals, quartering their water buffalo below the floors of their raised houses, rising before dawn to cook food for their pigs, ushering chickens up to the house to glean scraps from the floor, before retiring for the evening. And yet these well cared for animals are killed with a swift stroke of a razor-sharp knife each time ritual demands.

Meat is eaten in village communities only in the context of religious ritual. What is consumed by man is first offered to the controlling supernaturals, which inhabit the Toraja social and natural universe. The *deata* spirits are summoned at life rites, along with the ancestors of those long deceased. Food is provided at funerals for the soul of the deceased, and at special times is offered to the souls of all those in the vicinity who have recently passed away.

The *tominaa,* or priest of life, officiates at life side rituals. The *To makayo,* or priest of death, officiates at funerals, praising the soul of the departed and ushering it gently on its way beyond the confines of the settlement to the ancestral limestone burial grounds. Ultimately the rigidly segmented life rituals and death rituals are connected closely to each other. Souls of the deceased, in time, become revered ancestors who are summoned to share repasts at life rites with controlling *deata* spirits. The fact that increasingly elaborate gradations of life and death rituals present mirror images of each other suggests that it is through the mechanism of complementary duality that the people of Toraja ultimately express the coherent integration of their universe. At the zenith of the heavens is thought to reside "the white haired one," *Puang Matua*. This is the Toraja High God. Never seen, this immanence is believed to act through the vehicle of the *deata* spirits.

### The Funeral of Dena—A Toraja Priest

The funeral of the esteemed Toraja priest Dena was filmed by the BBC in September, 1976. This event was most unusual, not only because of the great age and wisdom of the deceased but because his unique lineage decreed a very special funeral procedure.

Dena was a special Toraja priest, a *tominaa* empowered to use the title *Tomenani*. Only one so entitled could be entrusted with carrying out the paramount life rites of the ancient religion. And so it had been for 40 generations for members of his family. Someone among the descendants of the ancestor Kambuno Langi (Shield of the Sun) always had been selected to master the sacred chants, to control the ritual procedure, to wear the sacred water buffalo headdress during the times when offerings were proffered directly to the High God.

So exalted was this family that in death the high positions of its members as paramount priests of life would be symbolically reinforced. The funeral of Dena thus took on the classic appearance of a ritual of reversal. Every taboo at a normal funeral would here become a ritual obligation. Normally dressed in black mourning cloth, funeral participants here would wear saffron yellow reminiscent of the color of ripening rice—symbols of life, fertility, and the rays of the morning sun. All processions would move from left to right, rather than the right to left normal during ceremonies for the dead. Indeed, chants and dances performed at this special funeral would be those drawn from ceremonies of life, rather than those from the ritual realm of death. Corn and millet—normal mourning foods—would be shunned in favor of rice, brought by the leaders of surrounding communities. The body of the deceased would be wrapped in yellow, once again symbolic of life. This was the way it was with the funeral of the aged Dena, greatest of the southern Toraja religious leaders.

## Summary

Accompanied by four students from Hasanuddin University in the south Sulawesi capital city of Ujung Pandang, my wife and I first traveled to Tana Toraja (Land of the Toraja) in early 1963. At the end of the 12-hour, 120-mile jeep trip we found ourselves in the cool Toraja highlands. The following day we were ushered into a traditional funeral ceremony being performed in a courtyard, surrounded by boat-shaped houses, in the midst of a large expanse of dry valley and rice paddies.

We conducted anthropological field work for over a year in Tana Toraja, and returned for six months in 1971 to film the Ma'bugi curing rite now documented in the film "Trance of the Toraja." Late in 1975, I was asked by BBC Director Malcolm Feuerstein to work, together with his film crew, on a Toraja religion segment for the series "The Long Search." Feuerstein had previously traveled in late 1975 to Tana Toraja and there had met an old man of great presence and wisdom. The BBC director's discussions with the aged Toraja priest Ne Dena had convinced Feuerstein that the one segment of his series to deal with primal religion would be filmed in Tana Toraja. The priest had been a guest in our house many times since 1968 and had consecrated our own home in the region in 1971.

Between the first discussions in December, 1975, and the work in August-September, 1976, the aged Toraja died. His long life had spanned the last of the precolonial wars in the 1930s (during which he had participated in head-hunting raids) to the coming of mass tourism to Tana Toraja in the 1970s. The commencement of BBC filming coincided with the funeral of Ne Dena. Would his passing signal the end not only of a renowned Toraja religious leader but also suggest metaphorically the impending demise of yet another primal religious tradition? As "The Way of the Ancestors" demonstrates, the accession of Dena's literate, sophisticated, youngest son, Tato, to the position of high priest of the southern Toraja districts gives some cause for optimism that the indigenous Toraja religion will be able to survive.

Perhaps more threatening than the monotheistic evangelism of the recent past is the influence of mass tourism in Tana Toraja at present. There is considerable danger that the primal rites of the Toraja may be turned into commercial spectacles organized, scheduled, and performed for affluent foreign visitors intent upon viewing a genuine agrarian rite in a modern world ever more lacking in authenticity.

The "Way of the Ancestors" amply demonstrates that the primal religion of the Toraja has tenaciously survived, at least to the present. The language, architecture, highland ecology, and well-developed dance and plastic arts of these people are unique in south Sulawesi province yet most familiar to students of Southeast Asian culture.

The efforts of a small group of dedicated leaders such as Tato, son of Dena, may well decide the future of traditional Toraja religion. For my own part, I am delighted to have been able to encourage adherents of this primal faith to persist in their ancestral religious traditions and to aid in some small way in making the culture of Toraja known to the world at large. The "Way of the Ancestors" is in all respects the religious path of primal man, as well as the unique heritage of a small group of mountain farmers in eastern Indonesia.

## STUDY QUESTIONS

The following study questions will help organize your thoughts after you have read this dimension of Primal Religions by Eric Crystal. Think through each question completely before checking your answers against the material in this Student's Guide.

1. Describe the differences and similarities between a world religion and a primal religion as defined by Dr. Crystal.

2. What are the major factors that are unique to primal religions?

3. In what ways will primal religions come under increasing pressure from without in the next 25 years?

4. Why is it important to preserve the primal religions in order to understand and protect mankind's cultural diversity?

5. In what way does the Indonesian national motto "Unity in Diversity" capture the essence of Southeast Asian culture?

6. How does the culture of the primal people of the plains differ from the culture of those of the mountains?

7. In what ways is the life-style different or similar among the primal people of the plains and those of the mountains?

8. What are the common characteristics of all cultures in Southeast Asia?

9. In what ways are the symbolic expressions of indigenous Southeast Asian religions vital to the life-style of the people?

10. In what way does Dr. Crystal believe that the Toraja manifest in microcosm the many Southeast Asian cultural patterns?

11. Why do death rituals and funerals play an important role in primal religions of Southeast Asia, such as the religion of the Toraja?

12. What significance is placed on geographic direction (north and south, left and right, etc.) in Toraja rituals?

13. Of what significance is the sacrifice of animals in the Toraja life rituals?

14. In what ways are the rigidly segmented life rituals and death rituals connected with each other?

# Chapter 2

# ZULU ZION

## A STUDY OF CHRISTIANITY IN AFRICA

Christianity is a universal religion, yet it can never be fully understood apart from the particular cultural contexts in which it has flourished. The Ganda people of modern Uganda have a proverb which emphasizes this fundamental point about Christianity and culture: He who never visits thinks his mother is the only cook.

You are invited to visit one of the cultural settings in which the Christian religion has taken root. To visit Zulu Zion, the voyager must travel light. Especially if visiting from Europe or North America for the first time, the traveler must abandon romantic and often fantastic images of the African continent; attitudes of paternalism or of superiority of Western culture, ideas, or technology; an unrealistic and probably unconscious expectation that, upon conversation to Christianity, the African somehow ceases to be an African. Unless such preconceptions are left behind, the visitor will not be prepared to meet Christians with their white robes and wooden crosses in hand as they serpentine at dawn through the streets of modern African cities; or to comprehend the pride of a Ugandan Christian who describes with hands waving how waters flowing from his native land carried the infant Jesus to safe shelter in Egypt 2,000 years ago.

It is not surprising, therefore, that man's long search for religious meaning includes a study of Zulu Zion—the independent Christian Churches of the great Zulu people of southern Africa. Zulu Christians represent but one small strand of African Christianity. But in a very real sense they illustrate a fundamental quality of the Christian religion, namely, that wherever adherents have claimed the name of Christ as their own, Christianity has been modified by the cultural milieu in which it took root.

## A PREFACE TO YOUR STUDY

An outline of the major concepts related to the study of Christianity in Africa begins your lesson. Use these to focus your study and to identify the main ideas contained in the material. A basic source of material for this study of African Christianity is provided by Dr. Paul Dekar, assistant Professor of Christian History at McMaster Divinity College in Hamilton, Ontario, Canada. The study questions will help assess your understanding of this material.

A different perspective on this topic will be revealed in the program "Zulu Zion" from the television series "The Long Search."

Another dimension of Zulu Christianity and traditional religions in Africa is provided by Dr. Yosef ben-Jochannan, who teaches religion at Cornell University and at Malcolm-King College in New York City.

The Questions for Thought section of this lesson leaves you with some issues and concerns which you will want to evaluate in applying them to your life and beliefs.

## IMPORTANT CONCEPTS

The major ideas in this lesson focus on the historic roots of Christianity in Africa and on the amalgamation process between Christianity and traditional African religious beliefs and practices. Look for these concepts as you study to organize your thoughts preparatory to reading and viewing.

The cultural settings, in which Christianity takes root, shape and influence the nature of tenets and beliefs.

Christianity is not alien to Africa but has a long and diverse history punctuated by Biblical foundations, missionary zeal, and nationalist aspirations.

What the European or North American considers essential to Christianity may be peripheral to what the African considers essential.

Christianity in Africa has had to amalgamate with traditional African beliefs and experiences.

## A CAPSULE VIEW OF ZULU ZION

For centuries Africa has nourished three great religious traditions of man: Christianity, Islam, and, for want of a better term, primal or traditional religion. Critics of African Christianity often claim that Christianity is alien to Africa. This is not true. From earliest Christian times, North Africa contributed substantially to the growth of the Christian religion. Many of the most celebrated church fathers—Augustine, Cyprian, Origen, Tertullian, and others—were African. For centuries after Islam swept through northern Africa, black Christians of Ethiopia and Sudan maintained intermittent contact with Christian centers in Alexandria, Jerusalem, and Europe. At the end of the 15th Century, Christian missionaries actively began to extend Christianity throughout the African continent. Initially, growth was sporadic. Elaborate conversions sometimes occurred, for example, in the royal family of the Kingdom of Kongo; however, rapid growth and vitality on the part of African churches have been more recent phenomena, and growth today is continuous. African Christians now number nearly 100 million. They include Adventists, Catholics, Copts, Orthodox, Protestants, and Zionists. By the year 2000, if present growth rates continue, there will probably be more Christians in Africa than on any other continent.

Zulu Zion lays claim to ancient promises of God to His people. Centuries ago the psalmists anticipated the universal acknowledgement of Israel's God: Princes shall come out of Egypt; Ethiopia shall soon stretch out her hands unto God (Psalms 68:31). Throughout Christian history, Egyptian and Ethiopian Christians have identified closely with that Biblical text.

Christians who call their churches by such names as the African Apostolic Church of Christ in Zion or the Ethiopian African Church

35

of Zion in South Africa have established a great and diverse number of churches throughout Africa, especially among the Xhosa and the Zulu of South Africa. The enthusiasm of many of their members attest to the reality of a great and spirited religious movement. In this capsule view of Zulu Zion you will explore the historical background of some 6,000 independent churches which originated in efforts by Africans to unite their traditional religious heritages with Christian teaching and practice. Special attention will be given to the Zulu Church of the Nazarites, founded in 1911 by Isaiah Shembe, and to his success in interpreting Biblical concepts to his Zulu disciples. There is responsible argument as to whether Zulu Zion has departed from Christianity, or demonstrates the universality and particularity of Christianity in the modern world.

## The Rooting of Christianity in Black Africa

In myriad institutional forms and individual ways, many Africans have made Christianity their own. Christian music, rituals, prophets, healers, village churches, and city cathedrals figure prominently in the religious topography of black Africa and catch the attention of even uninterested travelers. African Christians are presently assuming greater visibility in the universal church as well as in particular contexts of nation-building, economic development, and the struggle for human liberation. Missionaries from foreign lands continue important work throughout Africa, especially providing expertise in such fields as agriculture and medicine, which the Church has long considered integral to its mission. African churches originated largely in missionary societies, but these churches as well as the Coptic churches and so-called Zionist and Ethiopian churches are all entirely independent of missionary authority. African Christians now set the tone and control the future of African Christianity.

*The Early Missionary Era.* For centuries, African Christianity barely existed, apart from the venerable churches of Egypt and Ethiopia. A hundred years ago, only small Christian communities dotted the coastlines of black Africa, and much of the African interior remained uncharted and unknown to Western missionaries. The Christian communities which did exist were predominantly Protestant (Anglican, Baptist, Congregationalist, Methodist, and Presbyterian societies had organized in Britain and the United States at least a generation before Catholic missionary orders undertook work in black Africa) and consisted primarily of men and women rescued from slave ships. Mission leaders such as the Anglican Henry Venn, the Congregationalist Rufus Anderson, and the Catholic Francois Marie-Paul Libermann advocated a policy whereby African churches were expected to become independent (self-governing, self-supporting, and self-propagating were the phrases used) of missionary guidance as quickly as possible. Currents of racism and colonialism had not yet touched mid-19th Century missionaries, with the result that between 1825 and 1875 the development of many African Christian communities was entirely independent of direct missionary supervision and control.

*The Modern Missionary Era.*   Missionaries dominated African church life between 1875 and 1925. During that period, Catholic and Protestant missionaries partitioned the continent with all the resolve of the imperialists. Often missionaries paved the way for the imposition of colonial rule. This fact later became the major source of contention between African and Western Christians. Less well known are the instances in which missionaries successfully intervened to soften the blows of conquest and exploitation.

Whatever stance missionaries took toward political and other developments in Africa, their primary aim was the spread of the Christian religion. The old image of the missionary, with one hand holding a Bible and the other hand pointing at a smashed fetish, is quite apt. As a role model for the conquered Africans, the noble and pious missionary of the period from 1875 to 1925 hardly seems a probable candidate. But the missionary also went to Africa equipped with a quantity of goods which his Western culture provided: school books; medicine; printing presses; sawmills; manual skills; cacao, rubber, and palm seedlings; tins of food; barrels of secondhand clothing; and money to forge a new economic system. Unconsciously, the missionary activity frequently centered in educational, agricultural, and medical work rather than in evangelism or Bible translation. In terms of attracting potential converts to mission stations and rural outstations, and of assuring the cooperation of colonial authorities, the former activities certainly facilitated realization of the primary missionary purpose of winning converts to Christianity. The secondary activities, however, tended to shape converts in a characteristic "made in the West" mold, and the task of running institutions such as schools and hospitals also tended to strain missionary resources. Consequently, missionary societies entered into various financial arrangements with the colonial administrations, which ultimately detracted from the primary aim of evangelism. The missionary stations became major centers of social change as well as religious change. The number of Protestant and Roman Catholic missionaries rapidly grew to more than 12,000 by 1925. The net result was a massive assault on traditional African religion and culture.

***The Assault on Traditional African Religion.*** Africans did not react passively to this attack on traditional African religion and culture by the missionaries. Some resisted openly. For example, the Maji-Maji rebellion of 1905-1907 swept through most of southern and eastern Tanzania, a territory then known as German East Africa. Peasant grievances and the leadership of prophet-healers, who urged the restoration of what missionaries and colonists had corrupted, generated a mass movement in which more than 75,000 Africans died. Other campaigns to suppress African resistance, such as the savage war against the Herero in German South West Africa during the same years, were equally costly in human terms.

A more characteristic response by Africans to Christian proselyting and the introduction of Western ways was to make the best of the situation. After 1900 literally hundreds of thousands of Africans crowded into mission churches, schools, and other institutions. Missionaries often imposed strict rules upon potential converts, yet Africans earnestly resolved to change their lives and follow the Christian religion. One congregation boasted a waiting list of up to 15,000. The waiting process entailed at least two years of catechetical instruction; defiance of traditional customs, such as the destruction of ancestor skulls or the putting aside of all but one wife; committing to memory scripture passages such as the Ten Commandments or the Lord's Prayer; contributing out of one's meager resources to support building campaigns and village-to-village itinerant evangelism; and publicly attesting to one's acceptance of the rules and tenets of Christianity. Despite the rigor of this process, stories are legion of baptismal services during which a missionary stood in a river while two lengthy lines of adult converts streamed by the minister to be received into the Christian community.

According to the visionary policy of such men as Henry Venn and Bishop Samuel Ajayi Crowther, an indigenous African clergy was to guide an indigenous African church. After 1875 the implementation of this policy by younger missionaries who accepted Western ideas of evolution and imperialism was unthinkable. Consequently, the Anglican Church Missionary Society did not replace Bishop Crowther with another African, and everywhere the training of African clergy and the establishment of autonomous African churches proceeded very slowly. Only in isolated areas, and as a result of the courageous stand of certain outstanding missionaries, did the installation of African Christian pastors parallel the progressive growth of the African church. In 1913 the determined Alsatian Bishop Streicher pushed through the ordination of Victor Mukasa, the first Ganda Roman Catholic priest, and others followed. Similarly, the Anglican Arthur Shearly Cripps and the Methodist John White stood firm through the 1920s on the matter of the rights of native clergy in southern Rhodesia. Of course, the long period required to train priests and ministers, and such requirements as celibacy on the part of Roman Catholic priests, impeded the preparation of large numbers of clergy. Still, the greatest barriers proved to be the menial tasks assigned to native church leaders and the reluctance of missionaries to transfer their work into native hands.

***The Christianization of Africa.*** The period does offer outstanding evidence of the faithfulness of Africans to Christianity. The most prominent African churchman of the early 20th Century was a Fanti from Ghana, Emman Kodwo Mensa Otsiwadu Humamfunsam Kwegyir Aggrey. James Aggrey was his Christian name. His equally prominent biographer, the missionary anthropologist Edwin W. Smith, called Aggrey "an African of the Africans." Aggrey attained fame as a healer of black-white relations and as a Christian educator. He traveled widely, most notably with two Phelps-Stokes commissions which resulted in an enhanced role by missionary societies in the so-called solemn duty of the West to impart civilization to the poor, benighted African. Aggrey died in 1927, at the age of 50, while in the United States receiving a Ph.D. from Columbia University.

Aggrey was no revolutionary. As African passions began to stir against white domination, he remarked simply, "When I am worried, I go on my knees and I talk to God in my own tongue. . . . I plead with the Christian Church to make Africa the first Christian continent."

Fifty years after Aggrey's death, his plea for the Christianization of Africa was substantially closer to fulfillment. Much credit for that progress belongs to men like Aggrey and David Kaunda, Tonga Presbyterian headmaster of a pioneer mission school among the Bemba of Zambia. Kaunda's Christian convictions and zeal to spread Christianity were profoundly influential. His son, Kenneth Kaunda, President of Zambia, is one of several African statesmen whose political philosophies were shaped in Christian homes and institutions. The main burden of the progress of the Christian gospel in Africa, however, rested with men and women who lacked the educational qualifications of James Aggrey and David Kaunda. The vast majority of the dedicated and devout pioneer African evangelists will never be known.

One response by Africans to the missionary assault on traditional African religion and culture was the founding of independent Christian churches. The phenomenon appeared as early as 1819 in Sierra Leone, and gained momentum in Nigeria. At about the same time, at the end of the 19th Century, the movement started spontaneously and for varying reasons in South Africa, Cameroon, and elsewhere. Since the 1920s the phenomenon has appeared practically throughout the continent, and today embraces some 6,000 churches, millions of Christians and a vast literature. The independent Christian churches tend to have colorful, even exotic, names. Scholars describe them in many terms (for example, schismatic, sectarian, secessionist, heretical, dissident, quasi-Christian, post-Christian) which are often inaccurate and value-charged. Here we refer to them simply as independent churches, or Zionist and Ethiopian churches.

Some of these churches, particularly the first ones, broke from mission churches exclusively over the issue of congregational self-government. These churches generally mirrored their parent bodies on matters of church organization, worship, and belief. Some, notably in South Africa, received official recognition which permitted them to obtain land for schools and churches and allowed their ministers to perform marriages and other civil functions. Such permission was an outlet for the very profound frustrations of Africans over land questions, social relations between whites and blacks, the failure of missions to advance Africans to positions of genuine leadership. These churches posed little threat to the prevailing political order.

*Leaders of the African Independent Churches.* The great majority of the independent churches, especially those which did not originate in a break from the mission congregations, gathered around charismatic prophets and healers. Their followers' religious activity (physical trances, speaking in tongues, fasting and purification rites, careful observance of the Ten Commandments, baptism by immersion) also derived from contact with missionaries of various Pentecostal and faith groups; with Adventists and Jehovah's Witnesses who stressed Sabbath observance and millennial or apocalyptic expectation; and with black Americans such as the African Methodist Episcopal Bishop Henry M. Turner. The current of religious independency ran deep throughout Africa, and it aroused the suspicions of missionaries and colonial authorities alike.

Missionary critics tended to focus on deviation from patterns of Christian living in the West, for example, on the issue of polygamy. Western Christians have perceived in the independent churches a genuine movement of adapting Christianity to Africa, and have tended to blame missionary failure to express genuine Christian love for the African as the root cause of the phenomenon. As for the colonial critics, they tended to focus on the increase in nationalist sentiment, and either suppressed or drove underground many of the movements. This reaction against the independent churches as centers of potential political opposition continues to characterize the treatment of independent Christians by contemporary black African leaders, so that independent African Christians rarely articulate views on economic, political, or social issues. Sensing the essentially spiritual needs of their followers, the prophets, healers, and pastors have concentrated on an essentially spiritual message.

In short, the transplanted roots of Christianity began to take hold in African soil as a divergent but distinct species by the 1920s, largely through the work of missionaries from Western nations, African church leaders and parishioners, and independent prophets, healers, and adherents. African Christianity has been in the forefront among changes that have swept the continent in the last 50 years. Today, most of the mission bodies have granted full autonomy to the African churches, and the principle of independence, first articulated by missionary theorists over a century ago, has come full cycle. No less a spokesman for the universal church than Pope Paul VI celebrated this development in 1969, in speaking to African Christians at Kampala, Uganda, on the occasion of the dedication of a shrine to martyrs of the religious wars of the missionary period of African church history. The Pope declared, "You are missionaries to yourselves now. The Church of Christ is well and truly planted, suited to the tongue, the style, the character and the genius of the one who professes it."

*The Amalgamation of Christianity in African Churches.* The churches of Africa illustrate both the universality and particularity of the Christian religion. Balance between universality and particularity has often been difficult or even impossible to maintain. Thus, Cardinal Malula of Zaire had to go into temporary exile after challenging President Mobutu at the start of an "authenticity" campaign which required that Christians abandon baptized names, the celebration of Christmas, and catechetical instruction. In this instance, a distinguished African churchman believed there was danger to a principle integral to Christianity—Peter's injunction in Acts 5:29 that God rather than men ought to be obeyed. Similarly, many African Christians would object to consideration, in the following section of this Capsule View, of Isaiah Shembe as a representative of Zulu Zion. In this instance, Shembe's African critics are motivated by charges that Shembe is insufficiently Biblical and Christian. Their objection may or may not be valid, but there are definite reasons to examine Shembe's career. Not only is he one of Africa's best-known prophets, but his Church of the Nazarites brings into sharp focus the capacity of Christians to relate their faith to their cultural context without endangering their claim to being genuinely Christian.

## Zulu Zion

A century ago, Christianity had its strongest foothold among black Africans in the south. Dutch settlers arrived at the Cape in 1652, and the question of whether slave children should be baptized or not came up shortly thereafter. Some whites believed that indiscriminate use of the rite disgraced the name of Christ, but in 1665 the practice of baptizing black, Malay, and mixed children was adopted by ministers of the Dutch Reformed Church. For over a century, this denomination had a virtual monopoly on the religious life of the small white communities in South Africa, even though French, German, and other white immigrants began to arrive. The start of Moravian missionary activity early in the 18th Century broke this monopoly, but the Moravian Brethren, as well as the Anglican, Congregationalist, Lutheran, and Methodist missionaries who arrived in increasing numbers during the 19th Century, were more concerned with the unevangelized Bushmen, Hottentot, and Bantu-speaking peoples than with the white population. Famous missionaries such as John Philip, Johannes Theodore Vanderkemp, Robert Moffatt, and David Livingstone began to explore the vast southern African interior and opened stations to minister to the Griqua, Sotho, Tswana, Xhosa, and other peoples. Finally, the great trek of the Boer descendants of the first Dutch settlers, fleeing from British rule at the Cape in the late 1830s, brought whites into sustained relationship with the Xhosa, Zulu, and others.

White South African historians have generally described the wars of conquest of the Zulu as wars of liberating the Zulu from tyrannical rulers and freeing southern Africa from the menace of paganism. But the role of Christian missionaries in the conquest of the Zulu weighs heavily upon the Christian Church. Since the early part of the 20th Century the cry of the Zulu has been for the realization of God's promised blessing to the sons and daughters of Zion.

**The Zionist and Ethiopian Churches in Zulu Africa.**   Although the rise of independent Christian churches was by no means an exclusively Zulu or South African phenomenon, Zululand provided an especially favorable setting for the proliferation of Zionist and Ethiopian churches. A number of factors contributed to the success of Zulu prophets, healers, and other religious authorities in recruiting members to independent Christian churches. These factors included the failure of mission churches to minister adequately to blacks who experienced serious social dislocations as South Africa was industrialized and urbanized; the appropriation of black lands by whites; the establishment of a rigid color bar; the conspicuous denominational fragmentation of the mission churches themselves, especially as black American, Pentecostal, Adventist, and other missionaries undertook work in South Africa; and nationalist aspirations of the Zulu, who believed that Africa should be for the African.

*The Establishment of Independent Churches in South Africa.* The first schism which resulted in the establishment of an independent church in southern Africa was that of a Thembu, Nehemiah Tile, in 1883. Tile was an articulate, charismatic Methodist evangelist. He came into conflict with his white superior over his alleged political activity among the Thembu. Tile enjoyed a close, personal relationship with the Thembu paramount chief, Ngangeliswe, and when Tile left the mission church and founded his own church he attributed cosmic, religious significance to Ngangeliswe's supremacy. The establishing of a specifically Thembu church was immediately followed by intensification of Thembu political activity, including the signing of petitions protesting the intrusion of white magistrates into Thembu affairs and the imposition of onerous taxes. Tile's fame spread when southern African officials illegally arrested and subsequently released him, but the popularity of his movement waned after his death in 1891.

The significance of Tile's success in creating an independent political-religious movement was not, however, lost on other South Africans. A number of black evangelists and pastors undertook independent initiatives in political and religious spheres of activity. The idea that black African Christians should be free at least to worship as they pleased received legitimacy and other support from the black American churches and colleges, with which increasing numbers of South African blacks were familiar. In 1898 Bishop Henry M. Turner of the African Methodist Episcopal Church visited South Africa and ordained 65 black ministers of congregations in which the presence of whites was conspicuously absent. Even white ministers contributed to the ferment. Petrus Louis Le Roux, Edgar Mahon, and other ministers of the major Protestant churches, influenced by such diverse sources as the Revivalist and Pentecostal writings of Andrew Murray, the Salvation Army, and John Alexander Dowie's Christian Catholic Apostolic Church (founded in 1896 with headquarters at Zion, Illinois, near Chicago) broke with the mainline mission churches to establish their own denominations.

*The Perceived Nature of Zulu Christianity.* In 1905-1906 disturbances swept Zululand. The specific Zulu grievance concerned new taxes. Unrest incited the killing of white animals—white pigs, goats, and chickens—and an incident in which a small group of armed Africans shot at the police. Although virtually no Christians participated in the various protests, the fact that a few petitioners were members of two Zionist churches—the Zulu Congregational Church (founded 1896) and the African Presbyterian Church (founded 1898)—awakened white suspicion and hostility far beyond any danger the crisis actually posed. Especially ominous to whites was the fusing in Zionist sermons of two Biblical themes, those of the suffering servant and of the servant people. Thus, when white armies ruthlessly killed more than 3,000 blacks, Zionist pastors consoled their people by citing an Old Testament text, Deuteronomy 18:15, in their message: "The Lord thy God will raise up unto thee a Prophet from the midst of thee, of thy brethren, like unto me; unto him shall ye hearken." In the context of these and other troubles, the promise of a new Jerusalem, a new Eden, had found a new home in Zulu Zion.

During this time of affliction and rapid social change, the vast majority of Zulu practiced their traditional religion. This included vague recognition of God and lesser deities, but the vitality of Zulu religion centered in man's close relationship with the living dead (also called ancestors or shades) and departed chiefs and kings; in the diagnosis and cure of illness, impotence, and hardship; in rituals which facilitated transitions through the life cycle; and in resisting evil and manipulators of evil such as witches and sorcerers. The appeal of religious authorities such as Nehemiah Tile and the first Zionist pastors rested as much in their attention to such traditional concerns—communion of the living with the dead, healing, becoming mature men and women, purity, and danger—as in their advocacy of African rights or of a particular line of Christian thought. Thus it was that recognition of Isaiah Shembe's skills as a mediator between the living and the dead, as a healer, as a ritualist, and as a powerful foe of evil-doers distinguished him among Africa's religious leaders. Moreover, Shembe, who lived from about 1870 to 1935, was the person who, more than any other, reminded the Zulu of the promised Prophet of Deuteronomy.

One of the most serious difficulties characteristic of new religious groups is to ensure the ongoing life of the movement after the death of the original leader. The vast majority of Zulu Zionist churches either have not survived the death of the founder or have collapsed through a succession of schisms and leadership disputes. The transitory tendencies of these churches are the result of numerous factors, including overt opposition by missionary or political authorities and the nature of the appeal of charismatic figures who rely more on personality, life-style, and zeal than on bureaucratic skills to recruit followers. Isaiah Shembe again differed from other Zionist prophets by taking several steps during his lifetime to ensure an orderly devolution of leadership. He organized a church, trained fellow ministers, wrote hymns which were later collected and published, and, most importantly, provided for the education of his son, Johannes Galilee Shembe, who was born in 1904 and died in December, 1976.

Displaying many of the same gifts as his father, Johannes Galilee Shembe nevertheless communicated a sense of unworthiness to bear God's witness in the world, and a sense of sadness that he was not the equal of his father. Quiet, thoughtful, profoundly spiritual, Johannes Galilee Shembe won the respect of Nazarite church members and other Zulu as well, not only because he was his father's son but also because he demonstrated spiritual authority on his own and the particular skills of the modern, university-trained administrator, healer, judge, and pastor. Johannes Galilee Shembe frequently lamented that none of his sons appeared able to assume the mantle of leadership of the Church of the Nazarites. Whether or not Shembe will have successfully dealt with the problem of succession, as did his father, remains to be seen.

As this brief profile suggests, both Shembe and his father came to occupy dual roles: as prominent Zulu leaders, they won the devotion formerly directed to Zulu chiefs and kings; and as prominent religious leaders, they shepherded their flocks. Neither desired to enter the political arena, with the result that white authorities never interfered with their work. Like the great majority of religious Zulus, Isaiah and Johannes Galilee Shembe simply wanted religious independence. As Johannes Galilee Shembe put it, "The great African fault is imitation; we tend to give up everything to go with the Europeans."

## Conclusion

These short sketches of the rooting of Christianity in black Africa and of Zulu Zion have attempted to demonstrate two points. First, much of what Westerners consider essential to Christianity may be quite peripheral to Christians in another cultural setting. Many African and Western Christians, and even many African Zionists themselves, regard the Nazarites and other churches of Zulu Zion as non-Christian. This may be because these churches appear to have virtually no Christology, or because they give the impression that adulation granted to an Isaiah Shembe, for example, restores pagan Zulu practice. There are varied interpretations of such differences.

Second, African Christians have always affirmed that all baptized in Christ are without distinction, between Jew and Greek, slave and free, male and female. The conviction of Christian freedom has long animated the principle of religious independence on the part of African churches. Pope Paul VI's words to the African hierarchy gathered at Kampala in 1969—"You may, and you must, have an African Christianity"—cut to the core of the process by which African Christians have taken the name of Christ as their own.

## STUDY QUESTIONS

The following study questions will help organize your thoughts after you have read the Capsule View on Zulu Zion by Paul Dekar. Think through each question completely before checking your answers against the material in this Student's Guide.

1. Why did missionaries dominate church life in Africa between 1875 and 1925?

2. Because missionary work between 1875 and 1925 centers in educational, agricultural, and medical work more frequently than on evangelism, what effect did this have on African converts?

3. What two alternatives did the Africans appear to take to the massive assault by missionaries on traditional African religion and culture?

4. Even though indigenous African clergy were not to guide an indigenous African church after 1875, what events offer evidence of the faithfulness of Africans to Christianity?

5. Explain how the founding of independent Christian churches was another response by Africans to the missionary assault on traditional African religions and culture.

6. What was the effect on secular authorities and missionaries alike when the independent churches began to gather around charismatic prophets and healers?

7. What is the result today of this reaction against the independent churches as centers of potential political opposition?

8. How do the churches of Africa illustrate both the universality and particularity of the Christian religion?

9. In what ways can the current race situation in South Africa be partly explained in terms of the founding of the Zulu kingdom at the same time that white descendants of the first Dutch settlers began to move inland to escape British rule?

10. Why does the role of the missionaries in the conquests of the Zulu weigh heavily upon the Christian Church?

11. What factors contributed to the success of Zulu prophets, healers, and other religious authorities in recruiting members to independent Christian churches?

12. What was the significance of Nehemiah Tile's success in creating an independent political-religious movement in southern Africa in 1883?

13. In what context did the promise of a New Jerusalem, a new Eden, find a home in Zulu Zion in the early 20th Century?

14. How did Zulu Zionism combine Christianity with traditional African religions?

15. For what reason does Isaiah Shembe stand out among the leaders of Zulu Zion?

16. How did Isaiah Shembe ensure that his religious movement would continue after his death?

17. What was the one overriding factor wanted by both Isaiah Shembe and his son, Johannes Galilee Shembe?

18. What answer is given to critics who say that the churches of Zulu Zion are pagan?

19. What is the one tenet in Christianity that appeals to Africans, especially now in their move for independence?

## AS YOU VIEW

Another perspective on African faiths is provided by the television episode *African Religions: Zulu Zion*. To organize your thoughts in advance, study the program description below, and review the guiding questions based on "Viewing with a Purpose" at the end of the Guide. This will help you to participate more actively in the viewing experience.

This episode explores the black African response to the stimulus of Christianity. It examines the Zulu Independent Churches of southern Africa. When Christian missionaries took the gospel to Africa they also took the European culture. The attempt was made to suppress African religion. But since World War I, and with increasing vigor in the past 20 years, Africans have been rediscovering this lost religious culture. It has taken the form of independent churches with their own festivals, prophets, and rituals, and with a greater or lesser degree of devotion to Christ. One of the biggest independent church movements in southern Africa is the Zulu Shembe movement founded by Isaiah Shembe, who became its Prophet before World War I. His son, who succeeded him as Prophet, died just before Christmas, 1976. One of the questions addressed is whether or not the Shembe movement, with its emphasis on the Old Testament, should be represented as a Zionist church.

# QUESTIONS FOR THOUGHT

The following questions cover concerns or points of interest related to Zulu Zion and African traditional religions. They are intended to help extend your thinking about what you have learned.

1. What would African Christianity be today without the missionary zeal in the period between 1875 and 1925?

2. In what ways has Christianity amalgamated the beliefs and practices of other religions as it has done with the African traditional religious practices and beliefs of the Zulu?

3. How do you account for the fact that Hinduism is not a common religion on the African continent even though one of its major tenets is tolerance of other religious beliefs?

4. Would African religions, especially African Christianity, be any different today if the nations of Africa had remained under colonial rule?

5. What evidence have you seen of indigenous African religious influences on the religious beliefs of African-Americans? Have African-Americans influenced traditional African religions?

# TO EXTEND YOUR STUDY

The following books represent a sampler of some of the most engaging, recent literature on religion in black Africa, particularly African Christianity. Use them as a reference point and starting place to continue your study of religions in Africa.

Berglund, Axel-Ivar, *Zulu Thought-Patterns and Symbolism* (London: C. Hurst & Co., 1976)
> Enhanced by illustrations and informants' commentaries, this book will surely become a classic in the study of religion. Born and raised in Zululand, Berglund presents probably as accurate an account of an African religious system as is possible by an outsider.

Hastings, Adrian, *African Christianity. An Essay in Interpretation* (London: Geoffrey Chapman, 1976)

> A widely-known Roman Catholic priest with excellent ecumenical credentials, Hastings provides a lively, short introduction to the history and contemporary concerns of African churches.

Jules-Rosette, Bennetta, *African Apostles, Ritual and Conversion in the Church of John Maranke* (Ithaca, N.Y.: Cornell University Press, 1975)

> One of the best case studies of an independent African church, this book demonstrates the missionary zeal of African Christians. Jules-Rosette and her husband were converted to the Bapostolo Church. The last chapter of the book describes their activities in proselyting in the United States.

Mbiti, John, *The Prayers of African Religion* (Maryknoll, New York: Obis Books, 1975)

> Africa's best-known Christian theologian, Mbiti introduces an important dimension of African religion. The texts of more than 300 prayers reveal African insights and attitudes toward such themes as the nature of God and man, sin and thanksgiving.

Moorhouse, Geoffrey, *The Missionaries* (London: Eyre Methuen, 1973)

> A journalist, Moorhouse knows how to tell a good story without compromising historical accuracy. The book concentrates on the achievements of 19th Century pioneers such as Anna and David Hinderer, David Livingstone, and Cardinal Lavigerie.

Sundkler, Bengt, *Bantu Prophets in South Africa* (London: Oxford University Press, 1961) and *Zulu Zion and Some Swazi Zionists* (London: Oxford University Press, 1976)

> Originally published in 1948, Sundkler's first book broke new ground in presenting an accurate and sympathetic account of the independent churches of southern Africa. The second book provides valuable biographies of leaders of Zulu churches, including Isaiah and Johannes Galilee Shembe, as well as texts of hymns, prayers, and diaries.

Taylor, John V., *The Primal Vision. Christian Presence Amid African Religion* (Philadelphia: Fortress Press, 1963)

> An Anglican bishop and former missionary to eastern Africa, Taylor successfully brings Christianity into dialogue with traditional African religion.

West, Martin, *Bishops and Prophets in Black City* (New York: International Publications Service, 1976)

# ANOTHER DIMENSION TO
# ZULU CHRISTIANITY

*by*

Dr. Yosef ben-Jochannan
*African Studies and Research Center, Cornell University*
*and*
*Malcolm-King College*

Zulu Christianity is an amalgamation of the religions and cultures of three continents: Africa, Asia, and Europe. It is necessary to establish the same perspective for study as the perspective of people who live this religious experience. In this, another dimension of Zulu Christianity, you will be provided with a semantic frame of reference for your study. You will then focus briefly on the African roots of the Judeo-Christian-Islamic tradition. From there you will study the characteristics of a traditional African religion. Only then will it be possible to study the amalgamation of traditional African religion and the Judeo-Christian-Islamic tradition in Zulu Christianity.

## A Semantic Frame of Reference for Your Study

Before you enter into the study of any African religion, you should first be in the correct frame of mind. You should be circumspect about the terminology used as references to African traditional religion. Such a religion has been called everything from animism to fetishism. Neither term correctly describes the religious experience of the African people.

The word "fetish" is the cause of most, if not all, of the religious bigotry directed against African traditional religions. Yet its origin dates back only to the 17th Century, with the arrival of the first Europeans—the Portuguese—in Fete on the Gold Coast of western Africa. Noting that the indigenous Africans venerated trees, plants, idols, beasts, birds, fish, and even pebbles, much like spirits, the Portuguese called this "feitico," or "charm." This Portuguese derivative from the Latin "factitus" was to become further Anglicized to "fetish." The French, not wanting to be left out of this anthropological metamorphosis, added their own version and called it "faitis," which in English means "well-made" or "beautiful."

**53**

When the term is used today, however, it is most frequently in a derogatory way.

This all led to "fetichisme"—a term used for the African worship of terrestrial and material objects. Eventually it came to mean the general acts of primitive religions, with all external objects regarded as animated by a life that is analogous to that of humans. Now fetischisme," too, has been abandoned for the more modern word "animism," which is used in most of the non-African writings on African traditional religions.

Together with the use of other terms such as paganism, primitive, civilized, savage, and tribe, the use of fetichisme and animism has helped to create a religious bigotry toward African traditional religions.

## A Common Base for Study—What or Who Is God?

E. Bolaji Idowu, in his book *African Traditional Religion: A Definition,* offered this definition of religion and God:

> Religion results from man's spontaneous awareness of, and spontaneous reaction to his immediate awareness of a living Power, "wholly other" and infinitely greater than himself; a Power mysterious because unseen, yet a present and urgent reality, seeking to bring man into communion with Himself. This awareness includes that of something reaching out from the depths of man's being for close communion with, and vital relationship to this Power as a source of real life.

But, is it "god" or "God"? Is it a personified deity? Or is it Force? In the Zulu nation there is a belief in an all-encompassing Force. It is from this base that the religious experiences of this people grow. Any understanding of another religion comes through knowing the frame of reference of those people who believe in and experience that religion. You will not understand Zulu Christianity if you study it from only the Judeo-Christian-Islamic point of view. An exploration of the faith and tradition in the indigenous African experiences and beliefs will be helpful.

## The African Roots of the Judeo-Christian-Islamic Tradition

Rome and Greece were cultural centers for a heterogeneous group of people. They were the homelands of races or ethnic groups from many nations and three continents—Africa, Asia, and Europe. For example, Paul was a Roman citizen, yet he was a Hebrew. Seneca, the philosopher of politics, was a Spaniard. Lucius Septimius Severus, who became Emperor of Rome, was an indigenous African. His son, Caracalla, was of African and Asian parentage. Thousands of Africans of Rome made history during the Christian era. There were countless others, not so well-known, who were products of ordinary marriages and common-law relationships among Europeans, Asians, and Africans in Rome and Greece before and during the Christian era.

The entire world of Christendom owes its greatest successes, in part, to many indigenous Africans for their contributions before and during the Christian era. The first martyrs of Christendom were indigenous Africans, the first being Nymphamo. Tertullian, the first of the Church writers who made Latin the language of Christianity, was also an indigenous African. Likewise were Cyprian, who was bishop and martyr, and Augustine, one of the most famous of the "Fathers of the Church."

This African heritage has been almost lost as part of the Judeo-Christian-Islamic tradition, which has for centuries suffered from the cultural genocide that ethnocentrism brings to religion. Africans have suffered not only from colonialism but also from the reaction to colonialism. In the takeover of Christianity by the Roman Empire in 325 A.D. at the Conference of Bishops in Nicaea, the Africans were removed from positions of leadership and all the historic achievements of the African Christians were suppressed. African bishops and patriarchs (the first for the new religion that became known as "Christianity" at the Council of Antioch in 212 A.D.) were amalgamated into the European ethnocentrism that became part of European Christianity. The African Christian's Black Madonna and Child were replaced by the White Madonna and Child, a more comfortable image to European Christians.

Unlike other forms of Christianity, Zulu Christianity cannot be studied as a separate entity. One cannot avoid looking at Coptic Christianity in Ethiopia, that predated Roman Catholic Christianity by at least 124 years. Ethiopia "officially" became a Christian nation in about 188 A.D.; whereas Rome became "officially" Christian in about 312 A.D. when Emperor Constantine dropped his "divine symbols" and adopted Christianity.

It would be virtually impossible to avoid this aspect of Christian Church history and still be able to explain adequately why Zulu Christianity differs as much as it does from Protestant Christianity and Roman Catholicism. Cultural and ethnic considerations influence religion as much as they influence any other human endeavor.

Religions do not drop out of the sky; they go through historical evolution and revolution. Christianity is an outgrowth of Judaism, as much as Islam is an outgrowth of Christianity. But Judaism is itself an outgrowth of the religions of the Nile Valley and the Great Lakes regions of Africa. Thus, Zulu Christianity is also an outgrowth of an amalgamation of traditional African religion and the principles and beliefs of Christianity.

## An African Traditional Religion

It is wrong to assume that African religious concepts are invalid if they differ from Judeo-Christian theology. It is also erroneous to believe that African religions do not provide for Africans the type of closeness with their deity that the Christian experience provides for others. To understand this aspect of African religion, it is necessary to examine another type of African religious experience that is as much traditional to Africa and Africans as is the Judeo-Christian-Islamic tradition.

In any religion, beyond the basic concepts, we generally seek to examine how a religion functions. The African traditional religion in the past used, as it does in the present, rituals and rites to come into contact with the God of their universe. This universe has two worlds: the world of the living and the world of the ancestors. These are not necessarily the physical and nonphysical worlds. The world of the ancestors is, in fact, a theosophical dimension. The rites and rituals must have symbols or talismans to invoke the force of deity. There is no written scripture, so symbols and signs become the major focus of religious functions.

*Historic and Geographic Setting.* The Nile Valley and Great Lakes regions of Africa are the original site of a major African religion. Three branches grew out of it, as the Africans who created it migrated north, east, and west from their original geographic location. In this religious experience you can discover a new understanding of what God means to another group of people.

The original grouping, or national entity, is known as the Twa. The national groupings to the north are the Ta-Merrians (referred to by the ancient Greeks and Romans as Aegyptians). And the last branch or grouping call themselves Yorubas; those to the east are the Agikuyu and those to the south are the Amazulu.

*Major Concepts of the Religion.*  The religion which grew up in this region of Africa is not named for any godhead or spirit. The original Africans who created this religion based their faith on the following principles:

There is a supreme Force that created everything.

Good and bad are only extreme expressions of the Force's law of opposites.

All living things, that feel as humans do, have a redeemable quality.

The ultimate cause (death) is only another stage in the order of the Force.

These principles that originated in the teachings of the Twa of central Africa are found in the teachings of Pharaoh Amenhotep IV, who lived in the Eighteenth Dynasty, about 1350 B.C. It is believed that the ancient Egyptians migrated from central Africa and may have been influenced by the principles of this traditional African religion. In the Papyrus of Hunefer it states, "We came from the beginning of the headwaters of the Nile where God Hapi dwells at the foothills of the Mountain of the Moon." The beginning of the Nile is in Uganda, in central Africa. The "Mountain of the Moon" means "Kilimanjaro," which is located in Tanganyika.

*Concept of God.*  More than 40,000 years ago the Twa people created a concept of "God" with rituals, rites, and symbols that became the fundamental theosophical basis of many religions throughout the African continent.

The "Greatest Creator of all, the Unknown" is the only name by which the Twas referred to their deity, called *Ngai* in Kenya, *Aten* in Egypt, and *Olodumare* in Nigeria.

The Twas believe today, as their ancestors did thousands of years ago, that there is one all-encompassing Force that made everything. Here is a fundamental principle not in Judaism, Christianity, or Islam: the belief in a "Force" as a Creator rather than in a "God" who once assumed human form. To the Twa, the deity is neither male, female, nor thing. It has no shape, no description, other than a "Force." The Twas conceived of this Force as a power beyond all comprehension and thus impossible to be given a name, shape, or sex.

*Belief in Two Worlds.* The Twas believe that this Force created two worlds: one for the living, and one for the ancestors; and that these worlds did not have a beginning and will not have an ending. This concept differs from Judaism, Christianity, and Islam.

In the world of the living, we cannot physically visualize the world of the ancestors. There is, therefore, no physical description of afterlife in the world of the ancestors in the Twa theosophy. It is not heaven or hell. It is the place where life continues in another dimension. At the same time, the Twas believe that ancestral beings are always in their presence. This is why Twas provide food for their ancestors and make libations while invoking the intercession of ancestors with the Force.

It is one thing to recite rituals and participate in rites, but it is another to practice them in reality. The Twas practice their religion as a way of life. Each belief is put into daily life. Fertility rites and rituals are always the very first of the many a Twa child must learn. But here too, there is no separation between religion and secular functions in any Twa, Yoruba, or Agikuyu society. There is nothing that is religious that is not equally secular. Thus, there is no sabbath or special sacred day; at least not for the benefit of the Force. The Force needs no prayer from anyone to continue its existence. And since the Force gives nothing physically, and asks for nothing, there is no penalty or reward to be expected in the "world of the living" or in the "world of the ancestors."

*Changes in the Religion as It Migrated to Other Parts of Africa.* What we have been examining thus far is the original theosophical foundation of the Twas' religion. We must now examine how it changed as it arrived in places such as Kenya, Nigeria, and Egypt.

Among the Yorubas in Nigeria we find the Force has the name Olurum or Olodumare. The Force is recognized here as being the most powerful of all divinities. Across the entire continent of Africa, among the Agikuyu, we find this same Force under the name Ngai. The official resting place of Ngai is the "Mountain of Brightness"—the same "Mountain of the Moon" which is the home of God Hapi in the Egyptian religion.

The fundamental concepts of this traditional religion were carried by missionaries from Africa to other lands. As they spread, they changed in different environments. The ethnocentrism of each country also contributed to the alteration.

Signs and symbols of this ancient African religion are familiar. The gramadon is similar to the swastika. The ankh is similar to the cross. The Dog Star of the Four Corners, or Tuat, is similar to the Star of David.

## Zulu Christianity

Although Zulu Christianity was dedicated to the fundamental Christian doctrines and to the teachings of Jesus as "the Christ," it had to adopt local cultural and ethnic values that had existed for hundreds of years before organized Christianity came into southern Africa. This fact is vital to an understanding of the nature of Zulu Christianity today.

Western Christians should have anticipated the cultural revolution that was a natural result of Africans' winning their independence. To expect that African Christians would continue using the same "white Jesus" in their all-black churches was irrational. Zulu Christianity has begun to deal with this type of unreasonable expectation. In the future it will have to face criticism even from traditional African Christians, who will protest Zulu Christianity in much the same way they protested the violence used by African nationalists fighting to free Africa of colonialism. These traditional African Christians never once raised their voices against the colonialists until years of struggle, death, and destruction finally brought freedom and independence to certain African nations. Thus, as we move further into this mixed type of Uzulu philosophical concepts and European-style Christian concepts which we are now calling "Zulu Christianity," it is important to remember all the factors which brought the various forms of Christianity to northern Africa.

Is it at all possible that any Uzulu born and raised in the tradition of the Amazulu nation could in a few generations or more suppress his beliefs solely because he has been subjected to a set of religious doctrines created and developed by other people of a culture foreign to his own? Apply this question to American historical circumstance. How would European-Americans of the Christian faith react if they were forced to accept any of the American Indian religions, assuming the Indians had won the American-Indian wars?

In the setting of a Christian Church, an Uzulu must behave very differently than he does in his village. For example, the socio-political factors in the Christian church even denude the Uzulu male of his *induku* (carrying stick). This may seem unimportant, or perhaps even a little ridiculous, but it still is one of the many reasons why an Uzulu man will keep away from the Christian church, sometimes to his own economic hardship. An Uzulu who is unable to take his *induku* with him into church, or even walk with it on the Sabbath, considers himself nude; not nude in the sense that he is physically without clothing but nude in the sense that something that is part of his dress is denied him. He used his *induku* to ward off enemies, protect his family, kill snakes, and even enforce authority among the young. The *induku* may have been a possession of the Uzulu male for as long as the Amazulu nation has existed.

Practical things cannot be separated from religious obligations in the Amazulu nation in the same way that the Judeo-Christian society can separate the secular from the religious.


## STUDY QUESTIONS

These study questions will help you organize your thoughts and assess your understanding of this dimension of an African traditional religion. Think through each question completely before you check your answers against the material in this Student's Guide.

1. Based on the derivation of the word "animism," why is it not appropriate to apply it to Zulu Christianity?

2. Who were some of the early leaders in the Judeo-Christian world who were indigenous Africans?

3. In his paper, Dr. ben-Jochannan maintains that Africa suffered not only from colonialism but from the *reaction* to colonialism. What does he mean by that statement?

4. Why did early Christians discard the African Black Madonna and Child in favor of a White Madonna and Child?

5. Zulu Christianity is said to be an amalgamation of what two major religious experiences or faiths?

6. Indicate on a map of Africa where the African traditional religion discussed in this paper originated and where its three branches carried it.

7. What are the four major concepts of the Twa religion?

8. What evidence does Dr. ben-Jochannan advance that the religions of ancient Egypt may have had their roots in this traditional religion of central Africa?

9. The Twas refer to their deity as "The Force." What or who did this deity become in Kenya? What or who in Egypt? What or who in Nigeria?

10. How does the "world of ancestors" in the African traditional religion differ from the Judeo-Christian concept of afterlife?

11. In what ways is it more difficult for the Twa to distinguish between religious and secular than it is for someone in the Judeo-Christian tradition?

12. Why is there no sabbath in the Twa traditional African religion?

13. What forces in Zulu Christianity beliefs and practices are moving people away from the church?

14. In what ways is the Amazulu relation to their deity different from the European Christian's relation to their God?

# Chapter 3

# THREE HUNDRED AND THIRTY MILLION GODS

## A STUDY OF HINDUISM

Hinduism describes the loosely knit cults and beliefs of the majority of people in the Indian subcontinent. It can be considered a group of religions held together by certain shared features. Its ability to weave together different forms of religion and spirituality is unique. Hinduism operates within the social structure of a caste system in which the Brahmans are dominant. Sanskrit, the language of the Brahmans, is the vehicle of the scriptures and other sacred writings. Rebirth or reincarnation is accepted as a logical way to progress through the caste stages in various lifetimes. The stages of development within a person's lifetime are also described in Hinduism. The Hindu theme of "diversity in unity" is a way of approaching all religions, since for the Hindu they all point to the same Truth.

Hinduism has provided the social framework for Indian democracy, and, to some extent, has spread into other cultures. Through its adaptability and devotional power, Hinduism will continue to generate new forms of faith relevant to the scientific thought and social changes of the late 20th Century.

## A PREFACE TO YOUR STUDY

Your lesson begins with an outline of the major points of Hinduism. Use these concepts to focus your study of both the print and television materials.

Next, a capsule view of Hinduism is provided by Dr. Seymour Fersh, College of Education, Fairleigh Dickinson University. Dr. Fersh describes five features of Hinduism that characterize it as religious and social forces for a large part of the Indian subcontinent.

Use this capsule view of Hinduism as a reference for your study throughout this lesson.

You can continue your study of Hinduism by reading pages 14-89 in *The Religions of Man* by Huston Smith.

Another perspective on Hinduism will be revealed in the program "Three Hundred and Thirty Million Gods" from the television series "The Long Search."

Another dimension of the religions of India is provided by Dr. Fersh in an examination of the Jains, Parsees, and Sikhs. In this material included for your continued study, you can see more clearly how religious tolerance is in harmony with the Hindu belief.

The Questions for Thought provide issues and concepts related to Hinduism which you will want to consider in applying what you have learned.

## IMPORTANT CONCEPTS

The major points of Hindu theology and life include the adaptability of Hinduism, Hindu social groups, reincarnation, life stages, yoga techniques, and the nature of the scriptures. Take special note of these in the brief outline which follows.

You will find it easier to remember the major concepts of Hinduism if you compare them to what you know and will study about other religions.

*Adaptability of Hinduism.* More than most religions, Hinduism is able to accept new creeds without considering them necessarily a threat to established doctrines.

*Hindu Social Groups.* A caste system divides the Hindu population into hereditary social groups, each having its own specific code of prescribed behavior.

*Hindu Reincarnation.*   The doctrine of reincarnation affirms that humans are born, die, and are reborn in a continuing series of life cycles seeking ultimate release from the burden of rebirth.

*Hindu Life Stages.*   The Hindu believes in four stages of development within each lifetime—childhood, marriage, and beginning a family; maintaining and safeguarding the family; retirement from family and worldly responsibilities; and finally becoming a casteless, wandering ascetic, thinking only of God.

*Hindu Scriptures.*   The basic scriptures of Hinduism retain a direct hold on the individual, and their factual reliability is widely and profoundly accepted.


## A CAPSULE VIEW OF HINDUISM

Hinduism, as with most religions, describes the nature of God and the relationship of God to humankind. The social order, in the case of Hinduism a caste system, is derived from the sacred teachings. Within the caste system, each Hindu may proceed upward through a series of reincarnations seeking release from the burden of rebirth, and in each lifetime ideally proceeds through four stages of personal development. Together with a description of the Hindu scriptures, this capsule view will deal with these aspects of Hinduism.

### The Hindu Ideology

Unlike Judaism, Christianity, and Islam, Hinduism is not associated with a personal founder. It is not a revealed religion in the sense of having received its scriptures from a prophet or a divinity. There is no church official who describes what is right and what is wrong in Hinduism.

Hindus believe in the divine intervention of God in the affairs of humankind—not once or twice but many times, in the form of continuing incarnations. Hindus easily believe, therefore, that Moses or Jesus or Mohammed was heaven-sent, as their own Rama or

Krishna. Thus, many Hindus may accept new insights from other religions, but think it totally unnecessary to change their ancestral religious affiliations. New teachings do not replace the old ones; they are merely added to them.

Gandhi was a devout Hindu, for example, but he liked to learn about other religions and once said to Christian missionaries, "I do not want my house to be walled in on all sides and my windows to be stuffed. I want the cultures of all lands to be blown about my house, as freely as possible. But I refuse to be blown off my feet by any."

**The Caste System**

Indian life, especially in the villages where most of the population lives, cannot be understood without knowledge of the Hindu caste system. There are four general orders of varnas (social classes) from which more than 2,000 castes have evolved—each with its own specific code of behavior affecting one's marriage, occupation, social ranking, and social privileges and obligations.

Of the four general orders of varnas (social classes), the three highest are *Brahman* (priest), *Kshatriya* (warrior), and *Vaishya* (merchant). Only boys from these orders are eligible to undergo the "sacred thread," a significant Hindu initiation ceremony for adolescents. The fourth order is *Shudra* (laborer). Outside these classes is a fifth group, ranked lowest of all, variously referred to as "untouchables," "outcastes," or (by Gandhi) as *Harijans,* the "children of God." To orthodox Hindus, the untouchables rate so low as to be considered outside and beneath the caste system itself.

A major assumption of the caste system is that people are born *unequal* both in capabilities and in opportunities. Thus while an untouchable has few privileges, what is expected of him is much less than what is expected of a Brahman. In traditional, village-centered India, the caste system has contributed to continuity and survival by guaranteeing the village a steady, dependable supply of skills and a docile acceptance of the social order.

But today the system is considered by many Indian leaders to have outlived its economic usefulness and to be morally indefensible. It is not surprising that, when India gained freedom, the Constitution declared that the state cannot permit discrimination against any citizen on grounds of caste, religion, sex, race, or place of birth;

that untouchability was completely abolished and any practice of it punishable by law.

The most effective action against the caste system has been achieved, however, not by law but by changing economic and social conditions. Urbanization, industrialization, increased educational opportunities, movement away from the villages—all of these have loosened the foundation that supports the rigid structure of Indian Hindu society. The most important development in law, which will probably increase in importance in coming years, is universal suffrage. This has given the vote to all Indians, regardless of caste.

### Doctrine of Reincarnation

The status into which one is reborn is determined by *karma,* the doctrine of moral consequences, which says, in effect, that as you sow, so shall you reap. A Hindu figure of speech explains that "as among a thousand cows a calf will find its mother, so the deed previously done will follow and find the doer." Good behavior will bring promotion to a higher caste in the next life; bad behavior will surely be followed by demotion, perhaps to the level of a crawling creature. Living successive, exemplary lives will lead one eventually to Brahmanhood and thence to *moksha*—release from the burden of rebirth.

It should be noted that while the usual course to *moksha* is by a steady series of upward reincarnations, a Hindu may achieve this ultimate goal from any starting point—even that of untouchability—by virtue of having lived an extraordinarily praiseworthy life.

Humans are placed higher than animals in the evolutionary transmigration of souls, but the cow and, to a lesser degree, the monkey are regarded as very special or sacred.

While *karma* explains how one comes to be in a particular caste, *dharma* refers to the set of duties—the path of righteousness—that each individual should pursue in order to earn merits and avoid demerits. One's *dharma* should be in harmony with his nature and standing in life. "Better to do one's own *dharma* poorly than to do another's well" is considered sage advice. It would be a mistake, however, to consider the concepts of *karma* and *dharma* as fatalistic, for it is within a person's power to determine one's future—in the next life—by one's present actions. An eminent Indian philosopher has written that no other doctrine is so valuable in Indian life because it "inspires hope for the future and acceptance of the present."

One of the most significant passages in Hindu literature appears in the Bhagavad-Gita. This excerpt from W. Norman Brown sums up the way to *moksha*.

> The ways of God are various. One is by works, doing one's duty fully but doing it selflessly, without attachment, that is seeking no end except the performance of duty for its own sake.
>
> Another way is by knowledge, seeking and attaining perfect knowledge by means of intensive concentrated meditation, a way of the greatest difficulty, which only the rarest of men is capable of pursuing successfully. There is, however, still another way, which is easier and better, namely that of loving devotion (*bhakti*) to God. One who adopts that will be accepted by God. Devotion is thus the way by which all men can reach God. They need not be profound metaphysicians or iron-willed adherents to duty. . . .

The implications of the *karma-dharma* approach to life are in noteworthy contrast to the "you have only one (earthly) life to live" view generally held in the West. One might say that the traditional Hindu measurement of "progress" is in many lifetimes; the American in a single lifetime.

### Hindu Life Stages: Seeking the Ideal

The doctrine of dividing the ideal life of every man of the highest three orders of castes into four stages was fully developed by 400 B.C. (see Hindu Life Stages, p. 65). The ideal life of the Four *Ashramas* was seldom achieved; most men were satisfied to remain at Stage Two, the householder ashrama. An understanding of this hierarchy of values helps in appreciating the significance of the nephew's remark, to Ronald Eyre in the telecast, that the *sannyasin* (one who has achieved the Fourth Stage) "used to be my uncle." Why, if the uncle was still living, did the nephew use the past tense?

This same set of values is discussed by Gail Sheehy in her best-selling book *Passages*, in recognizing Hindu wisdom: "It is rather humbling to realize that such a view of life as a series of passages, in which former pleasures are outgrown and replaced by higher and more appropriate purposes, was set down in ancient India."

## The Literature of Hinduism

In traditional societies such as India, the importance of ancient texts is great because a religion such as Hinduism permeates and undergirds everyday life.

Of one of the Hindu epics, the *Bhagavad-Gita,* Gandhi once said, "To me the *Gita* has become an infallible guide to conduct. It became my dictionary of daily reference. Just as I turned to the English dictionary for the meaning of English words that I did not understand, I turned to this dictionary of conduct for a ready solution of my problems."

The *Ramayana,* for example, recounts the adventures of Rama and is a story which Indians never tire of retelling in words and drama form. Each character in the story and each event symbolizes considerations of morality, and has provided role models for countless generations of Indians. Also, the most joyous holidays in India are *Dussehra* and *Divali,* which commemorate the rescue of Sita by Rama and their return home after an exile of 14 years. The celebrations send forth the message that "light shall triumph over evil."

The scriptures of orthodox Hindus are the *Vedas.* There are four core Vedas, each with appendages. Most important of the appendages are the *Upanishads.* The *Vedas* are basically prayer books, whereas the *Upanishads* are philosophical works.

The Hindus believe their scriptures, called *shruti,* are divinely revealed in each world cycle to seers, called vishis. The word *shruti* in Sanskrit means "that which is heard," in contradistinction to *smriti* or "that which is remembered." *Shruti* is of utmost holiness because it is thought to have been supernaturally revealed—"heard" by the vishis as divine revelation. The *Vedas* are shruti. Hindu literature, including the lawbooks and the two great epics, the *Mehitharata* and the *Ramayana,* is, on the other hand, smriti, or that which has been remembered by human teachers.

## STUDY QUESTIONS

The following study questions will help organize your thoughts after you have read the Capsule View on Hinduism by Seymour

Fersh. Think through each question completely before checking your answers against the material in this Student's Guide.

1. In what basic way is Hinduism unlike Judaism, Islam, and Christianity?

2. What are the four general orders of *varnas* (social classes) and what are the distinctive features of each?

3. What is the major assumption of the caste system, and how does this affect religious and social practices among Hindus?

4. In Hinduism, how does one achieve *moksha,* or the end of the cycle of rebirths in reincarnation?

5. What are the four life stages in Hinduism, and why are they not observed faithfully by Hindus today?

6. What are the basic differences between the *Vedas* and *Upanishads* in Hindu literature?


## AS YOU VIEW

Another perspective on Hinduism is provided by the television episode *Hinduism: 330 Million Gods.* To organize your thoughts in advance, study the program description below, and review the guiding questions in "Viewing with a Purpose," at the end of this Guide.

This program traces the Indian religious experience in two highly contrasting locations. One is the bustling city of Banares, where millions come to bathe in the holy waters of the Ganges. The other is the small village of Bhith Bhagwanpur, in the flat, thirsty state of Bihar, unvisited except by professional storytellers and itinerant priests. Throughout, the program concentrates on the Hindu approach to God. But which God? For, as we soon discover, there is a choice of 330 million of them. The mind can either simply give up at such a thought or try to get at the reality behind it. By watching the annual festival in honor of the goddess of learning, a Vedic priest performing ceremonies for a healthy crop, a young Brahman boy going through the rite of initiation, and seeing old and young taking their morning ritual baths, we get a picture of the complexity and unity of the Hindu experience.


## AS YOU READ

Based on your study of the material in this Student's Guide, and from your readings in such sources as Huston Smith's *The Religions of Man* you should be able to answer these questions as a self-assessment of what you have learned.

### Study Questions for Reading on Hinduism

1. Do you agree with Hinduism's view that the wants of man are four: (1) *karma* (pleasure), (2) *artha* (wealth, fame, and power), (3) *dharma* (devotion to the community, the path of duty), (4) *moksha* (self-realization as eternal being, immortality). Also explain how self-development of the individual in one life, or many, leads progressively from the first two into the third and finally into the fourth goal of man. (Huston Smith, pp. 17-32).

2. Describe the four ways to moksha, the fourth and final goal of man. Which way would be most suitable for the intellectual type of person; for the emotional person; for the active person? (Smith, pp. 32-61) Raja yoga, as a way to moksha, was developed by the philosophical school of Sankhya Yoga but its techniques are used by others, including those whose way to moksha is predominantly intellectual. What aspects, if any, would you think valuable for a Westerner interested in meditation? (Smith, pp. 51-60).

3. Which of the four stages of life (ashramas) could be observed by men or women in our own culture in the U.S.A.? How would our attitude toward the *sannyasin* differ from the Hindu?

4. Compare the class structure of Hinduism with the American. How does the Hindu justify the difference between the privileges of the Brahman and the lack of them in the shudra *varna* (social class)? (Smith pp. 66-71)

5. Define *karma* and *samsara* (Smith, pp. 75-76) and explain their relation to moksha.

6. In what way does the evil in the world, personified by such deities as Kali, aid in the spiritual development of the individual?

7. Ramakrishna, founder of the Vedanta Society, thinks that all the great religions are pathways to God-realization. Which of these pathways did he experience himself? He did, however, think that the highest kind of self-realization was the experience of identity with the nirguna Brahman. What is meant by the nirguna Brahman? (Smith pp. 71-75)

## QUESTIONS FOR THOUGHT

The following questions raise concerns or points of interest related to Hinduism. Apply what you have learned about Hinduism by thinking through your answers to these questions.

1. In what way is Hinduism a truly ecumenical religion? How does Hinduism resolve differences between its tenets and those of other faiths?

2. How would your community or neighborhood change if all of the residents participated in Orthodox Hindu practices and social orders?

3. How would a life-style of ambition and material pursuit be affected by a new belief in reincarnation?

4. How does the Hindu concept of righteousness compare with that in the Christian faith?

# PRONUNCIATION GUIDE FOR HINDUISM

veda—váy-da
ashrama—ásh-ra-ma
kshatriya—sháh-tree-ya
vaishya—vý-shee-a
shudra—shóo-dra
upanishdad—uh-pán-i-shad
atman—áht-man
maya—mý-a
dharma—dúr-ma
sat chit ananda—saht-chit-áh-nun-da
tat tvam asi—tut tvum ah-see
vedanta—vay-dáhn-ta
samsara—sam-sáhr-a
nirvana—ner-váhn-a
Ramayana—Rah-máh-yah-na
Mahabharata—Mah-hah-bháhr-ra-ta
Bhagavad Gita—Bha-gah-vahd-gée-ta
Puranas—Poo-rán-a
Bhakti—bháhk-tee
guna—góon-a
trimurti—try-móor-tee
Rama—Ráh-ma
Shiva—shív-a
shakti—sháhk-tee
lingam—líng-um
moksha—mók-sha
jnana—ghýah-na
shankara—sháhnk-a-ra
darsana—dáhr-sha-na
nyaya—nee-aýe-ah
vaisesika—vy-shésh-ee-ka
sankhya—sónk-hee-ya
purusha—póo-roo-sha
prakriti—práh-kri-tee
mahatma—ma-hót-ma

harijan—háh-ree-jun
sannyasin—sahn-yáh-sin
japam—júp-um
raja—ráh-ja
samadhi—sa-máh-dee
ishwara—ísh-wah-ra
Brahma (creator god)—brúm-a
Brahman (the ultimate reality)—brúm-un
lila—lée-la
kali—káh-lee
jiva—jée-va

# JAINS, PARSEES, AND SIKHS
## Three Other Religions in India

*by*

Seymour Fersh
*College of Education*
*Farleigh Dickinson University*

India, where religion is an important part of everyday life, is also the place where many religions have begun and have been welcomed. This spirit of toleration is in harmony with Hindu belief and is reflected in the constitution of the new Indian nation, which guarantees freedom of religion. Of the 620 million people living in India, about 85 percent are Hindu. The next largest group are the Muslims, who make up 10 percent of the population. The remaining 5 percent are represented by 15 million Christians, 5 million Buddhists, 20,000 Jews, and three religious groups: the Jains, Parsees, and Sikhs.

The significance of the Jains, Parsees, and Sikhs is not in their number; there are only about 2.5 million Jains, about 90,000 Parsees, and about 12 million Sikhs. They are important because each represents a unique religious experience. From their teachings we can gain insights and stimulation for our own "long search." Together, they provide great contrasts. Jainism and Sikhism originated in India, but Jainism is of ancient origin, beginning around the 6th Century B.C., while Sikhism is relatively new, originating less than 500 years ago. The Parsees are descendants of a people whose religion was Zoroastrianism. Even older than Jainism, Zoroastrianism originated in Iran and was introduced to India in the 8th Century A.D. Not surprisingly, each of these religions perceives the world differently. Each has its own beliefs concerning the origin of the world and how we are to behave within it.

## The Jains

Mahavira, who established Jainism in its present form, was not the first *jina* of the Jains; there had been 23 great leaders before him. Their images are found in most of the 40,000 Jain temples in India. The Jains honor those who, through insight and action, revealed paths which others could follow, or exemplified behavior from which others could benefit. Mahavira taught that one's soul could rise through rebirths, if one exercised self-discipline and control, taking special care not to damage or hinder the souls of others; this included the souls in all living forms which are equally entitled to life-fulfillment. He also taught that personal salvation is one's own responsibility and within one's own power, inasmuch as advancement of the soul's journey upward comes not through prayer but through right conduct. Professor Heinrich Zimmer has cited some rules of behavior which a devout Jaina householder should observe. A Jain must:

1. Not destroy life.
2. Not tell a lie.
3. Not make unpermitted use of another man's property.
4. Be chaste.
5. Limit his possessions.
6. Make a perceptual and daily vow to go only in certain directions and for certain distances.
7. Avoid useless talk and action.
8. Avoid thought of sinful things.
9. Limit the articles of diet and enjoyment for the day.
10. Worship at fixed times, morning, noon, and evening.
11. Fast on certain days.
12. Give charity every day in the form of knowledge, money, or in some other way.

The Jains, because of their religion, have avoided occupations, including farming, which take life. Many Jains have become highly educated and prosperous, especially as merchants or bankers. Although they are few in number, the Jains have made large contributions—in money and in talents—to the national development of India. Their teachings have greatly influenced non-Jains, who have been impressed and attracted by the saintliness of Jain behavior. The best example of Jain influence is Gandhi. Nurtured in a part of India much permeated with Jain teachings, he took their concept of *Ahimsa* and applied it to political as well as personal action. In his autobiography, significantly in the final pages titled ''Farewell,'' Gandhi provides his own interpretation of *Ahimsa*. He also gives a modern application of this ancient Jain belief:

"My uniform experience has convinced me that there is no other God than Truth and that the only means for the realization of truth is Ahimsa. . . . To see the universal and all-pervading Spirit of Truth face to face one must be able to love the meanest of creation as oneself. . . . That is why my devotion to Truth has drawn me into the field of politics; and I can say without the slightest hesitation, and yet in all humility, that those who say that religion has nothing to do with politics do not know what religion means.

"Identification with everything that lives is impossible without self-identification, without self-purification; without self- purification the observance of the law of Ahimsa must remain an empty dream; God can never be realized by one who is not pure of heart. Self-purification therefore must mean purification in all walks of life. . . . But the path of self-purification is hard and steep. To attain to perfect purity one has to become absolutely passion-free in thought, speech, and action, to rise above the opposing currents of love and hatred, attachment and repulsion. To conquer the subtle passions seems to me to be harder far than the physical conquest of the world by force of arms. . . . I know that I still have before me a difficult path to traverse. I must reduce myself to zero. So long as a man does not of his own free will put himself last among his fellow creatures, there is no salvation for him. Ahimsa is the farthest limit of humility."

## The Parsees

The Parsees in India are perhaps the only people in the world who have directly kept alive the teachings of Zoroastrianism. We are familiar with many of the beliefs of Zoroastrianism because of their influence in early Hebrew and Christian doctrines. These ideas include the coming of a messiah, the resurrection of the dead, a last judgment, and everlasting life in heaven or hell. All of these doctrines sprang from the general belief that each person is part of the struggle between Ahura Mazda, the force for good, and Ahriman, the force for evil.

In this struggle, each person has free will to choose between the two, but ultimately Ahura-Mazda will triumph. As Ninian Smart observes, "So Zoroastrianism makes room for both individual destiny, which is highly dependent upon moral conduct, and that global destiny which is worked out in the last days." To help them, the

Parsees have the sacred writings, the *Avesta,* which they believe were revealed to them as a chosen people. This strong belief in their uniqueness has enabled the Parsees to maintain their religion almost without change, in spite of the fact that they left their original homeland more than 12 centuries ago.

Unlike the Jains, the Parsees do not encourage asceticism; they believe the world is here to be enjoyed and experienced. Most importantly, they emphasize practical moral living, designed to make the world a better place in which to live until it is eventually freed from evil. Their basic teachings include both monotheism and monogamy. Women have equal rights and status among the Parsees.

With the coming of the British in the 1600s, the Parsees began to prosper, particularly those living in Bombay. Well suited to work with the British, the Parsees shared with them similar religious values, were well educated, and maintained a strong interest and ability in trade and commerce. They soon became the most Westernized and wealthiest single group in India. Some of their members became leading shipbuilders, bankers, industrialists, and merchants. But the Parsees also remained loyal to India. One of them, Dadabhai Naoroji (the son of a Zoroastrian priest) has been called "the architect of Indian nationalism." In the 1800s, he was the first to "draw the plans and lay the foundations for India's self- government."

Currently the Parsees are facing the greatest challenge to their survival thus far, because of a declining birth rate and the fact that some of their younger members are leaving India. Among those who remain, a split is developing between two main bodies: a traditional, orthodox group that controls the institutions of religion and finance; and a reformist group which considers itself more modern and responsive to change. Recently, a controversy has developed over the ancient Parsee custom of disposing of the dead by exposing their bodies atop stone towers ("Towers of Silence") until vultures and the sun make it possible to pulverize the remaining skeleton, drop it into a well at the bottom of a tower and let it wash out to sea. The procedure is based on a religious doctrine, as explained by Mark Twain, who witnessed such an occasion in 1897:

> "The principle which underlies and orders everything connected with a Parsee funeral is Purity. By the tenets of Zoroastrianism, the elements of Earth, Fire, and Water are sacred, and must not be contaminated by contact with the dead."

The challenge to this custom drew a response from a high priest of the Parsees which characterizes the way in which the religion typically has responded to change: "We believe in long-standing tradition and will follow it. The only ones who raise a hue and cry are those against it, and they are a small number." He added that he was relatively unconcerned about the declining birth rate: "We believe in quality, not quantity."

## The Sikhs

Nanak, founder of the Sikh religion, was not the first to have a vision of the religion which was to become Sikhism; he was preceded and influenced by Kabir. The text also points out that Nanak was, however, the first in a succession of ten *gurus* who helped shape the religious doctrines and community that have served the Sikhs. More than any of the others, Nanak, with his spirit and confidence, gave direction and inspiration to the movement which resulted in a new religion. As Ninian Smart writes, "Nanak was not just a prophet. He was an original. He went about preaching the faith by singing, accompanied by his companion Mardana, whose stringed rebeck was in a sense part of the message. Nanak wore a mixed garb, to show he was both Hindu and Muslim or neither."

From the start, Sikhism provided a religious alternative to both Hinduism and Islam. The followers of Nanak's teachings were eventually forced to organize themselves into a militant group which could defend itself from the persecuting Mogul emperors. The Sikhs (disciples) retained beliefs that emphasized an individual's responsibility for his own behavior in harmony with God's will, while creating a community of believers in which all are equal regardless of class, sex, or other differences. Consequently, among the Sikhs, there is no priestly class; all members are considered competent to conduct services. The aspiration of the Sikhs to gain their own identity was furthered in 1966 when the new state of Punjab was created within the Indian nation. In this state, located in northwestern India, the Sikhs constitute a majority.

Nanak's example of traveling abroad has been followed by his disciples. Like Nanak, who went as far west as Mecca and as far east as China, Sikhs have been willing to leave their homeland, carrying with them their religious beliefs and behavior. Many of them, for example, were recruited by the British to serve in the Indian army because of their proven fighting ability and individual sense of discipline and commitment. In more recent times, Sikhs have continued to seek opportunities outside of India while devotedly maintaining their religious affiliation. It is estimated that there are now 120,000 Sikhs living in the United States and Canada.

Outside their homeland, the Sikhs have made adjustments in their appearances without compromising the essence of their religious beliefs. For example, among the five K's to be observed by the Sikhs (*kesh,* unshorn hair; *kachh,* special undershorts; *kara,* a steel bracelet worn on the right wrist; *kanga,* a comb; and *kirpan,* a steel dagger) some have been modified. The *kirpan* is now generally represented by a tiny dagger attached to the comb. In the case of unshorn hair, some of the Sikhs have substituted Western-style haircuts because, as one of them said, "Some employers have not hired Sikhs because they think they look like some sort of hippie class. But once he has hired them, he hires more and there are few firings. Sikhs have made a name by hard work and devotion to duty."

## STUDY QUESTIONS

These study questions will help organize your thoughts and assess your understanding of other religions in India. Think through each question completely before checking your answer against the material in this Student's Guide.

1. India is a place where many religions are practiced. In what way is this in harmony with Hindu belief?

2. There are relatively few people in India who are Jains, Parsees, or Sikhs in their religious affiliation. Why would their small population be a significant factor in the religions of India?

3. What are the basic tenets of the Jains as taught by Mahavira?

4. Why have the Jains avoided occupations such as farming?

5. In what way did the Jains influence India's spiritual and political leaders such as Gandhi?

6. Which religion in India has kept alive the teachings of Zoroastrianism?

7. In what ways do the beliefs of the Parsees parallel those of the Judeo-Christian tradition?

8. In what way do the beliefs of the Parsees differ from those of the Jains?

9. What factors threaten the continued existence of the Parsees as a religion in India?

10. In what way did Nanak influence and shape the religion of the Sikhs?

11. In what ways is Sikhism a religious alternative to both Hinduism and Islam?

12. Why is there no priestly caste among the Sikhs?

13. How have the Sikhs adjusted their religious beliefs and practices as they migrated outside their homeland?

Chapter 4
# FOOTPRINT OF THE BUDDHA

## A STUDY OF BUDDHISM

For much of the East, religious thought centers around the Four Noble Truths and the Eightfold Path of the Buddha. The Buddha himself, who lived in the 6th Century B.C., was evidently a person of great subtlety, intellectual power, psychological insight, and holiness. In due course the religion of the Buddha spread through most of India, and from there into Ceylon, southeastern Asia, central Asia, China, Korea, Japan, Tibet, and Mongolia. In the 20th Century, Buddhism has been drastically curtailed in those countries with Marxist governments, but it has begun to make a vital impact in the West.

When Western scholars first encountered Buddhist texts, they tended to look upon Buddhism as an ethical philosophy rather than a religion in the more popular sense. Buddhism includes philosophy, and also involves faith and practices meant to liberate people from the round of rebirth. Buddhism has been adaptable to the cultures through which it spread, and thus successful as a missionary enterprise. It does not repudiate the local gods and myths, but tempers them and uses them.

## A PREFACE TO YOUR STUDY

An outline of the major aspects of Buddhism begins the lesson. A capsule view of Buddhism is provided by Dr. Stanley Spector, Director of International Studies, Washington University, St. Louis. Dr. Spector describes Buddhism in terms of the philosophy of the Four Noble Truths and the guideposts on the Eightfold Path to Enlightenment. Use this capsule view of Buddhism to gain a basic understanding of Buddhism which you can extend throughout this lesson.

Additional in-depth material about Buddhism is found on pages 90-139 and 153-159 of *The Religions of Man,* by Huston Smith.

Another perspective on Buddhism will be revealed in the program "Footprint of the Buddha," from the television series "The Long Search."

The Questions for Thought found at the end of this lesson provide issues related to Buddhism which you will want to consider.

Buddhism and Hinduism share the same Vedic source. While a comprehensive understanding of Hinduism is not needed, reference to the material on Hinduism in Chapter 3 will be helpful to your study of Buddhism.

## IMPORTANT CONCEPTS

From more than 2,000 years of evolution of Buddhism as a faith, there are many aspects that could be studied. Certain major concepts about this religion, however, should be mastered before you expand your study to other aspects of religion. These points include a definition of Buddhism and its major concern; a description of Buddha and the role of Enlightenment in Buddhism; and knowledge about sects within Buddhism.

### Buddhism and Its Emphasis

Buddhism is a faith, a body of philosophy and wisdom, and a group of practices meant to relieve humankind of material, spiritual, and psychological suffering and to resolve the inevitable contradictions of life.

Buddhism's concern is not God or the *why* of life but rather *how* humans shall exist in this universe and give value to every breath drawn.

Buddhism is a religion rich in psychological insight, adapting well to widely varying cultural environments, accepting and absorbing local religious traditions.

### Buddha and Enlightenment

Gautama, or Sakyamuni Buddha, was not a god but a man who achieved what might be called divinity, or Enlightenment through complete self-realization based on right thinking and right living. Buddha was a teacher who, having found the way to Enlightenment for himself, stayed behind to help others along the path to Nirvana, where living beings are no longer caught up in the cycle of earthly existences.

### Buddhist Sects

Buddhism stretches south and east from India, its land of origin, to Sri Lanka and southeast Asia where it takes the form of *Theravadic,* or *Hinayana* (Lesser Vehicle) Buddhism, and northeastward in the form of *Mahayana* (Greater Vehicle) Buddhism to Tibet, Mongolia, China, Korea, and, especially today, to Japan.

## A CAPSULE VIEW OF BUDDHISM

In many ways Buddhism is a quite down-to-earth and modern religion. Perhaps that is why it addresses itself simply and directly to the individual being and seems to ignore the existence or nonexistence of God. It also does without so much of the community ritual often associated with religious practice.

This description of Buddhism will cover its background; philosophy; teachings, including the Four Noble Truths, the Eightfold Path, and the Doctrine of Five Aggregates; and five unique sects within Buddhism.

### The Background of Buddhism

Growing out of the Hindu traditions found in India around 500 B.C., Buddhism has spread throughout Asia and, in recent years, to some extent in the West. It has taken various forms and widely different emphases as time, place, and the needs of the people have demanded.

Like other major religions of the world, Buddhism has had a complicated evolution. Although it has been represented by widely varying sects and schools, its promise everywhere is the same, the easement of suffering.

Some religions ask what God can do for us or what we must do for God in order to meet some individual or social crises (droughts, wars, extreme expectations, loss of loved ones, the inevitability of physical death, the emptiness of life). Buddhism, on the other hand, offers a prescription for life and a philosophy which can meet the intellectual and emotional requirements of the most sophisticated thinker, as well as of the least educated believer.

### The Philosophy of Buddhism

Much of the complex metaphysical content of Buddhism is of historical origin and can best be understood in light of the Hindu concepts on which it was grounded. Buddhism was, after all, an assault upon and a challenge to the Oriental Indian "establishment," with its rigid caste society and its elaborate pantheon of rights and ceremonies for what has been called three hundred and thirty million gods.

But one does not have to be looking for a way out of the problems posed by the Hindu society and religion of 500 B.C. to know what it was that bothered the Buddha, Gautama (also named Siddharta, and also called Shakyamuni). He posed the same questions that have been asked by people in all periods of history: "Why am I here? What am I, really? What have I to do with the earth, the heavens, the universe, my fellow men? Why must I suffer? Must I truly die? What shall I do with my life? What happens after death?" In many cultures and faiths the answers to such questions are given categorically, often in the name of God or gods. Gautama Siddharta Shakyamuni tried, and his Therasaha followers still try, to provide more practical answers. What they sought was simplicity, yet ironically, in many cases, Mahayana Buddhistic philosophy developed some of man's most complex and rarified metaphysics.

Buddha's answers, based on his own real life trials and tribulations, are the fruit of his spiritual struggle to attain the Answer, or

Enlightenment. Another word for this is Truth. The attainment of such a state—or nonstate, for it involves utter detachment and the lack of a sense of being—has been described in many ways. But, we must be careful to remember, words and descriptions are only symbols and not the thing itself. Only those who achieve Enlightenment can know what it is, and this cannot be communicated. The best one can do is to help another to find it. Gautama, the Buddha, did this. That is why he is followed and sometimes even worshiped. Because he stayed behind to teach and help others, Buddha set the example for the Bodhisattva, the ideal in most Mahayana sects.

The heart of the Buddha's teaching has been transmitted to us in the form of the Four Noble Truths and the Eightfold Path. The Truths which constitute the basic items of Buddhist belief are based on a profound understanding of the human condition. The Eightfold Path is the road map provided as a guide along the journey to Enlightenment.

### The Four Noble Truths

These teachings are only the beginning, the simple basics. They reflect the spiritual and philosophic assumptions of the ages and societies which produced them. If learned and considered seriously, however, the Four Noble Truths can provide powerful insight into the way millions of people think and act. They may even help us to see ourselves in a clearer light.

The First Truth is that life is suffering (*dukkha*).

The Second Truth is that desire (*tanha*) is the cause of suffering.

The Third Truth is that there is a method for elimination of suffering.

The Fourth Truth is that the Eightfold Path is the way to eliminate suffering.

The great English writer, Joseph Conrad, once summarized human destiny like this: "Man is born; he suffers; he dies." Those who subscribe to this view might readily embrace the Four Noble Truths and rush to seek the Eightfold Path. But what of the young and optimistic who may feel that, "It is better to have loved and lost than never to have loved at all"? What of those who view deprivations, partings, and all the ills that flesh is heir to with equanimity, or at least with resignation? What of those who see the joys and consummations of life as outbalancing all the rest? Here the Buddhists' response might well be: "Go your way in peace and happiness, but should and when you need them, the Truths and the Path are there."

The realizations of the Truths and embarkation on the Path do not require the abandonment of other Gods or other faiths, as do monotheistic religions of the West. Therefore, Buddhism finds great favor, especially in China and Japan, as a complementary or supplemental religion.

In India, early Buddhism absorbed the old Vedic and Hindu myths and gods. Similarly, when Buddhism spread to China, Japan and Tibet, it acquired and sanctified legendary celestial hosts and terrestrial heroes. Such accommodation helps explain the ease with which Buddhism was accepted in alien environments. But if we wish to be rigorously logical (and such rigor is in keeping with Buddhist standards) it becomes apparent that attachment to any faith or gods, especially in the hope of salvation or immortality, is in itself a departure from the principle of nonattachment embodied in the Noble Truths.

## The Eightfold Path

There is little point in knowing the Four Noble Truths if one does not immediately follow up by consulting the guideposts of the Eightfold Path:

Guidepost 1. *Right knowledge.* Have sufficient knowledge of the key elements of Buddhist philosophy which are the Four Truths and the principles of impermanence, no-self, and suffering.

Guidepost 2. *Right thought.* Do not think greedily, lustfully, badly, or cruelly.

Guidepost 3. *Right speech.* Do not lie or speak vainly.

Guidepost 4. *Right conduct.* Do not kill, do not steal, do not misbehave sexually.

Guidepost 5. *Right livelihood.* Do not hurt others in the pursuit of your living.

Guidepost 6. *Right efforts.* Avoid or rectify evil thoughts. Conserve and develop good thoughts.

Guidepost 7. *Right mindfulness.* Meditate on the body, on mental activity itself, and on the thoughts and ideas in the mind. This involves the greatest degree of consciousness, as well as a constant awareness of these points: (1) the body is infinitely dissoluble; composed of impermanent, decaying, renewing, replacing parts; (2) mental activity may be lustful, hateful, and deluding; and (3) thoughts are mere mental constructs, impermanent, and motivated by craving.

Guidepost 8. *Right concentration.* Try to attain the highest or culminating stage of meditation which can grow from right efforts and right mindfulness. At this point, you are near the end of the road and you approach the intuitive and mystical experience called *samadhi,* or *nirvana,* which signifies the elimination of craving, hence eliminating the cause of suffering.

Using these guideposts, hundreds of millions of people, over a period of two and a half millenniums, have trodden with more or less success the Eightfold Path. But it is a long way between guideposts; it is like navigating by the stars. Many who made progress along the path have set down their experiences, following the example of Gautama Buddha himself. Some provided greater details or special cues; others offered shortcuts. Records of these experiences come from India, Burma, Tibet, Mongolia, China, Korea, Japan, Thailand, Vietnam, and even from the countries of Europe and America. They form one of the greatest bodies of literature produced by man.

Buddhism, in its analysis of matter and nonmatter, of being and nonbeing, reaches from the earliest intuitive gropings of man to the frontiers of modern physical and behavioral sciences. Hence Buddhism is like a crystal, each side showing a different facet and reflecting a new light.

## The Doctrine of the Five Aggregates

Early Buddhism, with its connection to the Vedic religion, was enmeshed in the ancient Hindu doctrine of *Samsara,* or endless rebirth. This presented problems and contradictions, since Buddha accepted the prevailing concept of rebirth. He tried to explain this through a complex doctrine known as the five aggregates (*skandhas*): body, feelings, perceptions, disposition, and consciousness. What man calls "self" is the combination of these *skandhas.* They are, themselves, changing from moment to moment. Hence, there is no permanent entity lying behind them, but they do provide continuity of a sort.

The conduct of anyone in his present life and previous lives is presumed to have produced a karmic matter which is stored and which, upon physical death, immediately passes to a new body. But karmic matter is both changeable and destructible. It changes from moment to moment, according to a person's conduct. Hence, it is not soul, which by definition is indestructible (and therefore rejected by Buddhism). In the Buddhist understanding, the karmic matter ceases to exist when one is freed from desire. At that point, there is no need for rebirth; nirvana has been achieved.

Acceptance of the Indian doctrine of rebirth is assumed in Buddhist religious philosophy. But for those who find such an idea, however rationalized, unacceptable, the Four Noble Truths and the Eightfold Path may still have great value, inasmuch as they address themselves to man's deepest apprehensions and oldest quests.

Modern Buddhism is broadly divided into two groups—Theravada and Mahayana—which may be distinguished by geography as well as by their names, principles, and practices.

## Lesser Vehicle: Theravada Buddhism

The older, basically Indian form of Buddhism represented the first great wave of Buddhist outflow to the neighboring regions of southeastern Asia, including Sri Lanka (Ceylon), Cambodia, Laos, Thailand, and Vietnam. It is commonly known as *Hinayana* Buddhism, or the Lesser Vehicle. It retains the evidences of its Indian origin more than the other major form of Buddhism. It emphasizes the role and activities of its monks and monasteries. For the average person, perhaps the best expression of Buddhist practice would be to help a monk attain his nirvana, or Enlightenment. This emphasis on a clerical group reflects the preeminence of the Brahmans, or priestly caste, among the Hindus. This is the only group under Hinduism eligible for *moksha,* or release from the burden of rebirth.

In its assault on the old Hindu establishment, Buddhism rejected the notion of anything so fixed and permanent as caste, yet it could not throw off the intellectual notion of *samsara,* or rebirths. It also could not easily rid its followers of prevailing social values. The priest retained his head start of ascendancy on the path to nirvana. There was, however, one difference: in Hinduism one was born into the priestly caste, but in *Hinayana* Buddhism any male could become a monk by submitting himself to the discipline of a monastic order, renouncing the world, and entering a monastery. Buddhism therefore widened the path enough so that at least every male could tread upon it.

If the layman felt the need, at any time, he could become a monk for as long or short a time as he desired. In Thailand today, every boy or young man spends some months or years as a monk in a monastery. In Burma, too, it is not uncommon for an active social or political leader who reaches an impasse to chuck it all, for a while, in favor of the quiet solitude of monastic life.

Theravada Buddhism focused on the activities of monks, so its teachings became very special or esoteric. This led to a division of labor. The monks became full-time devotees of their own salvation. The laymen patiently supported them, awaiting, as it were, their own turn in some life to come.

The monasteries of Europe in the Middle Ages provided sanctuaries where prayer inspired monks to noble works of art and literature. Similarly, in Asia, the Buddhist monastic tradition has given to the world monuments, temples, and sublime representations of the Buddha in all his aspects. The monasteries have been scholastic centers, providing basic and sometimes advanced education to children. Buddhism occupies a prominent place in the history of education in Asia.

## Greater Vehicle: Mahayana Buddhism

When Buddhism was carried north and east to China by a series of intrepid Chinese monks, it encountered peoples unfamiliar with the Hindu and Vedic sacred traditions. These were people whose basic view of life and whose social structures contrasted sharply with those of India. *Theravada* Buddhism was generally unable to surmount the Himalayan mountain range and penetrate the vast lands and populations of northeastern Asia. It was rather the existence of an alternate form, a simpler and more popular approach (some would call it more vulgar) called *Mahayana,* or Greater Vehicle, Buddhism which made possible the second wave of Buddhist expansion.

Wars, famine, endless dynastic struggles for the materialistic rewards of rulers, moral or rather immoral excesses, and a widespread feeling of malaise or ill-being and emptiness prepared the ground for the spiritual refreshment and relief that Buddhism had to offer. The people of northern and northeastern Asia were ready for Buddhism. To be accepted, however, Buddhism would have to strip itself of the accumulated ornaments and refinements of the particular culture and environment in which it had grown up, and come back to the essentials.

*Mahayana,* the Greater Vehicle, had accomplished this in India between the 3rd Century B.C. and the 4th Century A.D. It had concentrated on the basic message of compassion or loving-kindness which people everywhere, at all times, long to hear. As Christians find the central example of mercy or compassion in the willing self-sacrifice of Christ, people may find in the Buddha's staying behind after he attained Enlightenment a supreme example of the giving of one's self for the sake of others. Hence, the doctrine of the *bodhisattva,* or Enlightened Being, possesses the greatest possibility for mass appeal. It brings to those who are lost along the way the assurance that there were then and are now Knowing Ones among us, holding out their hands to guide us out of misery and suffering.

*Mahayana* Buddhism stresses the social aspect of the journey toward nirvana. The focusing of one's concern on the achievement of one's own selflessness (nonbeing, or nirvana) is the height of selfishness. Rather, this life should be accepted as an opportunity to help others gain Enlightenment and end suffering, and a next life should be welcomed as a further opportunity. But for the average person, unable to deal with the vagaries of Buddhistic metaphysics, another attractive alternative offers itself: to be reborn in nirvana. This concept is fairly universal in mankind's imagination. The bodhisattva was one who had the opportunity to enter heaven, but had put it off to help others. *Mahayana* offers many examples of such future Buddhas. They are all manifestations of the Buddha. There is historical evidence that such things happen, and a strong inducement to join the effort.

As Mahayana Buddhism passed different lands and ages, notably China, Japan, and Tibet, its most important philosophies, the Madhyamika and Yogacara (developed in India) were transmitted along with it. The treatises of these schools became doctrines of particular sects in China and Japan, but these sects were not popular. These philosophies were and still are today, however, the backbone of Mahayana thought in China, Japan, and Tibetan Buddhism.

*The Middle Way (Madhyamika).* The Middle Way stresses emptiness. Object or self is delusion; they are reducible to *dharmas,* which are impermanent. One should avoid one-sidedness; to say that something is real or unreal is not within the doctrine. The truth lies outside of these extremes. All dualities (life and death, impermanence and permanence, rebirth and nirvana) are identical. This may be related, strangely enough, to what Karl Marx and Mao Tse-tung have called "the unity of opposites." It is easy to see how such a concept can lead to the concept of Infinity or God. To grasp this concept fully requires meditation. Over the years, thousands of systems such as *karate,* tea-ceremony, and calligraphy, have developed to offer their own formulas for such meditation.

*The Consciousness Only (Yogacara).* Another approach, Consciousness Only, puts mind above matter. It stresses some particular attitudes for meditation in which mind overcomes body. Emptiness is pure consciousness. Feats of yoga are not aimed at making the body develop or do some physical feat, but rather at denying that there is anything but pure consciousness.

*The Pure Land.* The history and philosophy of Buddhism are enshrined in numerous canonical or classical works called *sutras.* Some are widely popular and well known. Others are the treasured secrets of particular monasteries and sects. One of the most popular and appealing is the *Lotus Sutra.* It stresses the kindly role of the bodhisattvas and presents the Buddha's vision of heaven or, to be more accurate, his vision of the 18,000 heavens which await those who have faith in his doctrine.

Here, then, is the seed for a vastly popular mode of Buddhist devotion—simple faith and sure reward. The Pure Land Sect, as this movement is known, would have to overcome only a few obstacles to be accepted in new environments. Demands upon the faithful are relatively few, for devotions can be as simple or as exacting as the student or teacher desires. The vision of the Pure Land, the fields of bliss, sometimes called the Western Paradise, have been celebrated in some of the most exalted prose, poetry, and painting of Asia. Moreover, to reinforce this, a further doctrine has developed which tells us that the Buddha, the Bodhisattva, will always stay behind until he has rescued every last individual. This doctrine exhorts us to have faith in *Amitabha,* the Buddha's name as Savior, and to repeat his name. If this is done, his compassion will bring ultimate release from suffering and entrance to the Pure Land, similar to the Western Paradise.

As you reflect on this optimistic reduction to formula of the Buddhistic edifice of philosophy and religion do not forget, however, that the Western Paradise, too, is in the end a mental construct. It is emptiness. Can we also call it God?

## STUDY QUESTIONS

The following study questions will help organize your thoughts after you have read "A Capsule View of Buddhism" by Stanley Spector. Think through each question completely before checking your answers against the material in this Student's Guide.

1. What does Buddhism offer that other religions do not?

2. In what ways did Buddhism develop as an assault upon and a challenge to the "establishment" in India?

3. In Buddhism, what is the significance of the "Four Noble Truths"?

4. What are the "Four Noble Truths"?

5. Name and briefly describe each of the eight guideposts of the "Eightfold Path."

6. How does Buddhism explain and assimilate the ancient Hindu doctrine of samsara, or endless rebirth?

7. What are the basic tenets of *Theravada Buddhism* (or the Lesser Vehicle)?

8. What are the basic tenets of *Mahayana Buddhism* (or the Greater Vehicle)?

9. What are the basic tenets of Middle Way Buddhism? How does this approach compare to the Consciousness Only approach to Buddhism or to the Pure Land approach?

## AS YOU VIEW

Another perspective on Buddhism is provided by the television episode *Buddhism: Footprint of the Buddha—India.* Study the program description below, and review the guiding questions in "Viewing with a Purpose" at the end of this Guide to help you participate more actively in the viewing experience.

We go to Sri Lanka (Ceylon) and India to discover the type of Buddhism practiced throughout southeastern Asia. Among those who help us are Buddhist monks (including one American), as well as school children, novices, and housewives. Each offers something from personal experience to help us come to grips with a religion that has high moral standards but does not believe in God. In the plantation town of Ambalangoda we attend a ceremony at which an eight-year-old boy becomes a novice monk, learn the meaning of Buddha statues, and watch monks at prayer and join them on their morning round of begging. Even if Buddhism does not officially accept the idea of a creator and personal God, many Buddhists turn to the local deities for their worldly requests. We visit the shrine of such a god and witness a trance ceremony. But the focal point of Buddhism in Sri Lanka is the monastery. At the remote hermitage of Waturuwila the cameras witness celebrations marking the end of the rainy retreat, and then travel to an even more ancient hermitage in the jungle where six monks live a life of meditation.

## AS YOU READ

Based on your study of the material in this Student's Guide, and from your readings in such sources as Huston Smith's *The Religions of Man,* you should be able to answer these questions as a self-assessment of what you have learned.

### Buddhism

1. Would you agree with the first of the Buddha's Four Noble Truths that life is suffering? Which kinds of suffering did the

Buddha mention? Do these still afflict mankind? (Smith, pp. 109-115)

2. What is the basic cause of suffering and how can it be overcome? (Smith, p. 123)

3. The final goal of Buddhism is nirvana. What is its meaning? Distinguish between God and Godhead. (Smith, pp. 123-127)

4. The Buddha promulgated the *anatta* (no-soul) doctrine. If the individual has no soul, what migrates from birth to birth? How does the karma accrued continue in subsequent lives? (Smith, pp. 127-128)

5. Suffering, no-soul, impermanence, according to the Buddha's doctrine, are the three Signs of Being. How is Impermanence related to the two other Signs of Being?

6. Explain the meaning of each item in the list of differences between Theravada and Mahayana Buddhism listed on page 138 in Smith.

7. What techniques are used in Zen for the attainment of self-realization? How are one's attitude and feeling towards the cosmos and others changed when satori is experienced? (Smith, pp. 145-153)

## QUESTIONS FOR THOUGHT

The following questions cover concerns or points of interest related to Buddhism. Apply what you have learned about Buddhism by thinking through the answers to these questions.

1. From the Buddhist perspective, is it possible for a Buddhist to be also a Christian?

2. Compare and contrast the role of Buddha in Buddhism with the Prophet Mohammed in Islam.

3. How are the elements of the Eightfold Path similar to or different from the Islamic, Judaic, or Christian principles guiding daily living?

# Chapter 5
# A QUESTION OF BALANCE

## A STUDY OF THE CHINESE RELIGIONS

China today attracts the attention of people interested in revolution, business opportunities, sources of untapped natural resources, possible solutions to social problems, and what is probably the world's finest cooking tradition. But why should one look to the land of "the heathen Chinese," to a society notable for its secular outlook, for insight on religion and its place in society? This question becomes all the more acute when we remind ourselves that since the establishment of the People's Republic of China in 1949, the Communist government of China has officially frowned upon the public practice of virtually all religions. It has sharply curtailed the maintenance of churches and temples, and practically brought to an end all religious teaching. To be sure, "religious freedom" has been guaranteed in the Constitution of the People's Republic, but it is only a freedom of silent thought and faith. The temples and churches one is allowed to visit today are commonly cultural museums. The few public religious ceremonies seem to be occasioned by visiting clergy, such as Buddhist priests from neighboring countries. Only the future can tell whether religion can for long be shut off by governmental decree or discouragement, yet the Chinese case is full of interest to the student of humanity and social behavior.

China, with its long history and the largest population in the world, is man's greatest single national social laboratory. Beyond considerations of sheer quantity and volume, however, are equally significant issues of quality. China's culture is unique and successful, responding to environmental challenges with the creation of a truly towering civilization.

In examining China's religious experiences and patterns, we shall see and come to appreciate more fully the interrelationships of men with deities, and the connection of daily living practices with devotions to the unknown and unseen. Also, we will examine how religion enters the realms of politics and social control while at the same time practical concerns shape and limit the domains of religion.

We shall explore, too, the way men hold some things to be peculiarly their own, even as they borrow new ideas and visions from their neighbors. The issues of *this world and the other world;* of state, society, and religion; of death, ancestry, and future, all have their particular Chinese resolutions. The Chinese puzzle, then, if only in the questions it raises in our minds, provides rich clues to the potentialities inherent in mankind itself.


## A PREFACE TO YOUR STUDY

Your study begins with an outline of the major points you should learn concerning the religions of China. Then, the key aspects of these religions are described in more detail by Dr. Stanley Spector, Director of International Studies, Washington University, St. Louis. In a capsule view of the Chinese religions, Dr. Spector examines both the historical context and the cultural environment which conceived and nurtured these religions.

Use this capsule view of the Chinese Religions as a frame of reference for your study of other material outlined in this chapter.

Additional material about Chinese religions is found on pages 160-196 and 197-216 in *The Religions of Man,* by Huston Smith.

Another perspective on the religions of China will be revealed in the program "A Question of Balance," from the television series "The Long Search."

The Questions for Thought found at the end of this lesson raise issues related to the religions of China which you will want to consider.

The material you studied in Chapter 4 should be reviewed before you begin your study of the Chinese religions. This background of Buddhism will help you to a better understanding of the concepts involved in the Chinese religions.


## IMPORTANT CONCEPTS

The vast scope of the historic and cultural base for the religions of China can be narrowed somewhat for your initial study by focusing on a few major concepts. Master these important points before expanding your study to other aspects of the Chinese and their religions.

The major concepts around which you should focus your initial study include the relationship of Chinese religions in a societal context; their plurality and diversity; and the relatively small impact of Islam and Christianity on Chinese religions.


### Chinese Religion and Secular Society

Chinese religious tendencies historically appear to have been subjected to the secular needs of the State and the social order.


### Plurality and Diversity of Chinese Religions

The Chinese have had no difficulty in developing and accepting several religions and ethical systems simultaneously.

For the Chinese there may be no conflict or contradiction in adhering, whether devoutly or casually, to such diverse, organized systems of belief as cults of deities, ancestor sacrifice, Confucianism, Taoism, and Buddhism, all at the same time.

It may be possible to refer to the whole set or group of Chinese beliefs not by individual designations but rather by the single term "Chinese Religions."

**Islam and Christianity in China**

The Chinese who responded to the relatively late arrival of Islam and Christianity, which are monotheistic and demand renunciation of all but the one faith, have been a small minority.


## A CAPSULE VIEW OF THE CHINESE RELIGIONS

This description of the major aspects of Chinese religions begins with an outline of Western misunderstandings of the Chinese religious experience and some of the reasons they occurred. The capsule view continues with study questions to help organize your thoughts. The major concepts related to these study questions are then described, and include: the roots of Chinese society; the relationship of Chinese religions to Chinese society; Chinese education; the eclecticism of Chinese religion; and Western thought and religion in the Chinese context. A pronunciation guide is provided to help you understand and use the Chinese terms in this chapter.

China became a very popular object of European curiosity during the Renaissance. This resulted, in part, from Marco Polo's dazzling, if unbelievable, accounts of China in the 14th Century, and was sustained by the reports of successive Christian missionaries. Over the centuries China enjoyed waves of popularity, depending on the fashions and fads of the time. China deeply influenced the European nobility, whose palaces and gardens invariably included Chinese themes. European philosophers, such as Leibnitz and Montesquieu, were fascinated by the views and concepts emanating from a high civilization so alien to their own.

Unfortunately, the cultural and physical differences between Europe and China were so great that there was inevitably a great deal of early misunderstanding of China. In spite of this, the views of educated and sophisticated Europeans toward Chinese institutions and esthetic and philosophic achievements were, generally, quite positive.

The views of European religious representatives tended to be mixed or ambiguous. These authorities found much to admire in the ethical and family system of China. They often envied the stability and discipline which they had heard were characteristic of the

Celestial Empire, as China was called. On the other hand, Chinese religion puzzled or dismayed them. Some Chinese seemed never to think or care about God. Indeed, it appeared that the greater the schooling and higher the position, the less did an upper class Chinese care about his immortal soul. Or if he was concerned about God, the concern did not stop at one god. The Chinese found additional comfort and assurance in having a whole battery of gods and deities to appeal to. Making matters worse, the Chinese seemed to worship their ancestors, performing exotic rites to nonentities, leaving God to shift for Himself.

To the common European, and later to Americans, the Chinese were strange (and therefore suspicious) and heathen. The "heathen Chinese," as they were called, could hardly be perceived as human, so widely did they vary from the norms one would expect from people. For one thing, so the story went, they did everything backwards. For instance, they read (if they were lucky enough to be able to read) from right to left, in columns going from top to bottom; they ate their soup last; they turned their backs on their teachers when they recited; and the men wore skirts, while the women wore trousers.

None of this should surprise us, because reports of strange and wonderful cultures make good reading and interesting listening. And what could be stranger than the fact that, so far as the alien European could learn, the Chinese did not even have the decency to engage in religious wars? Since the Middle Ages, the peoples of Europe and the Middle East, and even communities in North America, have taken seriously their obligation to "save" their neighbors from eternal damnation. Indeed, it seemed to be the ultimate test of one's own faith to engage in the destruction of another's! Hence, it was easy to conclude that because the Chinese did not kill and die for their faiths, they were either too lazy, too ignorant, or too benighted to have proper faith.

Today, most of us have a more enlightened view of China, and yet some of the old misconceptions remain. What we learn about China comes to us from a rather narrow information stream, and the interpretations we apply to this information are based quite naturally on our own logic of experience, which is necessarily biased in favor of our own culture. We must keep this in mind when we make judgments about China or any other culture, whether the subject is religion, government, communism, or human rights.

The subject of China also brings out a certain laziness in us, and we can hardly be blamed for this attitude. Rarely does it seem that what a Chinese does is important to us directly and immediately. Moreover, with so many thousands of years of history behind it, China poses a formidable problem for those who would like to learn just a little about her people, culture, and history. It cannot be done overnight.

Before you continue your study of the religions of China, examine the short lesson in the guide on pronunciation of some Chinese words and terms you will encounter in your study.

As we pursue our "long search" for knowledge about mankind's beliefs, we pass through the necessary dimension of time, for civilizations develop differently from fashions. As clothing fashions evolve, we can simply discard our old clothes and buy a new wardrobe. It is not that easy to follow the evolution of a civilization. Every existing element of culture or civilization developed out of some knowledge, belief or experience which existed before. Also, the process of borrowing from other cultures, when such adaptation is convenient or advantageous, is going on. The result at any given moment (and this is a process which never stops; it is happening even as you are reading this sentence) is that nearly all of our subject matter is complex as well as dynamic. We cannot avoid dealing with religions no longer practiced and beliefs no longer held. If we did, we would fail to see the basis for what now exists, as well as the full dimensions of the experiences of mankind today. Moreover, these experiences and understandings are built into our language. It would be impossible to communicate if we tried to limit ourselves to directly experiencing the present and dealing only with today. The older a civilization is, therefore, the more elements there are for us to comprehend. Small wonder that so ancient a nation as China is the object of so little true understanding.

The key to understanding China lies in the ability to focus on key problems rather than in the memorization of endless data.

Refer to the material on How to Study in the Introduction to this Student's Guide. There you are shown that an arrangement of material and concepts is important to organize your own questions about a religion and a culture.

Here is our suggested agenda of basic questions to start you thinking about China and its religions:

1. What were the physical conditions faced by Chinese people during their prehistoric and historic periods of development? (What was their original environment and how did it change?)

2. How did the environment encourage certain patterns of economic and political activity and discourage others?

3. Given both the environment and the kinds of activity engaged in for survival in such an environment, what kind of consciousness developed among people to give them security and to help explain their existence?

4. What methods were developed to ensure group unity and survival?

5. What special or particular features of the Chinese environment, or the response to this environment, produced special or particular social, political, religious, and intellectual characteristics?

6. How did changes in the social environment (native and foreign) give rise to change and development in the way the Chinese organized themselves, made their livings, and thought about man and the world around them?

To answer these six questions adequately might require many lifetimes of study. Yet, a few helpful generalizations can be made which might help with the basic task, which is to make sense out of whatever we do know, hear, see, or learn about China. These generalizations should not be accepted as permanent truths, but merely as ongoing attempts to understand data.

*Generalization 1.* The Chinese were able to organize an agricultural society and develop an agrarian civilization based on the availability of water in the region of the Yellow River Valley. This required the development of techniques of water engineering for irrigation and flood control, which in turn led to the development of specialists who later became priests and/or bureaucrats. This special need eventually made Chinese civilization unique in some ways. In other respects, as Chinese myth and legend show, the Chinese primitive organization and religion were not exceptional, and included the concept of deities working with or against man.

*Generalization 2.*   Control of religion became a State function early in Chinese history, accompanying and supporting military-political control. Eventually the emperor became the supreme offerer of sacrifices and mediator between man and heaven.

*Generalization 3.*   Many religions and cults which had their own priesthoods were developed in China or borrowed from other peoples, but the State tended to take them over and exploit or promote them for State purposes. Generally, therefore, the State favored its own bureaucrats over priests.

*Generalization 4.*   The State did not oppose earlier animistic beliefs and accepted the existence of popular local and national deities and beliefs, yet it utilized religion to support its political and economic goals. Hence *morality* was a primary State concern which dictated principles of obedience, loyalty, frugality, temperance, and responsibility in order to buttress the social and political order.

*Generalization 5.*   The principle thrust of Chinese education was secular. It strove to produce loyal and efficient bureaucrats and politically and socially harmonious subjects. Chinese education consisted principally of the teachings of Confucius, Mencius, and the followers of the various Confucian schools. The teachings of Confucius acknowledged and embraced traditional sacrifices and other religious practices, but the accent was on man in this world. From this point of view, many scholars conclude that Confucianism is not a religion but a school of political, moral, and ethical philosophy based on solid historical data. Whatever it may have been or may be, there can be no doubt that Confucianism, more than any other philosophy or religion, shaped the everyday Chinese social order. For this reason it has been under the severest attack by the Chinese communists and others who wish to overthrow the old social order.

*Generalization 6.*   Various Chinese philosophies and religions have usually been accepted and practiced simultaneously by the same individuals and groups. The Chinese do not see most different faiths and beliefs as antagonistic or contradictory, but rather as supplementary to each other. Taoism stressed man's place within the natural order and advocated acquiescence and acceptance as well as nonaction (we-wei). Taoism may be seen as a balance to Confucianism, which encouraged active participation (by the educated upper class) and whole-hearted cooperation in local and family affairs (by the uneducated lower classes). Confucianism produced prose; Taoism produced poetry. Confucianism required involvement; Taoism suggested retirement. Confucianism was for groups; Taoism was for individuals. Both were concerned, however, with getting through this world. Buddhism, when it came, had another aim: coping with the hereafter. It was therefore not only possible but reasonable for an individual Chinese to embrace the traditional practices of ancestor-veneration, honor the family or household god, follow the precepts of Confucianism, go to Taoist priests and temples, yearn to retire eventually as a Taoist hermit, and pray to Buddha for entry into the Western paradise. In the Chinese scheme of things religious, there is a time and place for almost everything.

*Generalization 7.* With a well-defined educated class, China has been a vast reservoir of philosophers and scholars. Consequently, China has known virtually every imaginable earthly and heavenly conception. *Mo-tze* came close to the conception of one God, and preached universal love. The Taoists formed into several cults and schools, some of which saw immortality as the result of alchemy or of secret (and group) sexual techniques. Chuang-tzu speculated whether life was real or a dream. Some Chinese came to worship Confucius as a deity, others gave godlike status to *Lao-tzu,* who was generally accepted as the founder of Taoism.

Each of these approaches is interesting, and the study of the details can enrich our own lives. But the main point is that the Chinese were eclectic, able to absorb many wisdoms rather than confine themselves to one wisdom. A useful analogy might be the Chinese conception of a meal, as distinguished from that of most Europeans or Americans. Whereas the European-American sees the main course as the essential one, perhaps accompanied by a soup, dessert, or side dish eaten in some rigorous order, the Chinese have no one main dish. They bring "main dish" after "main dish," all of equal value and importance, using one dish to balance or complement the other. The Chinese seem traditionally to strive for *balance* rather than *direction*. This is as true for the religious and philosophical life as it is for the diet.

*Generalization 8.* Although China achieved unity and political centralization more than 2,000 years ago, a nation which expanded and grew so vast over the centuries inevitably embraces a wide variety of subcultures and local religious sects. Specifically, this means that the practical expressions of religion vary from place to place. The unified culture of the educated upper class must be distinguished from the popular practices of the masses, for whom religion serves as a relief from the monotony of daily toil and gives meaning to the drudgery of life.

The popular aspects of China's native, localistic religion may seem a far cry from the sophisticated philosophic reasoning and speculation conveyed by most textbooks on Chinese thought and religion. The average Chinese has only a vague conception of the foundations of his religious observances, and generally grasps only the rituals and popular notions. The purpose of many of these rituals is to manipulate the gods and spirits by placating, threatening, or even driving them away. Religious observances on a national level also involve such practical objectives. Therefore, the distance between the rites performed by the emperor and the rituals of the villagers was not so great as might be imagined. If such ceremony is divorced from the rest of the complex of Chinese beliefs, it may appear to be superstition. But if we look at the matter from a Chinese point of view, one which admits and demands complementarity, we gain a better understanding of how religion can serve simultaneously as a source of family harmony, political order, poetic and artistic expression, simple festival-type amusement, hygiene, group therapy, and insurance against the unknown.

Christianity, Islam, and Marxism, which made their ways from the West to China, all demand exclusive control of the mind and spirit. Western positivistic science has also weakened the Chinese bias toward balance. Consequently, since the arrival of these newer religions and faiths, China has undergone torments of doubt and self-questioning. Old beliefs have been shattered, even while old practices and forms of behavior persist. The rise of Chinese nationalism in the late 19th and 20th Centuries has offered some replacement for the old sense of cultural security. For this reason Chinese Communism, despite its secular Marxist-Leninist basis, offers a new vehicle for expression of ancient beliefs. It has enjoyed remarkable acceptance. It offers programs of social justice which were implicit

**106**

in the idealistic writings of some Confucianists and other early religious philosophers. It offers a sense of accord with nature, as advocated by the Taoists. It offers political order and stability, as advocated by the Legalists. And it has a vision of an ultimate Paradise, though on earth and not—as the Buddhists would have it—in the void. Modern Chinese communism accepts and encourages traditional medical and hygienic practices. It offers a sizable, varied and well-developed body of classical literature. Vigorous attempts have been made to downgrade Confucius, yet Mao Tse-tung was elevated to the position of the great Teacher, pointing the Way. Just as a cult of Confucius eventually established itself complete with temples, relics, and a priesthood, so today a cult of the late Mao is developing. Whether or not this quasireligious tendency progresses further or is inhibited, it may be seen as the latest expression of the long search of the Chinese people for social order and meaning within a harmonious universe.

It is not easy to remember names or things when we cannot pronounce them. We do not have to be scholars or geniuses to remember Napoleon, or George the Third. Not only have we heard something about them but we can read their names, say them aloud, and recognize them when we hear them. Therefore, spend a little time to study this material so you can—more or less—speak Chinese.

### Pronunciation of Chinese Words Written in English Letters

*Vowels*

| | | | | | | |
|---|---|---|---|---|---|---|
| a | as in | *a*h | o | as in | torn |
| e | as in | *u*gh | u | as in | boot |
| eh, en | as in | *ye*t | au, ao | as in | cow |
| i | as in | *ee* | ou | as in | *owe* |
| ih | as in | *it* | ei | as in | *lay* |

*Consonants*

When the aspirate symbol (') is used after a consonant, the consonant is pronounced very much as in English. For example:

| | | | | |
|---|---|---|---|---|
| k' | as the "k" in English | ts' or tz' | as "ts" in English |
| p' | as the "p" in English | ch' | as "ch" in English |
| t' | as the "t" in English | | |

Without the aspirate symbol (') the consonants have a soft or unaspirate quality, as in the following:

p    becomes the "b" sound in English
     Thus the Chinese word *pan* is pronounced "ban"
t    becomes the "d" sound in English
     Thus the Chinese word *tang* is pronounced "dang"
k    becomes the "g" sound in English
     Thus the Chinese word *ken* is pronounced "gun"
ch   becomes the "j" sound in English
     Thus the Chinese word *chu* is pronounced "jew"

The letter j sounds like "rh" (with the tongue curled) in English.

All other consonants can be pronounced approximately the same as in English.

*Examples*

Shang-ti (god) is pronounced "shanng-dee"
T'ien (heaven) is pronounced "tee-en"
Chou (ancient dynasty) is pronounced "jo" or "joe"
Han Fei-tzu (legalist philosopher) is pronounced "han fay-dzugh"
Wu Ti (Emperor of Han Dynasty) is pronounced "woo dee"
Tao Te Ching (Taoist classic) is pronounced "dow dugh jeeng"

Now that you can make some Chinese sounds, you will want to remember that most of the words used in describing Chinese people and schools of religion or thought are combinations of Chinese root sound and Latin endings. "Confucius" is a hybrid of *Kung-fu* and (c)*ius*. The word for master or teacher in Chinese is *Tzu* or *Tze*; the Chinese put it right after the name. The Latin *ius* is the same kind of honorific. Therefore, when scholars came to give Chinese religious teachers and philosophers European names, they combined the name with the Latin honorific ending. (If your name were Bill, your honorific name, according to the system, would be Billius.) Therefore, we get names like Lao-tzu (the Master Lao) sometimes written Laotius (or Laocius); Mo-tze as Mocius, etc.

This system is simple, and usually works. A few minutes of practice in pronouncing names correctly will reward you amply, and make possible better understanding of anything you read or hear about China, past, present, or future.

## STUDY QUESTIONS

The following study questions will help organize your thoughts after you have read the Capsule View of the Chinese Religions by Dr. Spector. Think through each question completely before checking your answers against the material in the Capsule View.

1. Why did China become a popular object of European curiosity during the Renaissance? Why do misconceptions remain today?

2. In what ways did the development of an agrarian civilization in China contribute to Chinese religious development?

3. What was the relationship between the State and religion in early Chinese history?

4. In what ways did the State use religion to support its political and economic goals in China?

5. The thrust of Chinese education was secular. What effect did this have on the development of religions in the country?

6. How is it possible for different Chinese philosophies and religions to be accepted and practiced simultaneously by the same individuals and groups?

7. China is said to have had a vast reservoir of philosophers and scholars. What effect did this well-defined educated class have on the development of religious philosophy and practice?

8. China embraces a wide variety of subcultures. What effect does this have on its religious philosophy and on the practice of religion by the common person?

9. Why is it difficult for Christianity, Islam, or Marxism to gain strong support in China?

# AS YOU VIEW

Another perspective on Chinese Religions is provided by the television episode *Taoism: A Question of Balance—China*. To organize your thoughts in advance, study the program description below and review the guiding questions in "Viewing with a Purpose." This will help you to participate more actively in the viewing experience.

The rise to power of the communists in China brought about the end of organized religion on the mainland. Today, if you want to see something of the richness of Chinese religions you must go elsewhere. In our search for Chinese religious experience we go to Taiwan. There the temples are thronged and the government is concerned about the huge sums of money spent on religious ceremonies by ordinary people. A whole pantheon of gods, both local and imported from the mainland, is worshiped in thousands of Buddhist and Taoist temples throughout the island. The classical tradition of Taoism is dormant, but popular Taoism thrives.

Several strands make up the religious life of the village: a Confucian respect for the past and the ancestors; the cosmic pattern of the Tao that permeates all levels of existence and manifests itself through the oracles; the local gods who dispense justice and favors; the hungry ghosts of the dead who have to be placated. All of these strands come together as we watch a funeral near Tainan, where the ghost of the dead man is taken on a journey through the hells and back—and in the village of Meinung, where the pattern of family life with its attention to the courtesies to be paid to the living and the dead is unfolded for us.

# AS YOU READ

Based on your study of the material in this Student's Guide, and from your readings in such sources as Huston Smith's *The Religions of Man,* you should be able to answer these questions as a self-assessment of what you have learned.

## Confucianism and Taoism

1. Confucius was interested in creating a peaceful and harmonious society. His ethical principles for bringing this about can be organized around these basic ethical concepts:

    1. Jen
    2. The Ch'un-tzu
    3. Li
        a. Li as propriety:
        Rectification of Names
        The Mean
        The five key relationships
        The family
        Age
        b. Li as ritual
    4. Te
    5. Wen

   Define each of these concepts and show how it might have helped to bring peace and harmony to the society of Confucius' day. (Smith, pp. 166-187) Are these values relevant today to our society, which seems to be in much the same condition as China at the time of Confucius?

2. What seems to have been the religion of Confucius? (Smith, pp. 190-191) How did it resemble and differ from the religion in China in his time? (Smith, pp. 188-190)

3. The mystical philosophy of Taoism differs from that of Indian philosophical religion in being this-worldly, rather than seeking release from the world of nature; explain the preceding statement. What is meant by becoming one with the Tao? What are the Taoist values? Compare them with the Confucian values.

4. Explain the Taoist concept of the relativity of all values and of the related concept of the identity of contraries (the yang and the yin). (Smith, pp. 211-214)

## QUESTIONS FOR THOUGHT

The following questions cover concerns or points of interest related to the religions of China. They are intended to help you apply what you have learned.

1. Dr. Spector noted in this chapter that, as a result of great geographic and cultural distance, many Westerners have held a series of misunderstandings about the religions of China. In what ways might the Chinese misunderstand aspects of Christianity?

2. How does the political ideology of the People's Republic of China reflect aspects of the Chinese religions?

3. How is "balance" a characteristic of the Chinese religions individually or as a group?

# Chapter 6
# THE LAND OF THE DISAPPEARING BUDDHA

## A STUDY OF JAPANESE BUDDHISM

For the average person, including many a Japanese, Japan is a land of paradoxes: everything sooner or later seems to become its opposite. The Emperor was supposed to be divine (before Japan's surrender at the end of World War II) and the source of all power, yet he was virtually a prisoner and treated as a political puppet. Women were subservient, yet they controlled the purse strings. The Japanese were famous for their love of order and quiet, yet they endured centuries of internal political struggle. As soon as those political tensions were resolved, they organized foreign wars with shocking rapidity. They are a people of the most refined esthetic sense, who can weep inwardly at the sight of a flower, who flock to concerts and admire even Western musicians, and yet have tolerated and practiced harsh brutality. They talk of spontaneity, and live regimented lives. They have brought relaxation to the height of an art, and yet seem so often to be "up tight."

Today the Japanese have enthusiastically embraced science and technology and have achieved industrial wonders at a rate unparalleled in history. Yet they have also been the preservers not only of their own distinctive cultural tradition but also of much of the Chinese tradition, which either eroded or was deliberately destroyed in mainland China itself.

Japan is a land of sacred gardens, shrines, and temples. Practically every home has its own little altar. Yet, except for some evangelistic and even bellicose sects, few talk religion or practice public worship with any regularity.

How can we, as outsiders, understand anything at all about this distant and seemingly exotic land? Just when we believe we have removed the mystery, it reappears.

An exploration of the Japanese religious experience and approach to the Unknown will help us comprehend this mystery, and thus understand the Japanese people and ourselves a bit better. We will discover that the best Japanese religious practice may not be "religious" at all, in the sense that we commonly understand religion. For the Japanese, religion is best expressed in the small things they do in everyday life. What may appear to us as simple physical action or even nonaction is actually the ultimate expression of religiosity.

In recent years both Zen and Nichiren, two important Japanese branches of Buddhism, have come to enjoy wide interest and popularity outside Japan, especially in the western United States. What is it in these faiths that attracts so many Americans, and particularly the youth? The Japanese seem to be finding the questions, through nonverbal means, that many of us lack the words to express. If this is true, they have given not only Buddhism but even the intuitive Shinto a sense of the interrelatedness of all things in this world, some meaning for those of us confused by the irrationality of 20th Century life and conflict. Thus, Japan may be another finger pointing the way to our future.


## A PREFACE TO YOUR STUDY

An outline of the aspects of Japanese religions begins your study. Then, key aspects of Japanese Buddhism are described by Dr. Stanley Spector, Director of International Studies, Washington University, St. Louis. This material covering the major aspects of Japanese Buddhism will supply a base of experience necessary to continue your study of this religious phenomenon. Use this capsule view of Japanese Buddhism as a frame of reference for your study of other lesson material.

Additional material about Japanese Buddhism and other religions found in Japan is found on pages 139-153 in *The Religions of Man,* by Huston Smith.

Another perspective of Japanese Buddhism will be revealed in the program "The Land of the Disappearing Buddha," in the television series "The Long Search."

The "Questions for Thought," found at the end of this lesson, raise issues about the religions of Japan which you will want to consider.

There is a close relationship between the Chinese and the Japanese civilizations. Before attempting to understand the Japanese religious experience, it is important to review some aspects of Chinese religions. Therefore, you will want to review the material in Chapter 4 of this Guide titled "Footprint of the Buddha" and that in Chapter 5 titled "A Question of Balance." It is often difficult to show the interrelationships of the world's cultures and beliefs because of the organizational problems involved in textbook and study guide presentations. They deal with one topic at a time while historical developments proceed along many lines simultaneously. Your study will be more meaningful if you explore on your own the relationships between the Chinese and Japanese religions.

## IMPORTANT CONCEPTS

Your study of the religions of Japan will have more meaning if you focus on and organize your thoughts around certain key concepts. Once you have mastered at least these major concepts, you will be better prepared to continue your study of Japanese religions and to make comparisons with other religions of the world.

The key points you should attempt to master in your initial study of the religions of Japan include their plurality and dualism; the influence of three major religions; and the relation of Japanese religion to culture.

### Plurality

Japan is characterized by religious plurality at both the social and individual levels. An individual can observe the rites and believe in the principles of several religions at the same time.

## Dualism

The dualism of either animistic faith and sacrifices remains alive even after more complex and sophisticated faiths develop or are imported.

## Three Japanese Religions

Shinto, the distinctively Japanese national religion, deals with the origins of the Japanese kingdom and its people and proclaims the presence of divine spirits in all animate and inanimate objects.

Buddhism, the major Japanese religion, was imported from China and Korea, together with Chinese Confucianism and Taoism.

Buddhism expresses itself through several principal and many minor sects. The leading contemporary sects are Shingon, which emphasizes ritual; Pure Land, which emphasizes faith; Zen, which emphasizes meditation; and Nichiren, which emphasizes faith, scripture, ritual, and patriotism.

Christianity has also played an important role in Japanese history and intellectual development.

## Japanese Religion and Culture

Japanese artistic values, physical exercises, and special ceremonies are all deeply embedded in the Japanese approach to religion; they are part of Japan's long search to find meaning and give meaning to life.

New beliefs are absorbed into existing religious systems and acknowledged as part of the Japanese national system.


## A CAPSULE VIEW OF THE RELIGIONS OF JAPAN

Japan has a distinctive and original culture which reflects at every turn the influence of the vast Sinitic (Chinese) civilization to the west. The genius of Japan has been its success in adopting, at various stages in its history, key features of other cultures. The Japanese have not been ashamed of such borrowings. They are not mere imitators, and it would be a mistake to imagine that they have simply and mechanically stolen or transferred the heritages painstakingly developed by other peoples. In most instances, they have taken the achievements of other cultures and have raised them to new, higher levels. At the very least, the Japanese have responsibly preserved and given renewed life to traditions that have been neglected or grown moribund in other lands. In this sense Chinese civilization owes as much to Japan as Japan does to China. Especially today, when the communist regime of China is systematically attempting to eliminate manifestations of historical Chinese religions and borrowed foreign faiths, Japan has indeed become a treasury for the East Asian religious heritage.

The religions of China and Japan interrelate, making it impossible to study one religion without knowing something about the other. This is because of the dialectical process of intellectual and spiritual development which seems to characterize the growth of civilization. This simply means that ideas and beliefs inevitably call forth reactions and counterbeliefs. In time, resolutions of these contradictions are usually achieved, but this achievement in turn will sooner or later be subject to a counterresolution. As a result, over the centuries there can be a considerable accumulation of schools, beliefs, and sects. This process takes place universally when people engage in the long search for truth, and helps account not only for the breathtaking variety of approaches we encounter but also for many similarities.

The outsider, viewing a foreign religion or philosophy, looks for the big principles, but the insider may find the small differences to be just as significant. For a Hebrew the question of the virgin birth of Christ may be not only unimportant but completely irrelevant since he does not subscribe to the idea that Jesus had a special divinity, and may tend to consider differences among Christians on this issue as petty squabbles of the uninformed. In the same way there is the possibility of glossing over basic differences of tenet and practice among believers in Asian faiths.

Chinese tend to look at Japanese Buddhist schools and sects as being identical with the Chinese originals. The only important differences seen are in how the names are spelled in English (for instance, *Ch'an* Buddhism becomes *Zen* in Japanese; the Chinese *T'ien-t'ai* becomes the Japanese *Tendai;* the Chinese *Chen-yen* is the Japanese *Shingon*). Schools taking root in Japan also take on all the Japanese assumptions about man, society, nature, and about how men live from day to day. Chinese Buddhism was influenced by Taoism; so, when the Japanese inherited Buddhism from China, it was already different from what it had been in India. The same is true for the influence of Confucianism on both Chinese and Japanese religions. Moreover, when it became the turn of Confucianism to be revived in China and emphasized as a State moral code in Japan, Confucianism itself was already deeply "tainted" by Buddhism.

It has been the nature of religious development that spiritual leaders tried to restore particular faiths and practices to what they believe was original direction or expression. In time, of course, this restoration takes on its own special characteristics and also has to be "set right." This, too, is part of the dialectical process. Therefore, when we try to understand a religion, school, or sect we must find out not only from what it derives but also by what it is repelled. While it is possible that religious inspiration and experience may arise spontaneously, with no clear reference to anything known or seen before, more often we can trace very clear relationships to existing material and spiritual condition.

Whenever we touch or look at something we distort it to some extent. This is as true for observations in physics as in religion. Whenever we use words to describe something, we misrepresent it to some extent. This problem is not only one for science and metaphysics, it also happens to be at the heart of religion. It is one we must be conscious of, unless we simply decide to stop looking and keep quiet. Indeed, this is precisely what some schools of Buddhism have advocated. The Taoists in China, also, value the saying: "He who speaks of the *Tao* does not know it; he who knows the *Tao* does not speak of it."

Disregarding this warning, we can suggest the generalization that the Japanese religious approach is an interplay of ancient animistic beliefs culminating in the former national or established religion of Shinto and Buddhism. It is a fusion of Japanese belief and Chinese experience. It includes Taoism, Confucianism, and Buddhism. This fusion, moreover, consists of both combinations of early and pure forms and later, synthetic expressions.

A second major consideration must be that no matter how spiritual and other-worldly aspirations may be, the actions of human beings who have them are played out upon Earth. Monks may "withdraw from the world" and live in caves or monasteries, but these caves and monasteries take up physical space. The monks must eat, no matter how abstinent they try to be. Furthermore, monks— many of whom are scholars—have connections with other people who may be peasants, teachers, nobles, or kings. Sooner or later the monk, monastery, or doctrine will be perceived as having political utility. Crass economic, political, and psychological motives rarely can be excluded from any of man's activities, including religious activity. Devotion to a belief, even accompanied by the deepest spirit of unselfishness, may prove to be the most potent of all motives for starting wars, unleashing social chaos, or becoming unseemingly involved in the world of affairs. Both in China and Japan, in periods of social disorder, there were armed monasteries whose monks were not only skilled soldiers but adept at martial arts which they raised to the level of religious practice. In short, none of the religions and systems of belief we study exists in a vacuum. They rise or fall in a dimension of history and society.

Shinto was traditionally given first place in the hierarchy of Japanese religious belief. Not only was it a continuation of the early prehistoric attempts of Japanese to explain their existence and place in an incomprehensible world, and of their effort to placate the forces of nature which struck out against them with such devastating frequency, but also it was *Japanese*. A nation which was to borrow so much from others needed security of identity. Shinto's force or influence waxed and waned over the centuries in accordance with the needs of the ruling class for legitimacy on the one hand and of the people for protection on the other. The mythology of Shinto, like all mythologies, satisfied psychological needs, especially when, as in the Japanese case, it proved a happy basis for esthetic experience and inspiration. The way of looking at nature is something conveyed by a society to its members through countless formal and informal educational channels. Japanese sensitivity to nature ensured the vitality of Shinto as certainly as Shinto directed Japanese attention to the wonders of nature.

Shintoist mythology and legend ultimately provided ideal patterns for humans to follow in their earthly routines, creating an orderly procedure for social activities. Few societies have the equivalent of Shinto. What may be surprising is that Shinto was retained for so long, and is still retained even since Japan accepted such sophisticated religions and systems of belief as Confucianism, Buddhism, and Christianity. The reason, it would seem, is that just as the *kami* or spirits of Shinto permeate every animate and inanimate thing, so Shinto manages to permeate even a world of secular order, technology, and modern science. Shinto embodies a touch of the fantastic, the fairylike. It reminds us to lift our spirits. It brings the unknown and unseen into a familiar relationship with us. There is a Shinto shrine in Tokyo, and there people have their fortunes told. The fortune is given on a small slip of white paper. If people like their fortune, they keep the slip. If they do not, they fold it into a knot and tie it to the branch of a tree, so that the gods may take it back. Recently, in order to keep the shrine park clean, the authorities put up a sign which reads, "The people who 'sent back' their fortunes are educated people—students, doctors, lawyers, housewives, workers, and teachers—but they still go on tying rejected fortunes to the tree branches." It is just a nice custom, and besides, why take chances? This is the spirit of Shinto.

Buddhism was first brought to Japan from Korea, and slightly later from China. Indeed, during the T'ang Dynasty in China (618-907 A.D.) a succession of Japanese missions went to China to study Buddhism, as well as other aspects of Chinese culture. Buddhism entered Japan together with the Chinese written language, which remains today the basis of the modern written language of Japan. (Incidentally, to adopt something as important as a language or numerical system is highly significant inasmuch as it will critically control thought processes and ways of verbalizing and defining the world.) Simultaneously with Buddhism and Chinese language came Confucianism, which prescribed the elements of family, social, and political order. Buddhism was a prescription which the current state of Japanese society made most welcome. It taught resignation, compassion, and the hope of salvation, and it could tranquilize the people. Confucianism could produce good bureaucrats and good procedures, as well as a basis for advanced education to the court and the government. Of itself, however, Buddhism appealed intellectually and spiritually to all, from lowest to highest, including Prince Shotoku, who reigned from 596-621 A.D. and was the guiding spirit of the importation.

During the Nara Period (710-794) under royal and noble patronage, Buddhism grew in its new soil. But the influence of the Buddhist priests at the capital became so great that it began to threaten the power of the royal house. It is indicative of the strength of the Buddhist factions at court that the eventual solution to the problem

**120**

of the Buddhistization of politics was not to make the Buddhists move but rather to move the royal court from Nara, the old capital, to Heian, present-day Kyoto.

Despite this effort to deemphasize the role of Buddhism in politics, Buddhist monasteries thrived in the hills around Heian. Today when one wants to visit the great sites and temples of Buddhism, one goes precisely to Kyoto. During this so-called Heian Period (794-1192), the integration of Shinto and Buddhism had a profound effect on both religions. Each, however, continued to maintain its distinctions. Shinto adopted the Buddhist deities and Buddhism adopted the shinto gods. The shinto gods were incarnations of the Buddhas and bodhisattvas. Toward the end of the period a decline in the moral standards of the Buddhist clergy, a relaxation of principles, and a trend toward materialism under the seductions of court life led to what many view as a degeneration of Buddhism. Moreover, sectarian enmities, which had strong political overtones, led eventually to the fortification of monasteries and the development of warrior priests. Religion was challenging government.

The warrior priests and armed monasteries of Heian and the rise of a new class of militarists, imbued with Confucian secular doctrines of order and rational government, led to a decision by the new military ruling class to establish the governmental seat at Kamakura, not far from present-day Tokyo. Meanwhile the imperial court, remaining behind at Heian, lost its political relevance and became a living museum of Japanese etiquette and esthetics. The peace at Heian contrasted with the clouds of war which floated over Kamakura and eventually over all of Japan, as the warlords struggled for supremacy. Warriors developed new codes for themselves, while the distrait and distraught common folk yearned for a glimpse of something better than the earthly hell around them. Just as Buddhism offered security and comfort in the uncertain days of the wars among the Three Kingdoms in China, following the fall of the Han Dynasty in 220 A.D., so a simple form of Buddhism relying essentially on faith alone offered solace to a war-gutted Japan. Three sects offered new avenues of hope, respite, and salvation. These were the sects of Pure Land, Zen, and Nichiren.

All the major schools and sects of Japanese Buddhism, like those of China, belong to the Greater Vehicle, or Mahayana branch. In order to appreciate the development of Mahayana in Japan, we will briefly review the names and principal features of the earlier sects, noting their relationship to Chinese sects. We should bear in mind, however, that most of these sects have either declined considerably or entirely disappeared from the scene.

### Early Mahayana Buddhist Sects

*Sanron.* (In Chinese, *San Lun,* or Three Treatises) This sect used Taoist terms to expound a doctrine of emptiness. This is also known as the Middle Way.

*Hosso.* (Consciousness Only) A sect which preached that some people are too evil to be saved.

*Tendai.* (In Chinese, *T'ien T'ai*) This sect is named for a mountain in China where it originated. It attempted to synthesize the contradictory doctrines of various schools of Buddhism by arranging the different doctrines according to the chronology of the life of Gautama Buddha. It tried to demonstrate that the various doctrines were intended for different audiences at different stages of development, all adding up in the end to the same thing—the unification of Theravada and Mahayana Buddhism and salvation for all sentient beings. In Japan, Tendai produced a military clergy and was one of the wealthiest sects. It provided the basis for the three principal modern sects: Pure Land (amida-ism), Zen, and Nichiren.

*Kegon.* (In Chinese, *Hua-yen*) This sect linked the phenomenal world with the Buddha mind: all things are simply manifestations of the Buddha mind. Since the Buddha mind is in every being, every man can attain Buddhahood.

*Shingon, or True Word.* (In Chinese, the *Chen-yen*) This mystical and magical sect was based on the *mantra* of India, or magical symbols, which captured the essential mystery of Buddhism. It celebrated the famous *mandala,* or magical picture, which showed the Supreme Buddha surrounded by the Buddhas of the four directions. Elaborate secret rites as well as paintings grew out of this way of approaching Buddha, hence, this sect is closely related to the esthetic expression of Buddhism both in China and Japan. It claimed the power to produce miracles through the proper formula, such as rainmaking. Since *Chen-yen* could produce miracles, it could also easily seduce emperors and others who needed special power. Consequently, it gained great control of political power in T'ang China. The political demise of T'ang meant the decline of *Chen-yen* Buddhism, but not before *Chen-yen* suffered great persecution in the 8th Century at the hands of a concerned, jealous, and vengeful Confucian bureaucracy. Under the ministration of the Japanese monk-scholar Kukai, the sect found a new birth in Japan in the 8th and 9th Centuries. In Japan it was known as *Shingon*. Kukai believed the progression of religious consciousness consisted of ten stages. Among these were the stages of sensuous desire, Confucian morality, Taoist spirituality, Theravada self-denial, Mahayana metaphysics, and the final stage where one attained the True Word, the *Shingon* mystic truth. The attainment of this stage produced a sense of identity with the Supreme Buddha. This mystic truth was achieved through esoteric rites. *Shingon* still claims several million followers in Japan today.

**Major Contemporary Sects**

A sect can remain alive and vital through one of two means. It can have a rigidly controlled, disciplined, and well-supported body of priests, which alone possesses the means of salvation but keeps that means open and available to others. The alternative is to open its floodgates wide to the common person, guaranteeing him salvation if he exhibits simple but devout faith and performs some ritualistic formula which needs little practice or specialization to master. All of the major contemporary sects of Japanese Buddhism have satisfied one of these requirements.

*Pure Land, or Jodo.* (In Chinese, *Ch'ing Tu*) This is one of the oldest sects of Buddhism. It talks of the Pure Land, the Western Paradise, or Heaven of Bliss which all men may attain after death. It is represented by the *Amitabha* aspect of Buddha (in Chinese *A-Mi T'o-Fo*). It is the Buddha of Compassion who helps others attain salvation by leading them to the Western Paradise. The other popular deity who fulfilled such merciful functions was a Chinese, *Kuan-yin:* He was originally depicted as male, but later as female. The Japanese readily adopted *Kuan-yin* and Amitabha, which they called *Amida.* Pure Land devotees believed that by constantly chanting the name *"A-Mi-T'o-Fo"* they would be saved. In the 11th Century, the

Japanese monk Honen, reacting against the corruption of the monasteries of his time, formed a school of *Jodo.* His disciple Shinran formed a subsect, the *Shin,* or *True Sect,* which held that man was basically evil and therefore could not do good. Thus, salvation could not be achieved by good works. To be saved, to enter the Pure Land, one had to depend entirely on the compassion of Amida. The Shin sect differed from the rest of the Jodo school; it maintained that by uttering the divine name, and only by such invocation, could Paradise be obtained. No special practices were needed. One could simply live his ordinary life and be saved. It was not necessary to meditate, join a monastery, or become a priest. It did not matter if you were rich or poor, high or low; as long as you could breathe the word "Amida," you were saved. What a relief this must have been to people in that socially stratified, bureaucratic, and feudal society. In Japan today there are approximately 18 million *Shin-Jodo* members.

*Zen.* (In Chinese, *Ch'an*) It is the best known school of Japanese Buddhism outside of Japan because it offers concrete techniques for meditation and requires minimal knowledge of the scriptures of Buddhism. It is spreading under many names. Some of these bear no reference at all to Buddhism, although they have Buddhist as well as Chinese Taoist origins. The disciplines involved in judo, karate, flower-arranging, calligraphy, Japanese archery, gardening, the tea ceremony, transcendental meditation, and biofeedback, as well as dozens of other activities, are central practices of Zen.

Because Ch'an, or Zen, rejects language as misleading (since words are distorted symbols of reality) it concentrates on nonverbal communication. Action, even the action of sitting perfectly still, conveys more meaning than any words. There is no use looking for nirvana, for that is only a word, and the minute you think it or write it or say it, it is destroyed. No one can teach you about nirvana, and no one can tell you about Enlightenment. There are many schools devoted to such achievement, so you will want to refer to pages 592-598 in your text, where there are some excellent examples of what Zen is all about.

The discipline involved in the mastery of Zen techniques makes it a popular requirement of many Japanese companies today. They believe it produces better disciplined, well-composed employees. Military forces also find its martial arts techniques extremely useful.

*Nichiren.* This is a major Japanese reform movement named for its 13th Century founder. It stresses a Buddhist book of scripture, the Lotus Sutra, which calls for purity and proselytizing. It is generally less tolerant than other schools of Buddhism or Asian religion. It seeks to repurify Buddhism. The Three Great Mysteries involve worship of a *mandala,* their own special symbol of Sakyamuni Buddha's universal presence; constant repetition of the Lotus Sutra; and regarding as sacred any place where Nichiren ceremonies are performed. The third mystery implies that there is no need for special temples. The fulminations and intolerance of Nichiren resulted in the persecution of Nichiren, the man, and of the sect. In fact, one of Nichiren's doctrines predicts persecution of those who try to purify it, since by definition all other Buddhism is in a period of decay and decline preparatory to revival. Nevertheless, Nichiren still attracts about two-and-a-half million followers.

## Post-World War II Sects

The trauma of war and utter defeat in the mid-20th Century not only shook the faith of many Japanese in their traditional institutions and religions but also created a great sense of personal and national guilt.

Purity and cleanliness are characteristically supreme values of the Japanese. Indeed, much of Japanese ritual is concerned with purification, whether in the temple or the public and home bath. The war left the Japanese feeling dirty, as the "sick" literature of postwar Japan vividly demonstrates. But there can be only so much breast-beating and self-accusation before the human spirit revives. The Japanese set about to rebuild a newer and better Japan with grit, determination, and their usual spirit of discipline and self-sacrifice. They sought new answers from Western culture, technology, and religion. At the same time, as their national confidence returned, they looked once more to their heritage for new clues and inspiration.

The result has been the development of still more religious sects. Some rely on the traditions of Buddhism, imbued as it is with nationalistic Shinto values. An example of this type of sect is the *Soka gakkai.* It is based on Nichiren and embodies the techniques of Billy Graham and the Reverend Moon to enlist mass support. Others are combinations of Buddhism and Christianity, which often appear bizarre to the outsider. What is remarkable is that all of these new

**125**

sects have a wide appeal for the young, as well as offering hope and solace to the old and the bereaved. *Soka* gakkai is highly nationalistic and politically conservative. Its political arm, the Komeito Party, has had fair success in winning parliamentary seats. It uses modern mass media and public relations techniques such as rallies, badges, and uniforms to win mass support from the urban middle class. More recently it has moved into the countryside for rural support. Other sects have established temples and raised prodigious sums of money for the support of their teachers. Similar movements, of course, are not unknown in America and Europe. All of this is clear evidence that, with all its religious heritage and despite a generally secular climate, Japan's long search goes on.

## STUDY QUESTIONS

The following study questions will help organize your thoughts after you have read "A Capsule View of the Religions of Japan" by Dr. Spector. Think through each question completely before checking your answers against the material in the Capsule View.

1. Why is it a mistake to believe that the Japanese, through the years, have imitated other religions of the Far East?

2. In what ways do the religions of China and Japan interrelate?

3. In the study of a religion, why is it important to find out not only from what it derives but also by what it is repelled?

4. What does Dr. Spector mean when he says that the Japanese religious approach is a fusion of Japanese belief and experience?

5. How are the spiritual aspirations of a religion often tempered by the practical realities of living that religion here on Earth?

6. What features of Shintoism have contributed to its being accorded, traditionally, first place in the hierarchy of Japanese religious beliefs?

7. In what ways is Shintoism a basis for esthetic experience and inspiration?

8. How do Shintoist mythology and legend provide ideal patterns for humans to follow in their earthly routines?

9. What did Buddhism contribute to Japanese religious life? What was the contribution of Confucianism?

10. Why was the role of Buddhism deemphasized in Japan?

11. How was Buddhism integrated with Shintoist beliefs and practices?

12. What are the basic beliefs of the Pure Land school of Japanese Buddhism?

13. Why is Zen Buddhism so well known outside of Japan?

14. Of what significance is the Lotus Sutra to the Nichiren school of Japanese Buddhism?

15. In what ways did World War II affect the development of the religions of Japan?

## AS YOU VIEW

Another perspective on the religions of Japan is provided by the television episode *"Buddhism: The Land of the Disappearing Buddha—Japan."* Study the program description below, and review the guiding questions in "Viewing with a Purpose" to help you participate more actively in the viewing experience.

If the Buddha of Sri Lanka met the Buddha of Japan, would they recognize each other? We go to Japan to explore this question. The search takes us to Tokyo—and to a restaurant where all the staff must take part in regular Zen meditation sessions if they want to keep their jobs. Then we move on to more classical aspects of Zen—masters of calligraphy, swordfighting, archery, and the tea ceremony, all highly different acts unified by the underlying principles of Zen. Seeming less complex are the Buddhists of the Pure Land sect, whose faith in the godlike Amida Buddha is sufficient for their salvation and rebirth in the Pure Land. The apparently simple, however, turns out to be complex. The complexities of Zen are made simpler for us by one of Japan's greatest living Zen masters.

## QUESTIONS FOR THOUGHT

The following questions cover concerns or points of interest related to the religions of Japan. These questions are intended to help you apply what you have learned.

1. What would be the Zen master's answer to the question, "Does a cat have Buddha nature?"

2. In what ways is Shinto a unique religious expression, compared with many other religions of the world?

3. How might adherence to the combination of Japanese religious expressions change esthetics and life-styles of people in your community?

Chapter 7
# RELIGION IN THE ANCIENT NEAR EAST

## A STUDY OF THE FOUNDATIONS OF JUDAISM, CHRISTIANITY, AND ISLAM

The religions of the ancient Near East are important in their own right and because of the influences they exerted on three major religions of today—Judaism, Christianity, and Islam. The following account will emphasize the aspects of Near East religions that have exerted the most influence on these three living religions.

### A PREFACE TO YOUR STUDY

This chapter will provide the necessary background material for your study of Judaism, Christianity, and Islam. There is no episode in the television series "The Long Search" corresponding to the material in this chapter, nor is there any specific reading assignment in your text material. The Capsule View of the religions of ancient Egypt and the religion of Mesopotamia, Babylonia, and Assyria is provided by Dr. Grace Cairns, professor emeritus of philosophy and religion at Florida State University.

After reading the Capsule View, test your knowledge of this background material by responding to the Study Questions. It will be helpful to review this material before you begin your study of Chapter 8 (Judaism), Chapter 9 (Christianity), and again before you study Chapter 10 (Islam).

# A CAPSULE VIEW OF RELIGION IN THE
## ANCIENT NEAR EAST

Egyptian religion was focused upon a quest for the immortal, the permanent, the eternal. The pharaoh, who was its chief priest, was believed to be divine, an incarnation of the god of the sun, Horus, who was son of Osiris. From the earliest to the latest time in Egyptian history, Osiris was the most popular of all deities. The story of his death and resurrection is very old. He was said to have been the first king of Egypt and the one who gave his country its civilization. Finally he suffered death and later dismemberment at the hand of his enemies, led by Set, his brother. With the help of his wife and sister, Isis, Osiris rose from the dead and became king of the underworld and judge of the dead. Because Osiris was human as well as divine, his resurrection signified that every righteous man could likewise rise from the dead and have eternal life if he observed the proper procedures.

Osiris was also a fertility cult deity identified with Earth and its recurrent cycles of seasonal growth of vegetation. Above all he was concerned with the Nile and its rhythmic floods, that enabled Egypt to provide itself with food. Phallic emblems were used in his cult to symbolize this aspect of his nature.

Associated with Osiris was Isis. The kindly aspects of her personality are revealed in these passages from a New Kingdom (1580-1085 B.C.) hymn, quoted by Henri Frankfort, *Ancient Egyptian Religion,* Harper Torchbooks ed., New York: Harper & Brothers, 1961, p. 130:

> Beneficent Isis, that protected her brother, that sought for him without wearying, that traversed this land mourning, and took no rest until she found him! . . . She that revived the faintness of the Weary One, that took in his seed and provided an heir, that suckled the child in solitude, the place where he was being unknown; that brought him, when his arm was strong, into the Hall of Geb. . . .

Isis was also called the Enchantress, mistress of the magic arts. It was through her skill in this area that she was able to revive Osiris temporarily when Horus was conceived.

The Osiris-Isis cult, popular with the Egyptians, was spread all over the Greco-Roman world by the Ptolemies, who established the cult under the name of Serapis at Alexandria. Christianity, too, felt its influence. Wallis Budge, a noted Egyptologist, says, "In Osiris the Christian Egyptians found the prototype of Christ, and in the pictures and statues of Isis suckling her son Horus, they perceived the prototypes of the Virgin Mary and her child." (*Egyptian Religion,* New York: Bell Publishing Co., 1959, p. 105.)

Horus, son of Osiris, a sun god, was represented as a falcon behind the heads of the pharaohs in the monumental sculptures that still survive. Each pharaoh was a divine incarnation of Horus. In the afterlife Horus attained a mysterious oneness with Osiris, father of Horus, and his successor again became Horus. "As Osiris he was alive in the growing grain, in the rising waters of the Nile, in the rising moon." (Henri Frankfort, *Ancient Egyptian Religion,* p. 103.)

The other major deity was the sun, called Re (or Ra). Combined with the Theban deity Amon, he became Amon-Re, the leading god of the New Kingdom (1580-1085 B.C.). The sun god, too, like Osiris, typified immortality because he set every night but rose again every morning after his nightly sojourn in the underworld.

There were myriads of deities in Egyptian religion, of varying degrees of importance. Among the greater gods were those in the group of nine deities, the Ennead of Helopolis (capital of Egypt around 2380 B.C.). This Ennead was both a cosmology and a genealogy; a cosmology because it described the origin of the world, and a genealogy because it delineated the ancestry of the god, Horus, incarnated in every pharaoh. First in the Ennead was Atum, the father-creator god. Atum was spontaneously generated from the primeval abyss of waters called Nun. It was a common idea in the Near East that before creation there was an uncreated substratum, a primeval abyss of chaotic waters. In the Bible in Gen. 1:2 this was called the "deep." In the original Hebrew the word for "deep" is *tehom* and is equivalent to the word "tiamat" in Babylonian texts. In both literatures it means a chaotic mass of waters. In the Babylonian texts Tiamat was personified as a monster from whose body the god, Marduk, created an orderly universe. To return to the Ennead, Atum generated two children out of himself, Shu, the atmosphere, or air, and Tefnut, his female supplement. Then Shu and Tefnut had two children, Geb (Earth) and Nut (the sky). Shu separated Geb and Nut. Nut was represented as a huge cow, whose legs, with the help of other lesser deities, supported the sky. She stood between and separated land and sky. The stars studded her belly. Then Geb and Nut had four children: Osiris, Isis (whose name means "the throne"), Set, and Nephthys. These nine deities remained great gods throughout subsequent Egyptian history.

Other important gods were Ptah, an earth god who, in the theology of Memphis (ca. 3000 B.C.), created the world by his divine Word, which uttered what the deity thought in his heart. Ptah as the creator was not given nationwide acceptance. Associated with Ptah was the Apis bull, his herald. Hathor, a gentle deity, was goddess of the sky and of love, shown as a cow or with a cow's horns and ears. Thoth, god of wisdom, appeared variously as the moon, a baboon, an ibis, or an ibis-headed man. Maat was goddess of right, of order and law in the cosmos and in human social relations. Bes was god of childbirth. Anubis was shown either in animal shape as a jackal or with a human body and a jackal's head. He was the god of cemeteries, of proper burial, and master of embalmment; he weighed the heart of the deceased upon the scales of judgment in the afterlife. (See below.)

In various parts of Egypt certain animals were held sacred, probably because they had been revered in their respective districts before they became part of the great Egyptian civilization or before this civilization arose. The crocodile, the hippopotamus, the serpent, cats, dogs, the ram (sacred to Amon) belong to this group. Certain plants and insects (the scarab beetle, in particular, a sun symbol) were held sacred.

## Monotheism

In the 14th Century B.C., during a brief interlude in polytheism, the brilliant young pharaoh, Ikhnaton, became the first known monotheist in history. He proclaimed that there was only one god in the cosmos, and tried to eradicate worship of all other gods. He taught that Aton was the one god of the universe, the creator and sustainer of all. Though formless, Aton was portrayed as a sun disc, with emanating rays ending in human hands holding the symbol of life (the ankh). Ikhnaton composed poetic hymns to Aton. The following are excerpts from one of the most sublime; the hymn is called the most beautiful surviving work of Egyptian literature:

How manifold are thy works!
They are hidden from before us,
O sole god, whose powers no other possesseth.
Thou didst create the Earth according to thy heart
While thou wast alone:
Men, all cattle large and small,
All that are upon the Earth,
That go about upon their feet;
All that are on high,
That fly with their wings

The foreign countries, Syria and Kush,
The land of Egypt;
Thou settest every man unto his place,
Thou suppliest their necessities. . . .

Thou art in my heart,
There is no other that knoweth thee
Save thy son Ikhnaton. . . .

Ikhnaton's reform was much too sudden. No one was ready for this religious revolution. After Ikhnaton's death, at only 30, his successors immediately returned to polytheistic worship with Amon-Re as chief god.


## The Afterlife

As said above, the pharaoh in the afterlife attained a mysterious oneness with Osiris. Beginning with the First Intermediate Period (2180-2000 B.C.) commoners of the middle class also began to identify themselves with Osiris, who was alive in the grain, the Nile floodwaters, the moon, and the constellation Orion. The desire was to rise like the sun, rejuvenate oneself like the moon, repeat life (*uhm ankh*) like the flood of the Nile. (The *ankh,* symbol of life, is found everywhere in Egyptian funerary art.) To become Akhu, the goal was transfigured spirits, for an immortality "within the perennial movements of nature." This kind of immortality, Frankfort tells us, "was of immemorial antiquity in Egypt since it was expressed from the earliest times in the wish to become Akhu, transfigured spirits, circling as 'imperishable stars round the pole.'" (Frankfort, *Ancient Egyptian Religion,* pp. 105 f.)

**133**

To become Akhu, transfigured spirits, was the goal. Nevertheless the Egyptian saw no contradiction in thinking that it was necessary to preserve his mummified body in the tomb where his *ka* (life-force) existed and was to be maintained by offerings. Also he believed that his *ba* ("animation," "manifestation" is the meaning of the word) led a birdlike existence on Earth and in the nether world. He loved life, felt close to nature and desired to be immortal, but he thought concretely, not abstractly. He believed preservation of his body was necessary for immortality, even in its ultimate form, absorption "in the great rhythm of the universe" as a transfigured spirit. Also he believed that he must undergo the ordeal of judgment by the gods before Osiris could bestow the gift of immortality upon him.

The main features of judgment were: (1) reciting of hymns of adoration and prayer to the greatest gods Ra and Osiris; (2) entrance into the Judgment Hall and reciting the Negative Confession. When he entered the Judgment Hall of Maat, the Egyptian beheld the faces of the gods. Here were the Maati, Isis and Nephthys, who as the Maati stood for straightness, integrity, righteousness, truth. Also here were the 42 gods whose function was to watch sinners. Before this group, the Egyptian recited the Negative Confession, that is, he mentioned the sins he had *not* committed: robbery, murder, fraud, deceit, lying, vile or evil speech, anger, adultery, blasphemy, causing sorrow to others, pollution of land and water, insolence, avarice, showing favoritism in business or social relations, hypocrisy, pride. (3) Next comes the weighing of the heart on the scales. The heart was weighed against a feather, the symbol of Maat (justice, truth, righteousness). Witnesses of the judgment and weighing were many gods, in addition to those mentioned above. Included were Anubis (the jackal-headed god) who did the weighing of the heart, and Thoth, who wrote down the result of the weighing. Nearby was a frightful monster ready to devour the heart if the weighing proved it wicked. Also witnessing the weighing was the *ba,* soul of the deceased, represented as a human-headed hawk. (4) Thoth then pronounced the judgment, the result of the weighing. (5) If the judgment was favorable, the person was called "Osiris" and granted a homestead in the Field of Peace. He was identified with Osiris because all the rites and ceremonies were performed for him that had been performed by Isis and Nephthys to render Osiris immortal. The ancient belief in the magical potency of the word is brought out in the term *maa kheru,* now applied to the new Osiris. Maa kheru means "true of voice" or "right of word" and signifies that the one to whom it applies could now use his voice successfully to command invisible beings to do all the things for him that he has the right to expect. (6) With the judgment over, Horus led the successful candidate up to the place where Osiris was seated. He asked Osiris to be "an Osiris greatly favored," and Horus asked his father to let the new Osiris enter into the presence of the great lord, Osiris, king of the underworld, and to let the new immortal one "be like unto the followers of Horus forever." (Budge, *Egyptian Religion,* p. 175) (7) Then the successful person, now an immortal, was ready to explore the underworld and meet the gods therein. He might enjoy such things as following in the retinue of Re in his boat journey across the sky and in the underworld; or, as one of the Akhu, the transfigured spirits, he might enjoy circling as an imperishable star around the pole star.

As said above, preservation of the body was thought necessary for immortality. This was the reason for the extraordinary tombs built in Egypt to preserve the body from robbers or enemies. Most famous were the pyramids, tombs of Egyptian kings. Perhaps the most amazing of these structures of the ancient world, which stand today near Cairo, Egypt, is the Pyramid of Khufu, or Cheops, largest of the group. Its square base is 746 feet on each side and its height is 481 feet. Within it is an inclined passage that leads deeply into the interior, where the burial chamber is located. It has long since been robbed of its fabulous treasures of gold, precious stones, and religious artworks. King Khufu thought that the closing up of the passageway to the burial chamber by huge monoliths would make it impervious to robbers, but he was mistaken. The pharaoh was also a god, as we have noted. His tomb, therefore, was also a temple. A chapel for worship, with offerings, was part of the pyramid itself or of a separate building.

The Theban kings built for themselves underground tombs, but they also built temples as houses for their gods above the ground. The remains of the temples are imposing in their grandeur today. Some of the columns of these buildings still stand, after 3,000 years.

No other culture has taken a greater interest in immortality, in the permanent, the eternal than the Egyptian. This intense interest gave rise to some of the most amazing and enduring works of art in human history and to a great, unique art style in sculpture and painting. In religion the resurrection drama of Osiris and Isis, in the later cult of Serapis, prepared many in the Greco-Roman world for acceptance of belief in the resurrection of Jesus as the core-doctrine of early Christianity.

## THE RELIGION OF MESOPOTAMIA: BABYLONIA AND ASSYRIA

Assyrian religion was borrowed from the Babylonian. The Babylonians, a Semitic people, in their turn took over the culture, including the religion, of the Sumerians, a non-Semitic people. The Sumerian culture was very old; it took form around 3500 B.C. The Sumerians invented writing (the cuneiform style) and the monumental temple style called the ziggurat, and were first in many other aspects of civilization. (See S.N. Kramer, *History Begins at Sumer,* Anchor Books ed., Garden City, New York: Doubleday & Co., Inc., 1959.)

### The Gods of Babylonia

The Babylonian pantheon was based upon a standard list of deities drawn up by the Sumerians around 2500 B.C. First on the list were two triads of deities. In the first triad was *Anu* (not the supreme god, in Sumerian culture, but he became supreme around 2060 B.C. in the Babylonian religion). Anu was called "Father" and "King of the Gods." He was born from Apsu, the underworld ocean, and Tiamat, the primeval chaos. Anu lived in the third heaven. By historical times the consort of Anu was Ishtar, the great goddess, the most important deity in the ancient Near East.

The second deity on the list of gods was *Enlil,* a wind or storm god. He had both benevolent and hostile aspects in relation to mankind. In the myth of creation he slew the dragon of chaos, a role later assumed by Marduk, but he also showed his hostility to the human race in being the god chiefly responsible for bringing about the Great Flood. One of his main functions was as guardian of the

Tablets of Destiny. In Babylonian thought, this meant giving to each thing in nature, living or nonliving, its proper place in the created order. Enlil's chief messenger was Nusku, the fire god. In addition, Enlil had a large staff of lesser gods who were his doorkeepers, cooks, shepherds, and messengers. His famous temple was "The House of the Mountain" in Nippur, the center of his cult. "The House of the Mountain" became the name generally used for a temple.

*Ea,* the third god in the triad, was god of the land. His dwelling was thought to be in the apsu, the abyss of waters. This was the underworld ocean upon which the land rested. Ea was called "lord of wisdom" because he had all magical knowledge (he was "lord of incantations") and was the one who gave mankind its arts and crafts, all the fundamentals of civilization, including writing, building, and agriculture. His son was Marduk, who became the central deity of Babylonian religion, as Ashur became the chief god in Assyria. In astrological texts Ea is assigned most often to the constellations Aquarius and Pisces. His symbol was either a ram's head or a goat fish (head of a goat and body of a fish).

A second triad of deities next appears in the early god lists. This comprised Sin, the moon god, Shamash, the sun god, and Adad (or Hadad), the storm god. The female deity associated with this triad was the great goddess, Ishtar. Sin, the moon god, was lord of the calendar, a fertility deity as vegetation god, and responsible for the fertility of cattle. He rode a winged bull and the crescent was his symbol. His consort was Ningal, mother of the sun god.

Shamash, the sun god, was son of Sin. Shamash was popular with all the people. He was upholder of truth and justice in society. He is represented on the stele which gives us the famous law code of Hammurabi; the god Shamash is shown giving these laws to Hammurabi. Shamash and Adad were interpreters of oracles, through their priests. His symbol was the solar disk with a four-pointed star inside it and with rays emanating from between the points of the star. In Assyria his symbol was the winged disk.

Adad, the storm god, was widely worshiped throughout the Near East. In the Old Testament he is called Rimmon; and in the early stages of Hebrew religion Yahweh, himself, was a storm god. Along with Enlil, he took a part in the Great Flood. His symbols are the lightning shown in his right hand, while the left hand grasps an axe. His animal was the bull.

Ishtar, the most famous goddess of Near Eastern religion and the most widely worshiped, was the female divinity associated with this second triad. She became the consort of the high god, Anu, and absorbed the attributes of the more important goddesses so that she became known as "the goddess," or main female deity. Ishtar had two main functions. She was goddess of love and procreation and goddess of war. The planet Dilbat (Venus) was assigned to her, and her symbol was an eight-pointed or sixteen-pointed star. She rode upon a lion but is represented upon the Ishtar gate of Babylon with a dragon form, the *mushrussu*. At her chief center of worship, Erech, she was mother-goddess and goddess of love and procreation. Here her staff included both male and female hierodules, or temple slaves.

## The Tammuz-Ishtar Resurrection Myth

This myth is preserved in the Tammuz liturgies. The god Tammuz descends into the underworld (that is, he dies). His mourning sister-wife goes down into the underworld in search for him, and both return in triumph, bringing with them revival of fertility, of all vegetation, of life in the spring. The general theme is that of the vegetation god, who dies with the winter and revives, or is resurrected, to new life in the spring. The Tammuz cult was replaced in Babylonia by the New Year festival, which had a similar function, but the cult remained among the common people and was adopted by Syria and Canaan (the land of the Hebrews). In Syria, Tammuz was called Adonis. In Israel still, in Ezekiel's time (6th Century B.C.: Ezek. viii, 14) the women still practiced the ritual weeping for Tammuz and also, no doubt, celebrated his joyous resurrection.

## The Underworld and the Afterlife

The underworld, called the "land of no-return," was thought of as a gloomy, miserable place ruled by the goddess Ereshkigal and her spouse, Nergal. It was similar in conception to the Hades of Homeric times. The deceased became a mere shade in this land of sunless gloom, and had no hope of escape. The Babylonians were interested in a happy life in this world. The only man who attained immortality—and this was immortal life in an "Eden" in Mesopotamia—was the hero of the Flood story, Utnapishtim. The hero Gilgamesh, however, sought the gift of immortality. After many perilous adventures he was able to find Utnapishtim, who told the hero that immortality was not for mankind. He, Utnapishtim, received the gift because of what he did in a unique event, the Great Flood, sent by Enlil to destroy mankind. Enlil, in his gratitude that Utnapishtim had saved some men to continue the race, gave this "Noah" the gift of immortality. Utnapishtim offered a second best prize, the gift of eternal youth. This could be had by eating of a plant found growing in the bottom of the sea. Gilgamesh found the plant, but carelessly left it on the bank of a pool while he took a refreshing swim. A serpent came upon it and ate it. The serpent now could rejuvenate itself by shedding its skin, but mankind lost the opportunity of renewing its youth, through the carelessness of Gilgamesh.

Kings were not innately divine in Mesopotamia, as in Egypt. The king was called the tenant-farmer of the god and chief link between heaven and Earth. Professor Frankfort, in his book *Kingship and the Gods,* thinks it probable that the only kings deified were those who engaged in a sacred marriage with "the goddess." In an early text a king is ritually identified with a fertility god, Urash, before engaging in a sacred marriage with the great goddess Ishtar. Also at the New Year festivals the king ritually impersonated the god, Marduk, in the sacred marriage while a priestess impersonated the great goddess. Kingship, if not divine, was sacral throughout the Near East. Scholars tell us that more research needs to be done on this subject.

In conclusion, there was no desirable afterlife for mortals. The only "paradiee" was an Eden on Earth, sometimes called Dilmun (a paradise of the gods) which may have been the source of the Eden of Genesis. The land of no-return was similar to the Greek hades and the sheol of the Hebrews, a land of gloom and of souls that were miserable shades, mere shadows of their former lively selves. Some kings may have become divine through ritual when they "married" Ishtar, but were not innately so, as in Egypt.

### The Temple and Priesthood

The priesthood became very wealthy and influential. Everyone paid a tax to the gods who, in theory, rented all lands and services to mortals. Even the king was the main tenant-farmer of the god. The king, when he was powerful, could get what he needed from temple treasuries which seemed to remain full, for the most part. Temple staffs were often very large in number, about 730 persons in large temples, around 2600 B.C.; in later times the staff of the Marduk temple of Babylon numbered several thousand. The priesthood played a large part in national affairs of Babylonia and Assyria, but the king had the privilege of appointing his own candidates to the higher priestly offices. There was great variety in the duties of priests. The chief priest presided over and performed significant acts in the seasonal festivals; the *kalu* priests were musicians who chanted hymns accompanied by musical instruments; the *ashipu* priests performed rituals to protect the individual from evil spirits and to exorcise evil spirits which were looked upon as the cause of diseases and most of the afflictions of mankind; the *baru* priests were seers who interpreted dreams and read omens. The main function of the women priests was to serve as sacred prostitutes at the great seasonal festivals. This vocation was highly respected; several kings gave their daughters to temples for it. The priestesses were considered eligible for marriage and could move freely in society. Some Biblical scholars think that the wife of Hosea was a temple prostitute, for this institution was common also in Syria and Palestine.

The most spectacular and famous of temple building types was the ziggurat. The "Tower of Babel" story in the Bible probably was based upon it, more particularly upon the great ziggurat or temple-tower of the Temple of Marduk in Babylon, the religious capital of Mesopotamia. This building had seven stories of rectangular shape, each a smaller rectangle than the one below it. On the summit was a chapel in which the ritual of the sacred marriage was performed at the New Year festival. It was the central feature of a large complex of temple buildings.

## Ritual

The ritual of greatest significance in Babylonia and Assyria was the New Year. It was agricultural in origin. The New Year, or beginning of the year in the farmer's calendar, may have been the spring, when new growth appears, or the autumn, when the harvest is gathered. Both these times were celebrated as the New Year in some places, but at Babylon the festival was held in the spring during the first eleven days of the month Nisan; and, as Babylon gained in importance and became the religious capital, others followed suit and also celebrated it. The ritual of celebration of the New Year was very complex. The Epic of Creation was recited to create man and the universe anew. A drama was performed in which the main events of the Babylonian epic of creation were portrayed, namely, a contest between Marduk and the dragon of chaos, Tiamat, in which Marduk is the victor. On the fifth day of the festival, during the epic of creation drama, the king was brought to the statue of Marduk and left alone. Then the high priest entered, removed the king's royal insignia, struck him on the cheek, pulled his ears and made him kneel before Marduk, to recite a confession saying that he had not injured anyone in his city by any of his acts. The priest then blessed the king, who received again his royal insignia from the priest, who struck the king again on the cheek. The purpose of the blows on the cheek was to obtain an omen. If the king shed tears, the god was propitious; but if he did not, it showed that Marduk was angry, and disasters would follow.

The next rites of importance were the "fixing of destinies" and the sacred marriage. The former rite determined the prosperity of the New Year; the latter probably took place in the chapel at the top of the ziggurat. In this marriage the king represented Marduk, and a priestess of high rank represented the goddess Ishtar. This was a rite to insure the fertility of the land. In the sacred procession after this rite, the king "took the hand" of Marduk to lead him, and was followed by visiting gods, priests, and the people. A New Year festival after this pattern was celebrated throughout Mesopotamia; in the Baal cult of Phoenicia and Canaan, and in Syria.

## The Influences of Near Eastern Religions upon Christianity in the Roman Empire

We have already, in the section on Religion in Ancient Egypt, commented on the aspects of the Osiris-Isis cult that prepared Egyptian Christians, especially, for the acceptance of Christianity. The same was true for the Serapis, the cult in the Roman Empire.

Babylonian religion, with its concern for revival or resurrection of nature in the spring, although not related to the immortality of the individual, could be linked to it through acquaintance with the Serapis cult. According to Franz Cumont, in his book *Oriental Religions in Roman Paganism,* the most important contribution of Babylonian religion to Christianity was its interest in astronomy. In later times Syrian priests became disciples of Babylonian astrology, upon which they based a more scientific theology. Their astronomical studies led them to the idea that the supreme God dwelt above the stars and was eternal, almighty, and universal. They also believed in worship of the sun as the source of all life and of human intelligence. The idea of a transcendent, almighty deity influenced Christianity.

The Cybele-Attis cult from Asia Minor, similar to the Ishtar-Tammuz but far more violent in its ecstatic excesses, had some elements that may have been a bridge to Christian doctrines and practices. The priests of Attis and Cybele, at the celebration of the death of Attis, would emasculate themselves and flagellate themselves in emulation of the sufferings of Attis. Also there was a rite in which a bull was stabbed to death and its blood allowed to pour over the initiate to redeem him from his mortality and give him a rebirth into eternal life. A less extreme rite was another regeneration process which included eating from a timbrel (drum) and drinking from a cymbal. The idea of redemptive blood (of the lamb of God) and a sacramental meal in Christianity spiritualized these rites which the Romans knew.

Mithraism, a religion adopted mainly by Roman soldiers (a very large group) offered high morality, reward of a heavenly life for the virtuous, and punishment for the wicked. Life in the world was a conflict between the forces of the good almighty God, Ahura Mazda, and Ahriman's evil powers. Ahura Mazda would ultimately be victorious, and all on his side would live eternally in bliss.

The Oriental religions became so spiritualized and ethical that by the 4th Century, says Cumont in his book *Oriental Religions in Roman Paganism:*

> The members of the Roman aristocracy who had remained faithful to the gods of their ancestors did not have a mentality or morality very different from that of adherents of the new faith who sat with them in the senate. The religious and mystical spirit of the Orient had slowly overcome the whole social organism and had prepared all nations to unite in the bosom of a universal church.

## AS YOU READ

The following study questions will help organize your thoughts after you have read A Capsule View of Religion in the Ancient Near

East by Dr. Cairns. Think through each question completely before checking your answer against the material in this Student's Guide.

1. What were the three factors in the primary focus of ancient Egyptian religion?

2. What factors in the Osiris-Isis cult made it popular with the Egyptians and the rest of the Greco-Roman World?

3. What was the relationship between Egyptian pharaohs and the gods Horus and Osiris?

4. Among the myriad of deities in Egyptian religion, what nine remained major gods throughout subsequent Egyptian history?

5. Why were certain animals held sacred in parts of ancient Egypt?

6. According to Egyptian history and mythology, who was the first monotheist in history?

7. In what ways did the ancient Egyptian pharaohs prepare themselves for immortality in an afterlife?

8. What were the main features of the judgment undergone before Osiris could bestow the gift of immortality?

9. What in ancient Egyptian religion would explain the presence of pyramids with elaborate hidden tombs and passageways?

10. In what ways was Egyptian interest in immortality reflected in Egyptian art?

11. What was the basis of Assyrian religion?

12. The Babylonian pantheon was based on a standard list of deities drawn up by the Sumerians. Who were some of the Babylonian deities?

13. What was the myth preserved in the Tammuz liturgies and how did it relate to later religions, such as Christianity?

14. Compare the Babylonians' concept of the underworld with the Homeric conception of hades in previous times and the Christian conception of hell in succeeding times.

15. In what ways did the kings of Mesopotamia differ from the pharaohs of Egypt?

16. Why did the priesthood play a large part in national and religious affairs of Babylonia and Assyria?

17. What was the most significant ritual in Babylonia and Assyria? Why was the ritual important in both secular and religious terms?

18. Briefly summarize the influences of Near Eastern religions on Christianity in the Roman empire.

19. Why didn't the ancient Near Eastern religions have more influence on such religions as Hinduism and Buddhism?

# Chapter 8

# THE CHOSEN PEOPLE

## A STUDY OF JUDAISM

To many persons Judaism connotes the religion of a unique and particular people, one characterized by dietary laws, prayer caps, special festivals, and holidays. It is, in the eyes of some, more of a folk religion than a world religion.

Just what is Judaism? Why has it been able to endure after so many centuries of persecution? What message does it bring to mankind?

In what follows there is an endeavor to initiate you into the spirit of this living faith. You will explore its major ideas concerning God and man, and the mission that has been given to a people of bearing witness to the love and mercy of this God. The Torah as instruction or revelation from God communicating a way of life is investigated. This is done partially in an attempt to rid readers of misconceptions which would make of Torah simply a list of external performances, but more basically to provide an insight into Torah as a way of shaping the life of a people, both as individuals and as a community, from within.

Finally, there is an attempt to reflect on the significance of this people's survival despite terrible sufferings.

## A PREFACE TO YOUR STUDY

A short description of the major aspects of Judaism begins your study. These points are expanded in A Capsule View of Judaism provided by Dr. William May, Associate Professor of Religion, Catholic University of America. Dr. May explores the relationship between the Jews and their God, and describes the covenant established between God and the Jewish People. Use this capsule view to reach a basic understanding of Judaism which you can extend through your study of Judaism in the rest of this lesson.

Additional material about Judaism is found on pages 254-300 in *The Religions of Man,* by Huston Smith.

Another perspective on Judaism will be revealed in the program "The Chosen People," from the television series "The Long Search."

To give you another dimension on Judaism, Barry Tabachnikoff, Rabbi of Congregation Bet Breira in Miami, Florida, looks at the factors that make a Jew a Jew. In this paper he explores the essence of Judaism as a religion, a political entity, a homeland, an identity for the chosen people.

The "Questions for Thought" give you the opportunity to apply what you have learned about Judaism.

## IMPORTANT CONCEPTS

To focus your study of Judaism and help your basic understanding of this world religion, you should organize your thoughts around the following major concepts. They are grouped under the headings: The Nature of God; Torah; and The People and God.

### The Nature of God

God is both utterly transcendent, "wholly other," yet near to His creation, in particular His creature, man.

God is a moral being, as the paradigm of ethical conduct: a holy, just, and merciful being.

### Torah

Torah, "instruction" or "revelation," is the way of imitating God and becoming holy like Him.

**146**

### The People and God

The people are the instrument of God, His chosen vessel to bear witness to Him for all mankind.

The covenant is the alliance or pact between God and His people. It is an alliance to which He will be utterly faithful, no matter how faithless the people might be.

## A CAPSULE VIEW OF JUDAISM

Judaism is indissolubly linked to the life of a people. That people originated in this religious belief, when a nomadic Aramean named Abraham heeded God's call, almost 4,000 years ago, to leave his homeland and go to a land that would be given to him and his posterity. That people is variously called Hebrews (after Abraham the Hebrew) or Jews (after Abraham's great grandson, Judah) or Israel (after Abraham's grandson, Jacob, whose name was changed to Israel). That people became allied to its God in a special way when, after leading them from slavery in Egypt during the 13th Century B.C., He made a covenant or pact with them under Moses at Mt. Sinai. In the experience and history of that people (and perhaps even more significantly in its sufferings, for no people has been so terribly persecuted in history and survived) Judaism took root and grew. Today, after the horrible Holocaust that it suffered under Hitler, that people still lives, and among its members Judaism still flourishes as a way of life centered on God and His revelation or instruction (Torah) to His people.

This discussion will cover the nature of God in Judaism; Torah; Israel as a chosen people; three movements in Judaism; and Judaism and human suffering.

The God of Israel has disclosed Himself primarily in human history. Although He made His presence felt in the realm of nature, the more immediate or intimate disclosure of His being occurred in human actions and events, most particularly in the saving act of the exodus when He delivered His people from pharaoh's bondage. This act is brought vividly to mind for the people today in the liturgy of the Passover. This God, in His encounters with the people under

147

Moses at Sinai, disclosed the pattern and structure of communal and individual life, establishing a covenant or pact with them.

This God is, for the Jew, the one and only God, as the Shema, the daily prayer, bears witness: "Hear, O Israel, the Lord our God, the Lord is One." He is a being utterly transcendent in nature, the God upon whom all creation depends. He is a holy God, a being before whom man is to bow in adoration and stand in awe. Indeed, so "wholly other" is this God that His name is sacred. For a period of its history the people refused to speak the name that this God had disclosed to Moses, Yahweh, substituting for it such surrogates as "the Lord," "the Name," and "the Power."

This transcendent Creator, God, however, is not remote from His creation and, in particular, from man, the being made in His image and likeness. For God is a God in search of man, and in particular of the people whom He has chosen as His own, for His own purposes, in order to manifest Himself to them and carry out His providential plan for mankind. He is a God close to His people, whom He can never forget because they are His own. His Shekinah or presence comes to dwell in the hearts of those who believe in Him and do His will. The relationship between these two basic affirmations about God—His otherness or transcendence and His nearness—is well expressed in a Midrashic statement, "In every place that divine awesome majesty is mentioned in Scripture, divine abasement is spoken of too."

This God, moreover, is a moral or ethical or righteous God. Unlike the nature gods of the ancient Middle East, those nongods who were simply personifications of natural forces, He is not whimsical or arbitrary in His judgments or actions. He is the God of justice and mercy, the father of the fatherless and the protector of widows, the one who is "merciful and gracious, slow to anger and abounding in steadfast love and faithfulness, forgiving iniquity and transgression and sin."

This God is the "Giver of Torah," and it is Torah or "teaching" or "instruction" that confirms the events recognized by the community as the act of God. (When preceded by the definite article as in "The Torah," the term ordinarily refers to the first five books of the Bible, the Pentateuch; used as Torah, without the definite article, the term refers to the entire content of Judaism: its scriptures, its oral traditions and ethical obligations, its historical recollections and affirmations, its ceremonial and ritual observances, and the interpretations of its authoritative texts in the Talmud.) Torah, in other words, is the way of life given by God to His people. It is the way in which they are to be instructed if they are to be, like the God they worship, holy and just and merciful.

In the concept of Torah, then, Judaism's affirmations about God and man intersect as the daily ordering of human existence in the direction of the divine. God is not only the source of ethical obligation, He is Himself its paradigm. As God's image and particularly as one of His people, man is a morally responsible agent who is to look for God's presence in history and in nature and to be responsive to it. Basic to Torah is the notion that the people of God are to be imitative of Him. The theme, enunciated in the Scriptures and constantly insisted upon by the Prophets in word and dramatic action, is that the people are to be like God in their behavior, both as a community and as individuals. It is central to the whole rabbinic tradition. Torah is likened to bread coming from God; it is to be eaten daily so that the community can live in a way faithful to God and to His will.

Throughout the course of its history, the Jewish people has fed on Torah, the teaching or instruction of God as communicated in the Scriptures and in the entire Jewish tradition. During the long period of the Hebrew people's dispersion after the destruction of the second Temple in 70 A.D., until the contemporary period, when its life centers around the synagogues—particularly in central and eastern Europe—there was a process of democratization. Study of Torah became the concern of everyone in the community, and not simply of an elite within the community. According to Torah, daily existence could be made holy. The people sought to do this by regulating its life by Torah as interpreted in the Halakhic (rules of conduct) tradition and as mediated through the Talmud and its commentators.

It is true that on occasions Torah was rigidly viewed, and a static legalism prevailed. What is of greater significance in the life of this people is that this tendency to be inflexibly rigorous has constantly been held in check by the dynamism of rabbinic Judaism. Time and time again, under leaders like Saadia be Joseph (822-942), Maimonides (1135-1204), and in such movements as mystic Cabalism and Hasidism, the effort was made to reduce the hundreds

**149**

of precepts set forth in Torah to a small number which would express its ethical essence.

God gave His Torah to a people, and here we find another key notion in Judaism. The God of Judaism is a God who has chosen for Himself a particular people, binding Himself to them in a covenant of alliance and promising that He will be faithful to them.

The notion that Israel is a chosen people is a mystery. Yet the notion is central to Judaism. Its background is set forth in the Bible in the book of Genesis, which speaks of the disobedience of God's creature, man, and the spread of sin and disobedience over the globe. Man has turned from God, and God wills to bring him back to the path of righteousness and virtue. To achieve this purpose, God summons Abraham and the people of Israel who are descended from him. The divine choice is based on God's will, and not on any merits of people chosen.

The mystery of Israel's being a chosen people can perhaps be grasped only if we remember that it is God who does the choosing. A "chosen people" has, of its own self, no right to exist. History bears eloquent witness to the folly and tragedy that result when a particular group deems itself in some way better or nobler than another. A "chosen people" has a right to exist only if there is a God who cares for and speaks to man, a God who cares what man does. The choice of a particular people, then, can be conceived as choosing a particular people for a special mission. The mission imposes obligations on them and is given to them, not for their benefit alone but for all mankind.

This is the meaning that Israel's election has for Judaism. God's choice imposes a burden, an obligation upon the people with whom He has covenanted Himself. As the prophet Isaiah makes clear, they are to be God's witness and servant, the ones to bring knowledge of Him to the nations. They are to be the people who live by Torah and bring to others the justice and mercy of the God who loves them and all mankind. The fact that Israel was chosen does not mean that others are excluded from the divine presence.

Associated with the notion of the people as God's chosen elect is the notion of the Messiah. There have been divergent concepts of the Messiah, the anointed one of God, throughout the history of Judaism, and it is difficult to determine precisely what this concept means for Judaism today. At times he has been pictured as an individual who would restore the Kingdom of David and unite the people politically. At other times, a different view has prevailed. In contemporary Judaism, especially, the Messiah is no longer personalized by many Jews but is seen as a symbol of the age to come, when God's kingdom of mercy and justice will reign in the hearts of men.

The breaking up of the vast ghettos of Europe has brought new challenges to Judaism, which today is represented by three movements: the Orthodox, the Conservative, and the Reform. Orthodox Judaism, which prefers to be called Traditional Judaism, adheres to the traditional way of Torah, regarding both the Scriptural and traditional expression of Torah as binding, shaping daily life according to its teaching.

Conservative Judaism, which emerged during the 19th Century, stresses the need to be as faithful as possible to the way of Torah. It continually reassesses its particular directives in the light of present-day needs, adapting the traditional teachings in order to make prophetic Judaism come alive in a unique way.

Reform Judaism also emerged during the 19th Century. It broke with tradition in its attitude toward the binding authority of Biblical and Talmudic interpretations of Torah, stressing, instead, the ethical dimension of Judaic faith.

All three of these movements, despite their real divergences, have much in common. All stress belief in the unity of God and express the desire to bear witness, as a people, to the demands that He imposes upon mankind.

Partially as a result of Zionism, a movement initiated by the Austro-Hungarian journalist Theodor Herzl in the 19th Century, the people has regained its homeland in the Middle East, the modern state of Israel. Many religious Jews see in this development the hand of God. They view it as the beginning of a new development in the history of this people of the covenant. Others see this development as an indication that Judaism should rethink quite seriously the meaning of the people as God's chosen vehicle.

Judaism, thus, is wedded to a people. No people in history has suffered the persecutions, the pogroms, the slaughter that this people has suffered. Here, perhaps, lies the greatest mystery that Judaism presents to the human mind. It is worth pondering why this people has survived and why it has had to suffer as it has.

Judaism always has poignantly posed the problem—or the mystery—of suffering. The book of Job long ago posed it eloquently, grappling with it without leaving any satisfactory answer. The people sprung from Judah has experienced suffering as no other people has; confronted with the horror of Auschwitz, the people poses all mankind with the agonizing question: Why? Yet, in its sufferings, the people has kept alive the idea of a God who cares, a God who is good, merciful, kind, and just. This tells us something about Judaism and the mission of this people—at least it should, unless existence itself is absurd and meaningless. Throughout its centuries of suffering, Judaism bears witness to strong faith in God and to hope that He will, in His own time and through the mediation of mankind that walks the way of Torah, usher in a reign of justice and peace, a time when the wolf and the lamb shall lie down together, the nations will beat their swords into plowshares, and everything shall be recreated and refreshed.

## STUDY QUESTIONS

The following study questions will help organize your thoughts after you have read A Capsule View of Judaism by Dr. May. Think through each question completely before checking your answers against the material in the Capsule View.

1. In what way is Judaism indissolubly linked to the life of a people?

2. With what particular event or action of God have the adherents of Judaism identified most?

3. In the history of Judaism, why is it that the name of God was spoken more in surrogate substitutes, such as "The Lord"?

4. Describe the "otherness" and "transcendence" of God in the basic affirmation of faith in Judaism.

5. How does the God of Judaism differ from the nature gods of the ancient Middle East?

6. What is the difference between "Torah" and "The Torah"?

7. In what ways does the concept of Torah affirm the belief about God and man?

8. In what ways has Torah become a way of life for the Jewish people?

9. How would you explain the "mystery" of Israel's being the chosen people?

10. In what ways do Jews see the notion of the Messiah?

11. Describe the basic similarities and differences between Conservative Judaism, Reform Judaism, and Orthodox Judaism.

12. In what ways has Judaism posed the problem of suffering throughout the ages?

## AS YOU VIEW

Another perspective on Judaism is provided by the television episode *Judaism: The Chosen People.* To participate more actively in the viewing experience, study the program description below, and review the guiding questions in "Viewing with a Purpose."

What makes a Jew a Jew? In New York, Elie Wiesel, author and survivor of the concentration camps, tries to define it. In London, Norbert Brainin and the Amadeus Quartet carry the argument further, both in words and in music.

Inevitably the search takes us to Jerusalem where Dr. Pinchas Peli, sixth generation rabbi and sixth generation Jerusalemite, explains the meaning of prayer and acts as our guide through religious schools, synagogues, and the Yad Vashem museum to the memory of victims of the Holocaust. But do we find an answer to our question? Doctor Peli and his family invite us to join them at the traditional Sabbath meal, where the discussion goes on.

## AS YOU READ

Based on your study of the material in this Student's Guide and from your readings in such sources as Huston Smith's *The Religions of Man,* you should be able to answer these questions as a self-assessment about Judaism.

1. Describe the idea of God in Judaism. How does it differ from that of Islam or from the Nirguna Brahman of Hinduism? (Smith, 254-263)

2. What is the Hebrew view of man and his life in the world? Is it closer to the Hindu, the Buddhist, or the Islamic view, and why? (Smith, 281-285)

3. What are the scriptures of Judaism? Explain the concept of "revelation" with reference to authorship of the scriptures.

4. "The fourth component of total Judaism," says Smith, "is the nation." Besides the religious reason, there are four others for the establishing of the Jewish state in Palestine. What are these reasons? What do you think of their validity?


## QUESTIONS FOR THOUGHT

The following questions cover issues or points of interest related to Judaism. They are intended to help you. Apply what you have learned about Judaism.

1. How do the Jewish people in your community have an impact as a result of their faith?

2. In what ways is Judaism truly a world religion?

3. Is it easy to discover differences between Judaism and Hinduism or Buddhism? Can you think of any ways in which the religious experience of Judaism is similar to that of Hinduism or Buddhism?

4. Compare the impact which Judaism has had on the state of
   Israel with the influence which the Shinto religion has had on
   Japan.

# WHO ARE THE CHOSEN PEOPLE?
## Another Dimension on Judaism

*by*

Rabbi Barry Tabachnikoff
*Congregation Bet Breira*
*Miami, Florida*

What is the content behind the appellation "Jew"? What makes a Jew a Jew?

In this discussion of a definition of a Jew, Rabbi Tabachnikoff focuses on these major concepts. Use them to organize your thoughts as you study this dimension of Judaism.

It is the unique response of the individual to his fellow man, his environment, his acceptance of responsibility for self, his understanding of the Divine Imperative that makes a Jew a Jew.

This response is colored by the totality of Jewish experience, history, literature, faith, and doubt. It occurs in the context of daily living, as well as in the more recognizable formats of ritual observance and ethical teachings.

It is the unique affirmation of meaning and purpose in human life that comes from an awareness of the Jewish teachings that focus on the mutual relationships between creator and creature.

It is the answer of "the chosen people" responding to God's call. The response is as diverse as the understanding of those who perceive the challenge.

It is the struggle to overcome the limitations of human frailty in achieving a divine potential.

### Who Are the Chosen People?

To be a Jew is to be an enigma. Paradox is what makes a Jew a Jew. There is the conflict between being a "chosen people" and teaching the world that "all are equal." There is the tension between *The Torah,* that was revealed at a fixed time in history, and *Torah* (teaching), which is an on-going process of interpretation that changes in every age. There is the polarity between continuity and change, particularism and universalism, acceptance and protest.

It is ironic that in America today the present generation of Jews is probably the most educated in general studies, but in Jewish learning is perhaps the least literate. In the midst of economic prosperity and social acceptance, relative affluence and the potential for assimilation threaten the very Jewish identity that has survived hardships and endured martyrdom in other ages.

Jews in Russia risk their security and often their lives in order to cling to their Jewish identity. Many of those who have left Russia are totally ignorant regarding Jewish history and observance. All they know is their identity as Jews.

In Israel it is possible to observe a diversity of customs including Moroccan, Algerian, Bucharian, Indian, Syrian, Turkish, Falasha, Ashkenaz, and Sephardic origins. The variety is staggering.

In the face of almost incredible diversity, a thread of connectedness emerges that binds unique elements into an identifiable structure we call "Judaism." It defies a simple definition. People, nation, religion, or ethnic group won't work. But it is recognizable nonetheless. It is a functional, experiential working definition that emerges from an examination of the core elements of a life-response, a world perspective—*Weltanschauung.*

Traditional studies describe the spectrum of religious Jews and perfunctorily classify all others under the category of "nonobservant." The inadequacy of this system is clear when we observe that in the United States fewer than 30 percent of the identifiable Jewish people affiliate with any synagogue. In the State of Israel the observant population is numbered at less than 10 percent.

Obviously we require some other methodology for describing Jewish identity, other than "religious observance." Professor Michael Meyer of Hebrew Union College proposes the image of a rope whose definition and shape are in reality a collection of individual fibers. At various points a single strand may break without vitiating the rope as a whole. By analogy, Judaism has many fibers that combine to describe the totality. It is not necessary for all the elements to exist at any given point in the continuum. Rather, we require a minimal continuity that permits the form and strength of the strand to be transmitted.

## Religious Observance

A familiar element, with which we may begin our exploration, is religious observance. Rituals and ceremonies encompass the life cycle of the individual and the holiday cycle of the annual calendar. At one extreme the traditional (Orthodox) Jew follows many details with great care. At the other end of the spectrum the liberal (Reform) Jew may be quite selective and innovative in his approach to the same events. The particular details will vary widely, yet there is no essential difference among those who subscribe to some form of religious observance.

Judaism has never been a monolith. Competition and diversity of belief are hallmarks of Jewish history. Hillel and Shammai are quoted in the Talmud as differing on hundreds of issues. The Pharisees and Sadducees represented two schools of competing thought. They were succeeded by the Karaites, who contested the Rabbinic leadership, and later by the Hasidim, who competed against the Mithnagdim.

This tradition is still valid today. Among the traditionalists, an emphasis is placed on conserving the roots of the past and protecting the system of Jewish law (*Halacha*). At the other extreme, liberal Judaism searches for greater innovation and experimentation in a desire to derive relevance for contemporary society.

### The Religious Denominations Within Judaism

At the present, there are three major religious denominations within Judaism.

*Orthodox Judaism* clings to traditional observances and accepts the Bible literally (a fundamentalist position) as a guide book which instructs mankind with God's commandments. Orthodox Jews accept as binding the body of Jewish law and teachings that are collected in The Torah (Bible) and elaborated upon in the Talmud.

Orthodox Judaism embraces rituals such as dietary laws (kashrut) which carefully describe forbidden foods (pork, shellfish, scavengers), the separation of meat and dairy products, and the manner in which food is to be prepared (humane concerns in slaughtering animals for food, and details to assure hygienic preparation of food). Worship rituals are distinguished by the separation of men and women (to avoid distraction) and strict attention to minute details of ancient customs described in traditional sources. Prayers are recited exclusively in the Hebrew language, often repeated, and chanted to special melodies. Prayers must be recited at the fixed time

158

and with a prescribed, minimum congregation (minyan) in attendance.

*Conservative Judaism* is a more moderate expression of the traditional approach (neoorthodox) and while subscribing to the divine authority of Torah-Tradition it permits modifications and modernization of observances. It gathered adherents at the end of the 19th Century in the United States.

*Reform Judaism* revised the worship format by removing traditional garb (skull cap and prayer shawl) and eliminating the repetition of prayers and all references to the long defunct sacrificial system. It introduced musical instruments and the use of choir music in place of traditional cantorial chant; modified the liturgy; and introduced preaching by the rabbi as a focal point of the worship experience.

Reform Judaism does not accept Jewish law and tradition as divine in origin and therefore they are not regarded as obligatory. A rational approach is used to select those customs that are meaningful and useful in furthering the ethical ideals of Judaism and in retaining a broad identity with historical Judaism. Thus, Hebrew is used in some prayers as a link with the past, but the main portion of worship is in the vernacular.

The Bible is regarded as a historical repository of ethical teachings rather than as a divinely revealed text. Accordingly, many of the obscure commandments (Mitzvot) which are not of an ethical nature are ignored (e.g., Deuteronomy 22:11 describes a prohibition against wearing garments of mixed linen and wool. This commandment is observed by Orthodox Jews as "God's will" but is ignored by Reform Jews as lacking any moral purpose).

Reform Judaism has pioneered in granting full equality to women in religious rituals. In recent years the first women in Jewish history were ordained as rabbi and cantor by Hebrew Union College (the Reform Seminary).

### Religious Values

Another category—religious values—has a broad appeal that transcends the details of observance. Many people are "religious" without being "observant." They may not choose to follow the daily rituals and ceremonies, yet they identify with the broad value systems of Jewish tradition. This body of Jews is actually in the majority, although not within any denominational, religious category (Orthodox, Conservative, Reform). Its adherents identify with the ethical values which are incorporated in Jewish ritual and tradition and which are an integral part of Judaism.

Jewish worship focuses on three broad categories: creation, revelation, redemption. These ideas are significant for the nonobservant Jew as well as for the so-called religious individual. The Jewish response to these events has been at the core of Jewish teaching that results in a positive perspective on life. Whether accepted literally or taken as myths, they add meaning to life and relevance to man's strivings through essential values.

At the center of the creation story, the crowning work of creativity is man. This teaches the values of human life and the dignity of man. "Only one single man was created in the world, to teach that, if any man has caused a single soul to perish, Scripture imputes it to him as though he had caused the whole world to perish, and if any man saves alive a single soul, Scripture imputes it to him as though he had saved a whole world." (Sanhedrin IV, 5 Danby Translation.)

Man is a paradox, a creature of dust, yet he is "but little lower than the angels" (Psalm 8:6). Jewish tradition stresses the value of *pikuach nefesh,* saving a human life, and sets this goal above all other commandments. It places man's responsibility in the context of the challenge of *tikun olam,* perfecting the world.

The French poet Edmund Fleg summed it up by saying, "I am a Jew because, for Israel, the world is not yet completed: men are completing it." (Quoted from N. Glatzer, *The Judaic Tradition,* pp. 796-797.)

For those who subscribe to Judaism's values, the world is experienced not as an alien place but as the creative substance in which man and God together operate as partners. Judaism demands responsibility as well as obedience to cultic details. Ethical monotheism places freedom and responsibility in man's domain.

Judaism reaches beyond the experiences of the past to affirm the possibilities of overcoming evil and finding "meaning- salvation" in our lives. The liturgy constantly repeats the refrain: "From slavery to freedom" (*me-avdut l'cherut*) to stress that physical, intellectual, and spiritual redemption can be achieved.

The universal appeal of these religious values is underscored by the massive groundswell that draws individuals to some form of recognition of the importance of Passover (the Festival of Freedom or Redemption) each year. The universal need for atonement draws nonobservant and nonbelievers to the synagogue on Yom Kippur (The Day of Atonement). The same element is reflected in rites of passage when parents suddenly insist on a religious blessing for a newborn child, or for a youngster who has reached religious majority (at 13 a boy celebrates the ceremony of *bar mitzvah,* literally accepting responsibility for the mitzvoth, or commandments, when he is called to the pulpit and permitted to recite the blessings over the reading of The Torah).

### Anti-Semitism

A negative force, but one that has proven strong through the ages, is the influence of anti-Semitism. Perhaps as much as anything else, it clearly defines "what makes a Jew a Jew." World opinion does not allow total assimilation. Like the restraining walls of a jar that contains a gas which tries to escape, so anti-Semitism confines and constrains and ultimately helps define who is a Jew. In the process it often goads individuals to explore for themselves what makes them existentially Jewish. This was the case with Theodor Herzl who was spurred to organize a World Zionist Congress in response to the notorious Dreyfus case (in which a Jewish French officer was falsely accused of treason and convicted with falsified documents; he was later exonerated and the French government resigned).

In Nazi Germany a single Jewish grandparent was sufficient cause to condemn an individual to the death camps. It was a bitter irony that many who viewed themselves as "assimilated," and even voted for Hitler when he rose to power, later bore the brunt of hatred and brutality that is now termed the Holocaust.

While negative forces have reinforced Jewish identity throughout history, a variety of positive forces also influences the diverse expressions that collectively shape the people we identify as Jews.

### K'lal Yisroel (Community of Israel)

The category of peoplehood (*amcha*) has been complicated by the emergence of a national state of Israel after two millenniums of exile. A sense of national destiny has always been present, though long suppressed through the course of the Diaspora. "Next year in Jerusalem" is the cry that echoes on Passover. Worshipers face Jerusalem in synagogues around the world. Generations longed to go on a pilgrimage to the holy land of Israel. Old men treasure small sacks of soil, a precious connection with the revered homeland.

In our generation Israel has become a reality. Its citizens encompass Jews, Christians, and Muslims. But it is a national policy to offer automatic citizenship to any Jew who chooses to live in Israel, under the "Law of Return."

At the present time it remains unclear as to who has a prior claim to the term "Jewish people." In the Diaspora (world Jewry outside of Israel) it is a code word that links diverse communities on every continent. In Israel it conjures images of the Zionist dream of Theodor Herzl, who started the modern nationalist movement in 1897. Is one more Jewish because he lives in Israel? Can the "Jewish people" exist independent of the state of Israel? Can the state of Israel somehow guide, inspire, and lead the "Jewish people" throughout the world?

These are troubling questions that were never encountered before. The "Jewish people" lived in their land, Israel, and remained there until forced to leave. Wherever they went, they retained an identity and longed to return. Now, given the opportunity to return, a new option is emerging for those who are choosing "voluntary exile" (*Galut shel resut*). They affirm that a legitimate expression of Jewish, creative existence is possible outside of Israel, not as an appendage to Israel, but as a primary instance of *K'lal Yisroel,* the community of Israel.

Others, however, identify with the political facet of Judaism that was rooted in a national identity in the past, and now has reemerged in the state of Israel and the Jewish nationalist movement called Zionism. They express their Jewish identity as Zionists.

### Israel—Zionism

Zionism focuses upon the "Jewish people" but affirms that ultimate reality demands fulfillment of the obligation to live in *Ha-Aretz,* The Land. Often proponents of this ideal are in sharp conflict with fellow Jews who express their identity through religious observances or a general cultural identity.

A recent survey in California revealed parents expressing concern over their children's "becoming overly involved with Israel and perhaps moving, to live there permanently." Interest in Israel has always been part of Judaism and is an integral part of prayers and tradition. In the 19th Century, modern Zionism took root under the influence of national movements worldwide and the experience of anti-Semitism, which accentuated the need for a homeland and haven for the Jewish people.

Interest and concern for Israel's welfare touch the vast majority of Jews and focus upon a common goal, securing a place of refuge for Jews and rebuilding the homeland where Judaism was nurtured, thousands of years ago.

## Ethnicity

Positive forces also help to define and identify the meaning behind being a Jew. There is ethnicity that encompasses all aspects of culture—humor, literature, art, music, food. The emphasis on the priority of the family, inner-group-marriage, and folkways reinforces group identity. Even now, with the rising incidence of intermarriage and divorce, ethnicity acts as a shield to a total breakdown of Jewish identity. (See *Demographic Perspectives of Mixed Marriage,* Sergio Della Pergola in Encyclopedia Judaica Yearbook 1975-76, pp. 198-210.)

Other aspects of ethnicity encompass a personal identification with the body of Jewish history and the written heritage of the Jewish experience. The influence of the past is embodied in the great literature of the Bible, the rabbinic commentaries, wisdom literature, legends, and even the contemporary works (fiction and non-fiction alike) of such authors as Chaim Potok, Elie Wiesel, Isaac B. Singer, and James Michener.

Jewish identity is reinforced by a value system that not only tolerates doubt but actually encourages questioning and protest. Abraham protested to God against the impending destruction of Sodom and Gomorrah (Genesis 18:23-33). The root meaning of "Israel" (Prince of God) comes from Jacob's struggle with a mysterious night apparition described in Genesis 32:25-31. Because Jacob struggled and contested with God and prevailed, his name was changed to Israel (Prince of God, or homiletically, one who has struggled with God and prevailed). This theme is especially relevant

**163**

today when the spirit of protest has been exemplified throughout our society by the disproportionate leadership of Jews in the antiwar movement, the social action movements, the civil rights movement, the American Civil Liberties Union, and organized labor.

This common heritage is accompanied by an often unacknowledged but deeply felt sense of common destiny.

### Common Destiny

Though rarely articulated, this destiny has been imposed externally and internally. In our pluralistic society everyone has a dual identity. You are American and you are—something more. Sociologist C. Bazalel Sherman described it in *Beyond the Melting Pot*. It is the unique aspect that flavors our American culture. It is the longing to rediscover our roots. It is the existential awareness that ultimately no one can escape "who you are."

This sense of a shared destiny has been reinforced by the twin events that have shaped the Jewish experience in this century. The Holocaust and the rebirth of the State of Israel have given a new dimension and a renewed sense of purpose to Jews.

Albert Einstein described the essence of Judaism as an affirmation of life for all creatures. It is this positive life stance, this response to the world we live in, that makes a Jew a Jew. It is the ability to be concerned with perfecting our world (*tikun olam*) now, rather than waiting passively for salvation, that identifies a Jew. It is inherent optimism, in the face of overwhelming evidence favoring pessimism, that is the hallmark of being a Jew. It is the incongruous ability to strive for rational understanding while retaining the capacity to suspend judgment and rely upon the mystical experience.

Jewish mystic tradition describes a place where heaven and earth touch each other. It is in Jerusalem, on the Temple Mount, where the sacred and the profane, the immanent and the transcendent are joined. There one can stand both in heaven and on earth. If this can be done, then everything else is possible.

### Summary

Jewish identity can be expressed as a sense of common destiny, an appreciation of the Jewish heritage, an awareness of a unique place in history that transcends rationality or belief and is in some ways a mystique. Jewish identity has been expressed as belonging to a "chosen people" or even being aware of that chain of continuity which has survived 5,000 years of history throughout the world.

The positive facets of Jewish identity range widely. They include a gamut of religious observances; a sense of the community of Israel as a worldwide community; Zionism, which focuses upon the political and national aspects of Judaism; and ethnicity, which often influences individuals in their daily habits, life-style, and thoughts. In addition to ethical values and humanistic concepts which express the unique teachings of Judaism, there are negative influences which reinforce Jewish identity.

Anti-Semitism precludes assimilation and emphasizes identity with the larger category of identifiable Jews. It compels the individual to participate and often motivates him to a better understanding of his Jewish heritage.

Elie Wiesel has suggested that the survival of Judaism is a mystery. But its very existence implies a unique purpose. To be aware of this mystery and to know that one is part of it are significant aspects of Jewish identity.


## STUDY QUESTIONS

These study questions will help organize your thoughts and assess your understanding of this dimension of Judaism. Think through each question completely before checking your answer against the material in this Student's Guide.

1. What does Rabbi Tabachnikoff mean when he says that to be a Jew is to be an enigma?

2. In what ways is the Jewish identity partly described by religious observance?

3. What is one of the basic differences between the belief of the traditional (Orthodox) Jew and the liberal (Reformed) Jew?

4. What three factors are identified with the broad value system of Judaism?

5. How does the creation story relate to man and the value system of Judaism?

6. How is the world experienced by those who subscribe to Judaism's values?

7. Of what significance is Israel to the Jewish people?

8. Can the "Jewish people" have a creative existence outside of Israel?

9. How would you describe Zionism as another category of Jewish expression?

10. How does Rabbi Tabachnikoff explain the influence of anti-Semitism in defining what makes a Jew a Jew?

11. In what way has ethnicity helped to define and identify the meaning of being a Jew?

12. What does Rabbi Tabachnikoff mean when he says that the Jewish identity is reinforced by a value system that not only tolerates doubt but actually encourages questioning and protest?

13. What two events have shaped the Jewish experience in the 20th Century?

14. From the arguments advanced by Rabbi Tabachnikoff, what do you think makes a Jew a Jew?

# Chapter 9
# FATHER, SON, AND HOLY SPIRIT

## A STUDY OF CHRISTIANITY

Christianity is the most mysterious of the major religions. We identify it with certain messages coming out of the Bible. Yet it has proven to be diverse. It ranges from Eastern Orthodoxy, through Catholicism, to a great variety of Protestant churches and sects. Christianity is by no means as simple as it may seem.

## A PREFACE TO YOUR STUDY

There are three lessons in this chapter devoted to Christianity. In addition to an overview of Christianity as a faith, there are lessons on specific facets of Catholicism, Orthodox Christianity, and Protestantism. It is important that you study each of these facets of Christianity from the base of the major tenets and historic developments of the faith itself. The first lesson in this chapter, a general overview of Christianity, is provided by Dr. William May, Associate Professor of Moral Theology, Catholic University of America. The study questions and the section "As You Read" will help organize your study and focus your thinking.

The basic tenets of the Christian faith can be studied by focusing your attention on these key ideas or concepts about the Christian view of God, Jesus, the Church, and the Christian life.

### Basic Ideal of Christianity

Central to Christianity is a person, Jesus of Nazareth, a man, born of woman, who is believed to have been the Christ, the Holy One of God, the Son of the Father, the savior of mankind.

### The Christian View of God

The Christian God is a Trinity: the Father, who creates; the Son incarnate in Jesus, who saves; the Spirit, who sanctifies.

### The Christian View of Man

Man, made in the image of God, is destined for life with God. Yet man sinned and through sin is doomed to slavery and death and is in need of salvation and redemption.

### The Christian View of Jesus

Jesus the Christ is the Savior, the Redeemer. In and through Him God became one with man so that, believing in Christ, man can become one with Him and able to share eternal life.

### The Christian View of the Church

The Church is the community of those who believe in Jesus as the Christ and are guided by His spirit. This Church is to last until the end of time.

### The Christian View of Life

Christian life is to be one of perfection and holiness. Reborn in Christ, Christians are to love God in their neighbors, even in their enemies.


## A CAPSULE VIEW OF CHRISTIANITY

Many people are already familiar with Christianity, and many are Christians themselves. Yet there is always need, both for those who believe themselves familiar with something and those who are committed to a way of life, to reassess their attitudes and scrutinize their beliefs.

In what follows, an effort is made to articulate the major ideas central to a Christian understanding of God and of human existence. What is it about this faith that has appealed to countless millions of people from every nation on Earth throughout the past 2,000 years? Does it have anything to say to men and women of today? Are there needs, rooted in the human heart, to which it addresses itself?

Here, in capsule form, is an introduction to Christianity and to elements in its history.

## Historic Context

Essentially Christianity has three major expressions—one the Eastern, another the Roman Catholic, and the other Protestant. The first great division came between East and West.

That division was perhaps implicit in the early history of the Church. In its first three centuries the faith became widespread throughout the Roman Empire. Then, with Constantine, the Church achieved official success. But the Empire itself was beginning to break into two halves, one based on Constantinople and the other on Rome—the one Greek in tone, the other Latin. The Roman Church became the vehicle of Latin culture and struggled successfully to convert invaders. A new Western Europe was born, a synthesis between the Latin south and the Germanic north. But it was many centuries later, in 1453, that Constantinople was overthrown. So the historic situations of Eastern and Western Christians were very different. Moreover, the sudden conquests by Islam, in the 7th and 8th Centuries and after, isolated many Eastern Churches from Christendom.

Then, when Europe was beginning to show new strength and to begin its amazing overseas conquests, the Roman Church in the early 16th Century was split asunder by the Reformation. Much of northern Europe, and through it much of North America, became Protestant. These events ultimately were to precipitate modern capitalism, the scientific revolution, and modern humanism.

169

## Basic Tenets of the Christian Faith

Central to Christianity is a person. That person was Jesus of Nazareth, a Jew born in the First Century A.D. and believed by Christians to have been the Son of God and the savior of mankind.

Christians believe that Jesus was the Messiah, the anointed one of God, because of what He had to tell or reveal about God and man. The God revealed definitively in Jesus is, Christians believe, a God who is mankind's best friend. He is a God who cares. He is the one who will never betray man, no matter how frequently man may betray Him. He is the God who is true to His word, and He has given His word, Christians believe, through Jesus.

For the Christian, Jesus not only reveals who God is, but also who man is. Both Jews and Christians believe that man is made in the image of God, and is meant for life in communion with God. But because of human disobedience (epitomized and symbolized by the disobedience of Adam) sin came into the world, and with sin, slavery and death. Because of sin, mankind has become alienated from God. Because of sin, mankind is in need of redemption and salvation. God came to visit his people in Jesus to save them from sin and to bring them life everlasting. Despite sin, God still loves mankind and has made it possible, through Jesus, to share His life and friendship.

Christians believe that Jesus bought God's saving love through His own life, death, and resurrection. Condemned to death as a common criminal and a fomenter of riots, Jesus was executed on a cross, laying down His life for His friends and proving God's love for mankind.

The risen Christ, Christians believe, is still with us. He has not left mankind orphans, but in spirit lives today in His disciples, His faithful. They form His people, the Church, and their mission is to bear witness to Him.

Throughout its long history, Christianity has tried to understand the human significance of the saving acts of God brought about, in, and through Jesus Christ. The Christian faith has given rise to theology—faith seeking understanding—the effort of the mind to understand what the heart believes. This effort has had, as one of its effects, the articulation of Christian belief in creeds or statements intended to communicate, as well as possible, the principal doctrines that Christians hold about the God revealed by Christ. Among the most important Christian creeds are the Apostles' Creed, the Nicene-Constantinople Creed, and the Athanasian Creed.

In these creeds are expressed the mysteries or doctrines of the Trinity and the incarnation. Christians, reflecting on the saving acts described in the Scriptures and making use of precise terminology provided by philosophy, came to believe that the God revealed in Christ is triune in nature. There are not, for the Christian, *three* gods; rather the one, true, living God is so full of being and so personal in nature that this God subsists in a trinity of persons indissolubly one in being the Father, the Son, and the Holy Spirit. The son, personally, became the man, Jesus of Nazareth. In Jesus, God humanized Himself so that man could become divine—Jesus shared human nature so that man could be enabled to share His life. The life-giving Spirit, who *is* the love between Father and Son, is given to those reborn in Jesus to lead them to life eternal.

Throughout its history, too, Christianity has been mindful of the saving significance given to ordinary material things like water and bread and wine by Jesus' actions. This has given rise to the Christian ritual of the liturgy and to the teaching (and disputes) on sacraments, key human actions using the things of this world both to signify and to effect God's love.

Again, throughout its history, Christianity has sought to specify the meaning of Christian love by describing the way of life that ought to be characteristic of those who live reborn in Christ, and by specifying actions that are incompatible with that way of life. Disputes have naturally arisen among Christians over the specifics, but there is no doubt that there is a Christian morality and that this morality is closely related to the keeping of the Ten Commandments of the Old Testament. It is Christian belief that Jesus came to fulfill, not to destroy, God's covenant of grace with the Hebrew people and that Jesus related active love of neighbor to the Commandments.

Christianity is thus a religious faith and a way of life rooted in the person of Jesus of Nazareth. It is, moreover, an organized religious movement centered in the Church, the community of those who accept Jesus as their Lord. Indeed, Christians believe that it was Jesus' will to found a Church that was to last until the end of time.

Today, the Christian Church is divided into three major expressions, or "rivers" from which other rivulets flow. These three are the Roman Catholic, the Eastern Orthodox, and the Protestant.

Although these divisions of expression with Christianity are of long standing and have, in the past, been bitter, there are signs today that a healing process is underway, manifest in the ecumenical movement toward Church unity. A major step was taken during the Second Vatican Council, when the Roman Catholic Church, while maintaining its belief that it alone fully bears witness to the integrity of Christian faith, acknowledged abuses it had allowed and at the same time gave recognition to the Protestant Churches as truly being "Church," and not mere sects. Even more recently the Pope of Rome and the Patriarch of Constantinople lifted excommunications that their predecessors had hurled at one another.

Despite the real differences among Roman Catholicism, Protestantism, and Eastern Orthodoxy on doctrinal and sacramental questions, there is evidence today that the leaders in these Churches are willing to listen to one another, to learn from one another, to extend to one another the charity of life of Christ.

In addition, there is a growing recognition among Christians of the need for wider ecumenism, as this faith confronts the other major religions of the world. Under Christian ecumenism, the God who loves man in Jesus is the God of all men, not only of Christians; Jesus' saving death and resurrection are meant for all; and God's grace overflows the boundaries of the Christian Church to touch the hearts of all men. This, indeed, is something hinted at in the gospels, in Jesus' discourse about His last days. For the ones He welcomes into Heaven are not those who professed His name, calling Him "Lord, Lord," but rather those who fed Him when He was hungry, clothed Him when He was naked, gave drink to Him when He was thirsty, visited Him when He was in prison or sick. For Jesus, Christians believe, walks the world today incognito in the person of those we meet in our daily lives. They are His brothers and sisters and in meeting their needs Christians respond to His call to choose eternal life.

## STUDY QUESTIONS

The following study questions will help organize your thoughts after you have read A Capsule View of Christianity by Dr. May.

Think through each question completely before checking your answers against the material in the Capsule View.

1. Explain how Christianity came to have the three major expressions, the Eastern, Roman Catholic, and the Protestant.

2. In what way is Jesus central to the Christian faith?

3. To the Christians, who or what is God? How does the Christian explain the Trinity and still profess belief in a monotheistic God?

4. In what way is Christianity an organized religious movement centered in the Church?


## AS YOU READ

Based on your study of the material in this Student's Guide and your readings in such sources as Huston Smith's *The Religions of Man,* you should be able to answer these questions as a self-assessment of your knowledge of Christianity.


**Christianity**

1. Give a brief account of the life and the ethical teachings of Jesus. Compare them with the ethical teachings of Confucius and of Taoism.

2. Belief that Jesus was resurrected became the most effective aspect of early Christian teaching in making converts to the new religion. Why?

3. In what ways was Jesus the "Savior" of mankind according to the first followers of the faith? Discuss critically each of these four. Are they still accepted by most Christians today?

4. Christian theology centers largely around three doctrines: the Incarnation, the Atonement, and the Trinity. What is the meaning of each of these doctrines? How does the Nicene Creed

173

express these doctrines? Are they accepted by the three main divisions of Christendom, the Roman Catholic Church, the Orthodox Church, and most Protestant sects?

5. How does the Roman Catholic Church differ in organization from the Orthodox and Protestant divisions?

6. In what ways does the ritual of the Orthodox Church differ from the Roman Catholic and the Protestant?

7. Fundamentalism in Protestant Christianity seems to be gaining in numerical strength. What are its doctrines and why do you think it is gaining in popularity in this country?

8. In what ways do the meaning, purpose, and value of human and cosmic history in Islam, Judaism, and Christianity differ from the Hindu and Buddhist views?

# ROME, LEEDS, AND THE DESERT
## A Study of Roman Catholic Christianity

The basic idea in Roman Catholicism is that the Church founded by Christ is, in its full reality, visibly one and is under the leadership of the Pope, the Bishop of Rome, and those bishops throughout the world in communion or fellowship with him. For Catholics, the Pope is the successor to St. Peter and as such holds a primacy of both honor and jurisdiction with the Church. Like Peter, the Pope is to "tend the sheep" and to confirm his brothers in the faith.

## A PREFACE TO YOUR STUDY

Your study of Roman Catholicism begins with a capsule view of monasticism provided by James L. Ash, Jr., Assistant Professor of Religion, University of Miami. Additional material about Catholicism is found on pages 332-337 in *The Religions of Man,* by Huston Smith. Use the study questions in this Student's Guide to focus your thoughts and to organize your pattern of study for this material.

Another perspective on Roman Catholicism is found in the program "Rome, Leeds, and the Desert" from the television series "The Long Search." The Questions for Thought (later in this chapter) will help guide your thoughts for additional study of Catholicism and comparisons with other religions and sects.

## IMPORTANT CONCEPTS

In addition to the basic tenets of the Christian faith, there is one major concept on which you can focus your search in your study of Roman Catholicism:

The Church established by Christ through the Apostles is a visible, structured community with the Pope, the Bishop of Rome, and

**175**

successor of the Apostle Peter, as the visible expression of unity and of faith.

## A CAPSULE VIEW OF THE
## DEVELOPMENT OF CHRISTIAN MONASTICISM

The words monasticism, monastery, and monk come from the Latin word *monos* which literally means solitary or alone. In general usage in Western culture today, monasticism refers to a life-style in which individuals and groups withdraw from ordinary existence in the world in order to be alone with their God, thus to practice their piety more intensely. Christian monasticism has existed in many forms. Some monastics have remained withdrawn from the world to live a life of constant prayer, study, and mystical experience. Others have used their retreat as inspiration for service to others, living a life devoted to care of the poor and the sick, or teaching of the ignorant. Whether the emphasis is piety or service, however, the motivation is the same—denial of the self and complete submission to God. The means of self-denial for most monks have been vows of poverty and chastity, through which they renounce the world and announce their intention to conform their whole lives to what they perceive to be the will of God.

### The Beginnings of Christian Monasticism

Monasticism began as the logical extension of an ascetic attitude which had long been present in the Church. Early Christians practiced denial of the self through fasts (abstaining from food), sexual abstinence, and avoidance of other physical pleasures as a means of focusing on the spiritual. The attitude that the body was a hindrance to the spiritual life was present in a number of popular cults in the Mediterranean world of the first few centuries, and found its way into Christianity through the writings of Paul and others.

Perhaps partly as a result of this influence, sexual abstinence came to be especially venerated in early Christianity. Ancient docu-

**176**

ments clearly show that in most churches, by the end of the 3rd Century, a special class of women existed called "the holy virgins." These people were usually regarded as extremely spiritual because they had renounced sexual fulfillment in the context of a life of self-denial and service to God. Perhaps they were the first real monks.

## St. Anthony, Founder of Christian Monasticism

The first famous monk was St. Anthony of Egypt, whose biography was written by his younger contemporary, St. Athanasius. Anthony's life illustrates many of the central features of early monasticism. Born in the mid-3rd Century of well-to-do Christian parents, Anthony began wondering how best to serve God. While in his early 20s, this concern was unusually intense one day as he happened to enter a village church, where he heard a biblical text read. It was a passage which has since become the golden text of monasticism. The passage describes Jesus' response to a young rich man: "If you would be perfect, go and sell what you have and give to the poor, and come, follow me, and you will have treasure in Heaven." These words directly answered Anthony's questions, and he immediately obeyed them.

Anthony sold his farm, giving all the proceeds to the needy, and placed himself under the tutelage of an old Christian hermit near the edge of his town. Anthony's life consisted of manual work, prayer, and memorizing the Bible. Later he migrated into the desert, where he lived with the wild animals in an abandoned fortress, alone with himself, God, and the demons which constantly troubled him. His vivid religious experiences included visions of attacking lions, bears, serpents, and scorpions, and an appearance by Satan himself, trying to tempt Anthony away from his life of holiness. Anthony's reputation as a holy man spread and he began to attract disciples. Within a century the eastern deserts had numerous colonies of monks and hermits, many of whom practiced extremes of asceticism that strain the imagination. One Macharius of Alexandria, for example, is said to have stayed awake for 20 nights, stood upright during the whole of Lent, and eaten only cabbage leaves. Another sought to be devoured alive by wild beasts; but when he entered a cave filled with wild hyenas they would not touch him, and he was greatly disappointed. Some holy men spent their entire lives sitting on the top of tall pillars, where they would deliver pronouncements and prophecies to a variety of prestigious clients, many of whom had traveled hundreds of miles for the spectacle.

## Communal Monasticism

Extreme forms of asceticism appealed to individualists who sought radical means of retreat from ordinary life. But Anthony's hermit-type of monastic living was soon replaced by another style. The new type of monasticism was founded by another Egyptian, Pachomius, about 40 years after Anthony's death. Pachomius tried the hermit life, but felt the need for a community. About 320 A.D., he founded the first organized Christian monastery in southern Egypt. There all the monks formed a single family. They followed the same schedule, with hours assigned for work, prayer, and eating. They lived in small cells close to one another. This setting originated the kind of monastic ideal which later dominated Western monasticism, namely, the totally Christian society untainted by the worldliness of secular life or the moral compromises increasingly characteristic of the Church at large. By the time of Pachomius' death, ten of his monasteries had been established in Egypt; one had more than a thousand inhabitants. Thus the trend became clear: communal monasticism was to be more long-lived and continuous because it was more institutionalized and stable. Individual hermits came and went, but large monasteries lasted for generations. Communal monasticism also tended to discourage extremes of asceticism, practicing instead a tamer and more regulated form of Christian piety.

## St. Benedict, Reformer and Organizer of Western Monasticism

Since monasticism began in settings dominated by Eastern Christianity, with its mystical and contemplative characteristics, it seemed strange and foreign to Western Christians at first. By the 5th Century, however, monasticism in both communal and hermit forms could be found throughout the West. Lacking a monastic tradition, the Western monasteries had problems. Some were very strict in their requirements, others notoriously lax. Someone was needed who could bring the Western aptitude for order and organization to monasticism.

That figure was Benedict of Norcia. Born about 480, he studied for awhile in Rome, but the evils of the city discouraged him. He decided to become a hermit monk, at about the age of 20, and took up residence in a cave in a mountainous area east of Rome. The fame of his sanctity caused disciples to gather, and he was offered the headship of a nearby monastery. He accepted the offer, but left when the monks there refused to obey his strict rules. Benedict then founded his own monastery, where he could have absolute control. It was called Monte Cassino, and it became the mother monastery of what was later the Benedictine Order. At Monte Cassino, Benedict constructed his famous *Rule* for regulating the monastic life. The Rule still forms the basis for life in a Benedictine monastery.

Benedict's Rule viewed the monastery as a self-contained and self-supporting fortress of God's soldiers. The semimilitary discipline was in the hands of its head, the abbot (literally meaning father). The abbot had to be obeyed in all things, but he was obliged to operate according to consensus on most matters. The Rule emphasized worship as the major duty of a monk, and provided for seven daily devotional periods totaling at least four hours. Almost as important as worship were manual labor, usually in the fields, and the regular reading of Scripture and devotional texts. Benedict's Rule gave to Western monasticism a legal and authoritarian structure that made it possible for Western monasticism to become a major institution in European culture in the Middle Ages.

### The Historical Significance of Monasticism

During the first three centuries of the faith, when its adherents were sometimes persecuted by the State, the highest ideal was that of martyrdom. One who died for his religion was assured of great heavenly rewards. The holy martyrs became saints, the subjects of prayer and veneration. But after Christianity gained official government toleration in the early 4th Century, how could an intensely pious person ever expect to die for the faith? Other means of self-sacrifice were bound to surface. Thus, after the Church became popular and tolerated, monasticism took the place of martyrdom as the highest form of service to God.

The popularity of the Church was a mixed blessing. Once the emperor was a Christian, it became socially and politically advantageous for any aspiring public figure to profess Christianity. This new development meant that the Church quickly became a mixture of the pious and the ambitious, its original fervor diluted. In a setting where Christian ideals sometimes took second place to social and political goals, the Christian concept of a holy life completely devoted to God had to be pursued outside the normal life of the Church. Monasticism thus began as a movement away from the worldliness of the Church. The monasteries kept the ideal of holiness alive and provided a setting and structure in which it could be pursued.

The emergence of monasticism was a manifestation of the fact that the truly intense piety of Christianity moved outside the normal life of the Church. Visions, revelations, and ecstatic experience migrated from the jurisdiction of the churchman-bishop to the jurisdiction of the monk-abbot, playing less and less a role in the public life of the Church. It was no accident that the location of every major reform movement of the Church in the Middle Ages was the monastery, for there the religious experiences that so often gave rise to prophetic fervor were given relatively free rein.

It was during the Middle Ages that the golden era of monasticism occurred, for then the Church was at the center of European life. Almost anyone who was extraordinarily serious about Christianity took up the monastic life. During the period often known as the Dark Ages, when much of Europe had lapsed into the cultural insularity and backwardness of feudalism, monasteries were the guardians of learning. From the fall of Rome to the establishment of the great universities in the late Middle Ages, the monasteries preserved historical records, copied ancient manuscripts, and kept literacy alive. Practically all the achievements of the Renaissance and the Reformation depended directly on books that the monasteries had preserved. The ideals and institutions of Anthony, Benedict, and the other heroes of the monastic tradition played a crucial role in guarding and preserving Western culture.

## STUDY QUESTION

The following study questions will help organize your thoughts after you have read A Capsule View of the Development of Christian Monasticism, by Dr. Ash. Think through each question completely before checking your answers against the material in the Capsule View.

1. How would you define monasticism?

2. In what way is monasticism a logical extension of an ascetic attitude of long standing in the Christian Church?

3. In what ways does the life of St. Anthony illustrate many of the central features of early monasticism?

4. In what ways was communal monasticism of the 4th Century similar to or different from the individual monasticism of St. Anthony?

5. What events in the life of Benedict of Norcia contributed to the establishment of a monastic movement that became known as the Benedictine Order?

6. What is the historical significance of monasticism? In what ways did it replace martyrdom and other personal sacrifices in the Church?

## AS YOU VIEW

Another perspective on Roman Catholicism is provided by the television episode *Catholicism: Rome, Leeds, and the Desert.* To organize your thoughts in advance, study the program description below, and review the guiding questions in "Viewing with a Purpose" at the end of this Guide.

Catholicism, especially since the Second Vatican Council of the early 1960s, had undergone many changes. In this program, filmed in Rome, Spain, and England, we discover the diversity and the unity of religious experience that go under the label of the Holy Catholic Church. We meet members of the Little Brothers of Jesus, one of the smallest Catholic orders, who single out for themselves the simplest manual jobs wherever they live. Their inspiration is the years in Jesus' life before His ministry, when He worked as an unknown carpenter. The Little Brothers are filmed at work in Leeds, England, and at their training house for novices in Farlete, Spain. Also in Spain we see the Benedictine Abbey of Montserrat, a pilgrimage center with its remarkable statue of the Virgin Mary and its famous boys' choir. As a focal point of the worldwide Church a solemn High Mass, celebrated by the Pope and 19 Cardinals on Ascension Day, is filmed in St. Peter's, Rome.

## TO EXTEND YOUR STUDY

The following resources will provide you with the material for a more in-depth study of Christian monasticism. Use these as a reference point and starting place to continue your study.

St. Benedict. *The Rule of St. Benedict.* Translated with introduction and notes by Anthony C. Meisel and M.L. del Mastro. (Garden City, New Jersey: Doubleday Image Books, 1975)
> The classic organizing principles of Western monasticism, written by its founder.

Bede Jarrett. *The Life of Saint Dominic.* (New York: Doubleday, 1964)
> A good biography of the founder of a major medieval order, illustrating the characteristics of medieval monastic piety.

David Knowles. *Christian Monasticism.* (New York: McGraw-Hill, 1969)
> A popular account of the history of monasticism by its leading scholarly interpreter.

# THE ROMANIAN SOLUTION
## A Study of Orthodox Christianity

Eastern Orthodox Christianity (or the Orthodox Churches of the East) separated from Western (Roman) Christianity in the 9th through 11th Centuries. The basic idea of Eastern Orthodoxy is this: External unity between local churches and the universal Church is helpful but not necessary so long as the local churches preserve internal unity by recognizing Christ as the true invisible head, by administering the sacraments properly, and by professing the faith as articulated in the first seven ecumenical councils of the universal Church (all held during the first millennium). Eastern Orthodoxy regards local churches in communion with patriarchal churches (those founded by apostles) as autonomous in their jurisdiction. They grant the Pope, as Bishop of Rome, a primacy of honor but not of jurisdiction.

## A PREFACE TO YOUR STUDY

Your study of Orthodox Christianity begins with a Capsule View provided by James L. Ash, Jr., Assistant Professor of Religion, University of Miami. Additional material about Orthodox Christianity is found on pages 337-342 in *The Religions of Man,* by Huston Smith. Use the study questions to focus your thoughts and to organize your pattern of study for this material.

Another perspective on Orthodox Christianity is found in the program "The Romanian Solution," from the television series "The Long Search." The Questions for Thought at the end of this section in Chapter 9 will help guide your thoughts for additional study of Orthodox Christianity and comparisons with other religions and sects you have studied.

## IMPORTANT CONCEPTS

In addition to the basic tenets of the Christian faith, there is one major concept on which you can focus your search in your study of Orthodox Christianity:

The Church is a visibly structured community that expresses its faith most vividly in the liturgy, with an equal independence among all local churches in communion with an apostolic see.

## A CAPSULE VIEW OF ORTHODOX CHRISTIANITY

Eastern Orthodoxy is the general term for the group of Christian churches that formally severed relations with Western or Roman Catholic Christianity in 1054 A.D., after centuries of disputes over political and theological issues. Today Eastern Christianity survives in many areas north and east of the Mediterranean, including Greece, Asia Minor, eastern Europe, and Russia. Most of these churches look to the Patriarch of Constantinople as their spiritual leader. Their relationship to him, however, is not obligatory or carefully defined, which contrasts with the Western Churches' relationship to the Pope. The two groups have always agreed on the important central dogmas of the Christian faith, but different styles of piety, forms of organization, and patterns of theology have made complete harmony impossible since the earliest Christian centuries.

### The Early Divergence of East and West

Actually the distinctions between East and West go back to the fact that there were two cultures coexisting within the Roman Empire during the years that Christianity was taking over the Mediterranean world. The Eastern or Greek-speaking part of the Empire was wealthier, more populous, more culturally diverse, and more cosmopolitan. The Western, or Latin-speaking part, although Rome was its capital, was by comparison modest and somewhat provincial. The Roman aristocracy illustrated the cultural inferiority of the

West by its refusal to speak Latin, the tongue native to the area, in official proceedings, until the latter years of the Empire's existence. Instead, Greek, the language of all educated people in the Empire, adorned public temples and official documents. The fact that the Empire was a combination of two regionally centered cultures meant that, as Christianity expanded into the Empire, different thought patterns produced different theologies, and different social customs produced different liturgies in the Eastern and Western Mediterranean worlds.

Other distinctions also arose. The Eastern Churches showed remarkable ability to accommodate themselves to the nations which they entered, translating their services into the native tongues of the people. This friendliness to local customs made it easy for the Eastern Churches to become nationalistic and independent within each nation, a fact illustrated by the names of the various Orthodox Churches—Greek, Russian, etc.

In some areas such nationalism occasionally meant that the Church was in practice simply a department of the State. Western churches, by contrast, emphasized uniformity and universality, keeping their liturgies in a single language (Latin) regardless of the region. Western churches were controlled by a more authoritarian organization centralized in the Roman papacy, and tended to be much more loyal to popes than to kings. Sometimes they even proclaimed that kings should be subject to the pope, an idea that was never adopted in the East. Thus, one would not hear of a French Catholic Church or a Spanish Catholic Church because in the West there was, strictly speaking, only one Catholic Church, the *Roman* Catholic Church.

## Contrasts in Theology

A major consequence of the cultural distinctions between East and West was the emergence of two patterns of thinking about the Christian faith. The West tended to think in legal or judicial terms, whereas the East tended to think in philosophical or mystical terms. A good example is the theologies of salvation.

The Western Churches viewed salvation as a change in one's legal status before God, the elimination of the just penalty for disobeying God's law. It meant that one was excused from the terrible punishment of an eternal hell which he rightly deserved. The Eastern Churches, however, viewed salvation as a reestablishing of man's lost communion with God, a mystical participation in the divine being of God. It meant that one was progressively being restored to a relationship of intimacy with his Creator.

In the East, sin was not so much the disobedience of divine law as the turning away from union and fellowship with God. The consequence of sin was not legal guilt in God's court of justice but a loss of fellowship with God and the replacement of immortality with mortality. There was relatively little speculation in the East about what happens to sinners after death, no elaborate definition of hell and purgatory as in the West. Instead, damnation was self- explanatory; it meant separation from God, mortality, and utter loneliness.

Another example of these contrasts is the theology of the Eucharist, or Lord's Supper, the central event in the liturgy of both East and West. The West tended to view the Eucharist as a fresh participation in the forgiveness of sins which Christ's death brought about. But the East followed the thought of St. Ignatius, who saw the Eucharist as the "medicine of immortality," a key to the restoration of one's mystical union with God.

Thus the West's legalistic theology centered on defining the rules for what might be called "getting right with God." It had a more pervasive sense of the sinfulness of man and a more carefully detailed doctrine of grace. The East, however, centered its theology not on obtaining forgiveness for definitely recognized evil deeds but on a mystical transformation of man's inner nature.

### Contrasts in Church Organization

The differences in theology had their counterparts in the ways in which the Churches were run from day to day. Alongside the West's legal mentality was a genius for practical organization. An authoritarian administrative structure knit the Western Churches tightly together. At the top of the structure was the pope, who often conceived of himself as the monarch of the Church. This organization never developed in the East, partly because the East was so much more diverse than the West in the early centuries of Christianity. The East had several strong centers of Christian leadership and influence competing for power, whereas the West had only one real administrative leader, the Bishop of Rome, later called the pope.

In the East there was no pope, no single figure who could represent the Church and stand up to the emperor if necessary. The result was that the Eastern Churches were often susceptible to imperial control. After Emperor Constantine effectively moved the capital of the Roman Empire to the Eastern city of Constantinople, by taking up residence there, it was natural for the bishop of that city to enjoy a prominence similar to that of the Bishop of Rome. But the fact that the bishop, or patriarch, of Constantinople was under the emperor's nose meant also that he could be under the emperor's thumb. Constantine's move left the pope free to expand his powers without rival in the West, but ensured that the Eastern Churches would have little independence from the secular government. This development may have proved helpful to the Eastern Churches, for Eastern Orthodoxy has shown amazing ability to coexist with oppressive and sometimes even non-Christian governments.

## The Controversy Over Icons

A major Christian dispute between East and West occurred in the 8th Century over what might seem now to have been a minor issue. The incident shows the continuing friction between diverse styles of piety in the East and the West. The question concerned the use of icons—images of apostles, saints, and martyrs. In many churches the icons were used as aids to worship. If one were praying to a saint, for example, it helped to look at the icon while praying.

Emperor Leo III, probably in an effort to gain the support of Jewish and Muslim factions in his troubled army, published a decree in the year 725 proclaiming the use of icons in worship as idolatry and forbidding it. The result was widespread religious revolt, for the icons were a popular feature of Christian worship. The pope called a synod at Rome in 731, threatening excommunication of anyone who condemned icons.

The dispute continued through the careers of several popes and emperors, until the ascent to the throne of an emperor who saw the folly of repressing such a popular practice. This emperor was Constantine IV, who in 787 summoned the Seventh General Council of the Church. The Council approved the use of icons, and seemingly the dispute was over.

The legacy of the dispute remained, however, in the repressed Eastern Churches' reluctance to use the third dimension in religious art. To this day Orthodox Catholics can have only two-dimensional representations inside their churches; paintings, mosaics, and stained glass are as far as Eastern art can go. The West, beyond the emperor's grasp during the icon controversy, continues to use the third dimension freely in its art and architecture, with statues of Christ, Mary, and the saints having a prominent place in Western Catholicism.

## The Formal Breach Between East and West

By the 11th Century, Christianity had conquered virtually all of Europe. The last nations to convert were the Scandinavian countries, to Western Christianity; and Russia, to Eastern Christianity. The missionary success of both branches meant that the ecclesiastical map of Europe now reflected the continuingly divided states of Christendom. But in the 11th Century both branches were still in communion with each other and there was, at least in theory, one universal church.

The official cleavage came in 1054. The precipitating event was another episode in the perennial jealousy between Roman Popes and the Patriarch of Constantinople. The patriarch had issued documents condemning Western practices, among them the custom of forbidding its priests to marry. He also closed all the Western Churches in Constantinople and ordered all Western monasteries to adopt Eastern practices. He even allowed the bread at a Western Eucharist service to be thrown to the ground and trodden under foot. Finally, in retaliation, a papal representative at Constantinople placed on the high altar of Saint Sophia a sentence of anathema against the patriarch and all his followers. Four days later, in the same place, the patriarch excommunicated the pope and his followers. The breach was now complete and official.

Since the formal breach, the two communions have gone their separate ways, but in recent decades signs of reconciliation have appeared. Roman Catholicism softened its attitude toward Orthodoxy as a result of the ecumenical spirit of the Second Vatican Council. An outgrowth of the change was Pope Paul VI's journey to the Holy Land in 1964, during which he met amicably with the Patriarch of Constantinople. A year later Rome and Constantinople issued identical statements regretting the harsh language of the separation of

1054 and removing the sentences of excommunication. Today most of the Orthodox Churches are comembers, with most Protestant groups, of the World Council of Churches, whose meetings are now attended by Roman Catholic observers as well. It is clear that the Eastern and Western branches of Christianity have come closer than they have been in centuries. Whether a formal reunion between them can ever occur is still a question.

## STUDY QUESTIONS

The following study questions will help organize your thoughts after you have read A Capsule View of Orthodox Christianity, by Dr. Ash. Think through each question completely before checking your answers against the material in the Capsule View.

1. With what broad geographical area is Orthodox Christianity associated?

2. Describe the two cultures which coexisted in early Christianity, within the Roman Empire.

3. What were features of the Roman Churches that associated them more closely with Rome? How did the Eastern Churches show ability to accommodate themselves to other nations?

4. Describe the basic, divergent patterns of thinking about the Christian faith that one finds in the Western Churches, centered around Rome, and the Eastern Orthodox Churches.

5. In Eastern Orthodox Christianity, there is no pope and the Western pope is recognized only as the Bishop of Rome. In what other ways do the political organizations of the churches differ?

6. How has the major Christian dispute over the use of icons in churches been resolved by the Orthodox Christian Churches?

7. What were the events that led up to and precipitated the cleavage between Western and Eastern Churches in 1054? How is this breach being mended today?

## AS YOU VIEW

Another perspective is provided by the television episode *Orthodox Christianity: The Romanian Solution*. To participate more actively in the viewing experience, study the program description below, and review the guiding questions in "Viewing with a Purpose."

The Orthodox Churches in Eastern Europe seem to be bound to the communist states in essentially loveless marriages. In Romania, however, there seems to be some genuine regard between the partners, and occasionally the old spark. It is not uncommon for members of the Romanian Communist Party to be churchgoers and even communicants. The government permits the building of new churches, and gives financial aid for the restoration of historic church properties. The Romanian Orthodox Church is still seen as an important aspect of Romania's cultural heritage and ethnic identity. Churches are packed to overflowing, and the construction of many churches in new industrial suburbs is financed by public subscription. This television program takes us through Romania from city to village, witnessing the Romanian religious experience. Easter week is spent in Moldavia, with its beautiful and unique "painted" churches, and then we go over the Carpathian Mountains into Transylvania. The Orthodox Christians preserve some of the oldest—and longest—liturgies in Christendom; a normal Sunday morning service takes three hours. Spirituality is intensified by the Byzantine splendor of the setting and the beauty of some of the most inspiring choral music to be heard in any church in the world.

## TO EXTEND YOUR STUDY

The following resources will provide you with material for a more in-depth study of Eastern Orthodox Christianity. Use them as a reference point and starting place to continue your study.

Ernst Benz. *The Eastern Orthodox Church.* Translated by Richard and Clara Winston (Garden City, N.J.: Doubleday Anchor Books, 1963)

An excellent translation of a German scholar's comprehensive survey of Eastern theology and practice.

Jaroslav Pelikan. *The Spirit of Eastern Christendom (600-1700).* (Chicago: University of Chicago Press, 1974)

A detailed and scholarly study which concentrates on the historical development of Eastern theology.

Timothy Ware. *The Orthodox Church.* Second edition. (Baltimore: Penguin Books, 1969)

The standard survey treatment in English.

## QUESTIONS FOR THOUGHT

The following questions cover concerns or points of interest related to Orthodox Christianity. They are intended to help extend your thinking about what you have learned.

1. How is the Orthodox view of salvation, as a mystical participation in the divine being of God, possibly related to Hindu or Buddhist metaphysics?

2. Compare and contrast the relationship between the Orthodox Church and Constantine's Empire with the relationship between the Shinto religion and the State of Japan.

# PROTESTANT SPIRIT: U.S.A.
## A Study of Protestant Fundamentalism

Although the term "Protestant" means precisely that—a pro-test against what Roman Catholicism was doing to Christianity in the 16th Century—Protestantism began as a reform movement within the Roman Catholic Church itself. Luther, Calvin, Zwingli, and other reform leaders wanted to prune away what they believed to be human errors introduced into the Church by Roman theologians. There is an element of individualism within Protestantism, yet it would be an error to think that Protestantism champions a rugged individualism. It recognizes that the Christian life is to be a fellowship of believers; it simply believes that the authority of the Biblical word takes precedence over the human authority of the pope.

## A PREFACE TO YOUR STUDY

Your study of this aspect of Protestantism begins with a capsule view provided by Dr. James L. Ash, Jr., Assistant Professor of Religion, University of Miami. Additional material about Protestantism is found on pages 342-348 in *The Religions of Man,* by Huston Smith. Use the study questions to focus your thoughts and to organize your pattern of study for this material.

Another perspective, on the influences of fundamentalism in Protestant Christianity, is found in the program "Protestant Spirit: U.S.A.," from the television series "The Long Search." The Questions for Thought later in this chapter will help guide your thinking for additional study of Protestantism and comparisons with other religions and sects you have studied.

## IMPORTANT CONCEPTS

In addition to the basic tenets of the Christian faith you have studied in Roman Catholicism and Orthodox Christianity, there is one major concept on which you can focus in your study of Protestantism:

The Church, although in some ways structured and visible, can never stand between the individual person and the redeeming Christ. As redeemer, Christ speaks to the believer through the word of God revealed in the Bible.

## A CAPSULE VIEW OF THE INFLUENCES OF FUNDAMENTALISM IN PROTESTANT CHRISTIANITY

Fundamentalism began as a coherent movement among American Protestants in the first decades of the 20th Century. As its name implies, it was a vigorous assertion of certain doctrinal tenets which the leaders of the movement regarded as "fundamental" and essential. Among them were the verbal inerrancy of the Bible, the literal truthfulness of Biblical miracles, and the virgin birth of Christ. The Fundamentalist movement was essentially a defensive action aimed against modern currents of thought, which seemed to undermine the structure of traditional Protestantism. Fundamentalism was adopted in varying degrees by conservative Protestant demoninations. Today it forms to some extent the ideological basis for most of the rapidly growing American religious groups.

### Historical Roots

At the center of Fundamentalist thought is a peculiar view of the nature and the role of Scripture. From earliest times, Christians viewed their Scriptures as sacred and God-inspired, although the lists of authoritative books varied at first from region to region. The precise nature of scriptural inspiration was never officially defined. This was largely because, until the Protestant Reformation of the

16th Century, Scripture did not have exclusive status as the primary arbiter of Christian doctrine. Luther and the other reformers elevated the function of Scripture by embracing the principle of *sola scripture*—scripture only—stating that Scripture had to be the Church's primary guide in matters of doctrine and practice, and that traditions of the Church, when in conflict with Scripture, should be changed.

With this exalted view of the Bible, it was inevitable that questions about the nature and function of Biblical inspiration would eventually come to the fore in Protestantism. Actually it took quite a long time, because the theology of the early reformers generally eliminated such questions. Scriptural inspiration was connected to the mysterious workings of the Holy Spirit, the Third Person of the Trinity; it was claimed that one could detect and understand such inspiration only when the same Holy Spirit mysteriously enlightened one's heart. Thus, for the early reformers, the inspiration of the Bible could neither be proved nor disproved by empirical or scientific means. It could be verified and understood only in the inner religious experience of one who, in John Wesley's words, had had his "heart strangely warmed."

## Nineteenth Century Threats to Protestantism

By the 19th Century, some Protestants saw such grave perils on the horizon that they began to abandon the earlier views in favor of a more objective and rationalistic view of Biblical inspiration. The first threat was a new method of Biblical study spawned in German universities called "higher criticism" (the German word "criticism" simply meant "study"). Using sophisticated linguistic analysis, Julius Wellhausen and other "higher critics" asserted that the first five books of the Bible were not written by Moses, as virtually all Protestants had been taught since childhood, but by many authors, writing in different centuries, whose works were combined into single narratives as late as the 3rd Century B.C. These scholars and their rapidly growing circle of American disciples claimed that the Bible was a book influenced by the same kinds of historical forces that had shaped all books. In other words, their naturalistic assumptions led them to treat the Bible as they would any other ancient document. This attitude was very alarming to many Protestants, some of whom had even been taught that the Bible was written in a special divine language that no culture had ever spoken!

The second threat to Protestantism was Charles Darwin's theory of evolution, which gained widespread popularity among American scientists within a decade of the publication of *The Origin of Species* in 1859. (It would take longer for the majority of British and European scientists, more conservative and traditional than their American counterparts, to embrace Darwin's edeas.) Darwin disturbed conservative Protestants because his theories contradicted their literal interpretation of the accounts of creation in the Bible. Again, the doctrinal foundation and central symbol of Protestantism, the sacred Scriptures, seemed under attack. Could there be no certainty that these holy documents were indeed the word of God?

The views of the early reformers provided no help against evolution and higher criticism, because Luther and the others had implied that the inspiration of Scripture could be known only in subjective experience and could not be objectively proved. If help was to come against the new currents of thought, it would have to come in the form of a new theory of inspiration, which could enable Protestants to place absolute confidence in the literal truthfulness of the Bible.

## A Conservative Response

Such a new theory was formulated at Princeton Theological Seminary in the early 1880s. Professor A.A. Hodge, joined by his colleague B.B. Warfield of Western Theological Seminary, published an article claiming that the original manuscripts of Scripture were verbally inerrant and logically flawless. The original manuscripts had been long since lost, so this move enabled its proponents to disregard as copyists' errors the textual contradictions pointed out by critics. The Hodge-Warfield definition of inspiration also provided its adherents with a mood of absolute certainty, with which they could dismiss evolution as a delusion of infidels, based solely on conjecture.

Not all Protestants took this militant, defensive approach. Liberals found other ways to counter the threats of the new ideas, or they revamped their theologies to accommodate Darwin and Wellhausen. They spoke of adjusting theology to the findings of science, of tentativeness, of the necessity of uncertainty, and of the primacy of mystical experience in knowing religious truths. The conservatives displayed an intense desire for absolute certainty that has always characterized Fundamentalism. They viewed the liberals as turncoats and labeled them "modernists." Many liberals were proud of the label. By the time Shailer Mathews published *The Faith of Modernism* in 1924, the term was a rallying cry for much of the liberal wing of American Protestantism. The label "modernist" is significant because it demonstrates contrasting views of the two emerging Protestant parties—Fundamentalist and Modernist— toward modernity. The Fundamentalists were quite consciously looking backward. In spite of the fact that their theology was based upon a novel view of Christian Scripture, they saw themselves as defenders of ancient truths, the fundamentals of the faith.

### The Fundamentalist Controversy

The Hodge-Warfield definition of Biblical inspiration as verbally inerrant and logically flawless—or in technical terms, the concept of plenary (complete) verbal inspiration—gave intellectual precision and clarity to notions of the Bible's literal trustworthiness that had long been present in popular American Protestantism. Conservative spokesmen at Bible institutes and prophecy conferences during the 1890s, and afterward, enthusiastically proclaimed plenary verbal inspiration, and sternly denounced the "infidelity" of modernism.

The Fundamentalist movement got its name from the publication of a series of books called *The Fundamentals,* between 1910 and 1915. Subsidized by two wealthy businessmen and widely circulated, the books contained articles on numerous theological topics. Most of them were, to some degree, defenses of Biblical inerrancy and literalism. By the time Americans were experiencing President Harding's "return to normalcy," following the turmoil of World War I, the issues raised by *The Fundamentals* began to echo loudly in the pulpits and publications of most of the major American Protestant denominations.

What historians call the Fundamentalist-Modernist Controversy was largely confined to the decade of the 1920s. In June of 1922 a popular Protestant leader, Harry Emerson Fosdick, delivered a fiery sermon from the pulpit of New York's First Presbyterian

Church, entitled "Shall the Fundamentalists Win?" His answer was a resounding "No!" that precipitated a vitriolic controversy. Fosdick criticized the Fundamentalists for their intolerance of other Christians. He denied that their so-called fundamentals, focusing on a theory of Biblical inspiration, were truly central to the Christian faith at all.

The battles that ensued were complex and numerous. Spokesmen on both sides were slanderous and irresponsible. Perhaps the most visible manifestation of the controversy was the famous Scopes trial of 1925, in which a biology teacher in a Tennessee high school was convicted of violating a state law against the teaching of evolution in public schools. Speaking for the prosecution, the aging but popular William Jennings Bryan defended the antievolutionary view of the Fundamentalists, basing his argument on an appeal to Biblical literalism. Although the teacher, John T. Scopes, was convicted, the spectacle was a tragedy for the Fundamentalists. The press coverage was massive, and most reporters saw Bryan as representative of an ignorant and narrow-minded religion of the past. This distorted caricature of Fundamentalism has persisted to this day, particularly among scholars, and has been responsible for much misunderstanding of the movement.

Bryan's role as prosecuting attorney in the Scopes trial symbolized the militant and uncompromising actions of many Fundamentalist leaders during the 1920s. In numerous Protestant denominations, Fundamentalists succeeded in instigating heresy trials against prominent liberals, but in the end the liberals maintained control of most Protestant institutions. Fundamentalism was forced outside the mainstream of American Protestantism, but its theology was by no means dead. Its most sophisticated defender was the scholar J. Gresham Machen, whose *Christianity and Liberalism* (1923) advanced the thesis that the liberals had in fact deserted the Christian faith.

## Recent Developments

Defeats suffered by the Fundamentalists in the 1920s insured that few Protestants would ever again call themselves Fundamentalists. But the theology of Fundamentalism has survived, in varying degrees, in the more conservative Protestant denominations. Most of today's heirs of the Fundamentalist perspective prefer to be known as "evangelicals." In independent Bible churches, interdenominational seminaries, and some larger conservative denominations the literal infallibility of Scripture is a prominent tenet of faith. This belief provides its proponents with the same absolute certainty that the early Fundamentalists displayed, and makes vigorous evangelism possible.

The presence of the Fundamentalist view of Scripture in many of the successful Protestant revivals of recent decades illustrates the view's usefulness and appeal. The strictest Fundamentalists are rationalists; they maintain that persons know God by an intellectual activity, studying the Bible. They are suspicious of religious mysticism and critical of revivals which emphasize an inner experience. More moderate Fundamentalists, however, manage to combine a revivalistic view, that God is known primarily in the warmed heart, with a rationalistic view, that God is known primarily in the mind as it comprehends the statements of Scripture. This somewhat contradictory, or at least paradoxical, theology can be found in most of the rapidly growing Protestant groups today. Thus the modern heirs of Fundamentalism have been able to combine central aspects of both liberal and conservative thought that gave rise to the Fundamentalist-Modernist controversy. They have warmed hearts and infallible Bibles as well.

Perhaps the best explanation for the recent growth in conservative Protestant churches is the presence of these same two factors— the tremendous motivating power of intense religious experience, and the absolute certainty of the Fundamentalist view of Scripture. Taken together, the Protestant groups that share the view of an infallible Bible are growing rapidly. Those groups that do not share this view, taken together, are losing members. Whether the trend will continue is another question, but it is clear that the influence of the early Fundamentalists will be with us for a very long time.

## STUDY QUESTIONS

The following study questions will help organize your thoughts after you have read A Capsule View of the Influence of Fundamentalism in Protestant Christianity, by Dr. Ash. Think through each question completely before checking your answers against the material in the Capsule View.

1. What doctrinal tenets were considered fundamental by the leaders of the movement that became known as Protestant Fundamentalism?

2. What is the Fundamentalist's view of the nature and role of the Scriptures?

3. Why did 19th Century Protestants begin to adopt more objective and rationalistic views of Biblical inspiration?

4. What influence did Charles Darwin's theory of evolution have on the widely-held 19th Century belief in the inspired nature of the Scriptures?

5. In what ways do the views of the early Modernists and Fundamentalists differ? In what ways are they the same?

6. What were the roles of such people as New York's Harry Emerson Fosdick and Nebraska's William Jennings Bryan in the Fundamentalist-Modernist controversy?

7. In what ways did the theology of Fundamentalism survive the defeats of the 1920s and how is it manifest today?


### AS YOU VIEW

Another perspective is provided by the television episode *Protestant Spirit, USA*. Study the program description below, and review the guiding questions in "Viewing with a Purpose" to help you participate more actively in the viewing experience.

Churches with the seating capacity and styling of deluxe movie theaters, services conducted with the professionalism of television spectaculars, and congregations that occupy every seat at four staggered services every Sunday morning are features of a churchgoing boom in the United States. We visit Indianapolis, in this television episode, and witness the many-faceted approach to religion and community of what has been called a modern Protestant revival. We try to find out what is beneath the sheer vigor of the religious expression of black and white American Protestants. This feeling of community and service comes over tellingly in the Fundamentalist and Episcopalian Churches and in the special deliveries of food and drink for the needy from the soup kitchen of a black church on Thanksgiving day. We find that organized religion is not in a state of apathy in America. In some quarters it is even big business, and the dynamism of the black churches in liturgy and thinking has been an inspiration to white America.

## QUESTIONS FOR THOUGHT

The following questions cover concerns or points of interest related to Protestant Christianity. They are intended to help extend your thinking about what you have learned.

1. Compare the role of the scriptures in Fundamentalist Christianity with The Torah in Judaism or with Islam's Koran.

2. Protestant Christianity has been described as a more personal faith than Roman Catholicism or Eastern Orthodoxy. Support or rebut this perspective.

3. Two groups in the Fundamentalist movement are the revivalists, who state that God is known primarily in the warmed heart, and the rationalists, who state that God is known primarily in the mind. Relate these concepts within Fundamentalism to the "East-West" split, covered elsewhere in your study.

# TO EXTEND YOUR STUDY

The following resources will provide you with material for a more in-depth study of Fundamental Protestantism. Use them as a reference point and starting place to continue your study.

Normal F. Furniss. *The Fundamentalist Controversy, 1918-1931.* (New Haven: Yale University Press, 1954)
> An adequate account of major events, but tends to view Fundamentalists as necessarily pathological.

C. Allyn Russell. *Voices of American Fundamentalism.* (Philadelphia: Westminster Press, 1976)
> Excellent biographical studies of early 20th Century Fundamentalist leaders which illustrate the good and the bad in the movement.

Dean M. Kelley. *Why Conservative Churches Are Growing: A Study in Sociology of Religion.* (New York: Harper & Row, 1972)
> A study of the common characteristics of churches which share aspects of Fundamentalist ideology.

Ernest R. Sandeen. *The Roots of Fundamentalism.* (Chicago: University of Chicago Press, 1970)
> The best historical and scholarly study to date, advancing the questionable thesis that Fundamentalism grew out of British and American millenarianism.

# Chapter 10
# THERE IS NO GOD BUT GOD

## A STUDY OF ISLAM

In Islam, there is only one God, the creator and sustainer of the universe. Among all His creations, man is supreme, with everything else subservient to God.

The prophets are God's messengers, to whom He revealed the truths of the unseen realities and the truth of the coming life which will be lasting and worthy. The series of prophets began with Adam and concluded with Mohammed.

Man, the servant of God, should seek to please Him through obedience to His law and teachings. Because God alone is the Divine Being, no man may claim divinity or supremacy over others. All are equal—men and women of all races and colors.

Islam is a complete guide, defining God's relation to man and man's relation to other human beings. The Islamic law, known as *Shari'ah,* covers family, commercial, and criminal law, as well as other areas.

The *Qur'an* (Koran) is the sacred book revealed through Mohammed. United in its original Arabic form, it is believed by Muslims to be the word of God and is treated with the greatest veneration.

## A PREFACE TO YOUR STUDY

An outline of the major points related to Islam begins your lesson. Use these to focus your study of both the printed and video portion of the lesson. A frame of reference for your study of Islam is provided by Dr. Muhammad Abdul-Rauf, Director of the Islamic Center at Washington, D.C. Dr. Rauf describes God, the prophets, man, social law, and the sacred scriptures of Islam. This overview will give you a perspective and basic groundwork to organize your thoughts for a study of the Islamic religion. Use this capsule view as a reference for the other portions of this lesson.

Additional descriptions of Islam will be found on pages 217-253 in *The Religions of Man* by Huston Smith.

Another perspective on Islam will be revealed in the program "There Is No God But God," from the television series "The Long Search."

As additional help, the Glossary offers short definitions of terms unique to Islam. The "Questions for Thought" section at the end of the lesson leaves you with some issues and concerns in Islam which you will want to consider.

# IMPORTANT CONCEPTS AND TERMS

To assist in your study of Islam, there are basic points you should look for and remember. These include the nature of God the Prophet; Islamic teachings and law; Islamic life; Islamic worship; and the articles of Islamic faith. Once you have mastered these concepts, you will be better prepared to continue your study of Islam and to compare it to other religions.

## God and the Prophet

In Islam there is only one God, unified and unique, the creator and sustainer of the universe. Man is to submit completely. No idols or images are permitted. God's Arabic name is *Allah*.

*Mohammed,* born at Mecca in 570 A.D., was the chief Prophet who preached the religion of Islam. He was the last of a series of prophets which began with Adam. He is most deeply venerated but not worshipped by Muslims.

## Islamic Teachings and Law

The Qur'an is the Holy Book of Islam, believed to be the word of God. It survives as it was delivered through the Prophet, in its original Arabic text, and is the main source of Islamic teachings.

*Hadith* is the body of words and practices traced to the Prophet which supplements the Qur'an as a source of Islamic guidance.

Shari'ah is the canon law of Islam, which is to be observed by Muslims in all situations. It covers family, commercial, criminal, and others types of law.

## Islamic Life

There are uniformity and permanence in Islamic traditions. Modern movements toward reform aim at restoring the original purity of the faith. Islam affirms the equality and dignity of mankind with a consequent blindness to color and race.

There is no religious rank or hierarchy in Islam. Each person has direct access to God. Sins are to be repented but should not be confessed to a mortal. Public announcement of violations of the law is considered harmful and is therefore prohibited.

Muslims believe in a moderate way of life, which satisfies both spiritual and physical needs. Marriage is primarily for procreation and companionship, but sensual enjoyment within it is legitimate and virtuous.

*Sufism* is a way of life more rigorous than the ordinary; it aims at further purification of the soul, based primarily on Islamic teachings.

Islam advocates the avoidance of pork and its extractions, and abstention from alcohol.

## Islamic Worship

The *Ka'ba,* a rectangular structure in Mecca, is the focal point of worship for all Muslims. They face it while praying and make pilgrimages to it.

The *mosque,* the Muslim house of worship, is the rallying point of a Muslim community. The floor of the mosque is covered with clean mats or rugs and contains no images or forms.

### Five Articles of the Islamic Faith

The five articles of the faith are: declaration of the religion which marks a Muslim from others; performance of the five daily prayers; payment of a religious tithe called *Zahat;* fasting the ninth month of the lunar calendar called *Ramadan;* and *hajj,* going on pilgrimage to Mecca once in a Muslim's lifetime.


## A CAPSULE VIEW OF ISLAM

This section will explore the nature of God, of man, and man's relationship with God; the Qur'an as the source of all Islamic teachings; the role of the Prophets in Islam; details of each article of Islamic faith; and special features of Islam in America.

Islam is the religion revealed through the prophet Mohammed of Mecca. Mohammed taught at Mecca from 610 A.D., when he was 40, until he moved to Medina, a town about 280 miles north of Mecca, where he died in 632. The nearly one billion adherents of Islam, called Muslims, are centered mainly in Asia and Africa, although some 25 million live in Europe and another 2 million in North America.


### God

Islam is based upon a firm belief in the existence and unity of God, the creator and sustainer of the world. God alone exists absolutely; everything else may exist only through His will. God is One, the One; He has no peer or equal. He reveals Himself continuously in nature and in creation. He has no human traits. Time and space cannot contain Him. Since God is not a body, form, or substance, He possesses no bounds or limits.

It is stated in the Holy Book that the God whom Muslims call Allah is also the God of the Jews and the Christians. Muslims from all walks of life—simple people, thinkers, scientists, philosophers— have clung to this primary belief, of experiencing the unity and uniqueness of God. This is the central feature of the creed of Islam.

A Muslim is always conscious of God's presence, and repeats his praise of God whenever he makes a move. Although he knows that he is endowed with free will, a Muslim is aware of his dependence upon God, who determines things in the interest of the whole world.

Idol worshiping and veneration of objects or forms which represent God are inconsistent with Muslim belief.

## Man

A Muslim is aware that he is a tiny but integral part of the universe, which was and is being created by God, on whom the universe is dependent. Likewise dependent are his fellow men, whose relationship to God is the same. All men are equal, regardless of their color or origin. Man, endowed with an intellect that enables him to communicate and to formulate values, is seen as the supreme creation, with everything else being created for his service.

Muslims constitute a brotherhood in which there should be no religious ranks or social castes. Every individual has direct access to God, so no one may intercede on behalf of another. There is no division of secular or spiritual domains, which are one and the same. "Religion," for the Muslims, is a term which covers all aspects of life.

## Righteousness

A Muslim seeks the pleasure of God and deliverance on the day of judgment through obedience to God and His divine law, known as Shari'ah. The Shari'ah law covers all human activities—social, economic, and religious. It provides rules and guidelines observed in all commercial activities; a law of marriage and the family; a criminal law; and even laws controlling military activities and international relations.

While a good deed is promised a tenfold reward in Paradise, an evil or lustful thought is not punished unless it is translated into action. Disobedience to divine law is a sin against God, and unless God forgives the sinner he will be punished in hellfire.

God is most merciful and forgiving of sins unless they encroach upon other human beings. In this case, forgiveness depends upon the victim. Divine law is not enforced so much through visible agents as through the individual's awareness of the watchful "eye" of a God who knows what is in the individual's heart.

It is also believed that every individual has a register on which his words and deeds are recorded by two angels who accompany him.

Islam thus accompanies the believer and should be a guide to the practicing Muslim everywhere—in the market, in the office, at home, in the street, in the house of worship. To a Muslim, God is real, though He cannot be perceived through the physical senses. He is close; closer than a jugular vein.

Until the recent European conquest of the Muslim lands, the Shari'ah law was dominant. Since that time European economic and legal systems have prevailed except in the area of family law. Only Saudi Arabia and a few Gulf states still adhere to Shari'ah law in areas other than family law.

There is now agitation in other mideastern countries for the full restoration of that law. A popular belief is that current problems in these countries are manifestations of God's displeasure over the neglecting of His law.

The moral code of that law prohibits murder, adultery, fornication, theft, extortion, usury, cheating, telling a lie, rancor, and backbiting, as well as the consumption of pork or any intoxicating drink. Any other harmless food or drink is lawful.

Modern European influences have led to certain types of behavior inconsistent with Islamic teachings. To counteract this trend, new laws have been enacted. A law recently passed in Egypt prohibits the sale of intoxicants to Muslims in public places. In addition, institutions known as "Islamic Banks," which make loans without charging interest, are on the rise. Charging interest on loans is believed to be like usury.

### The Qur'an

The essence of all Islamic teachings is enshrined in one book revealed to and transmitted to mankind by the Prophet Mohammed. The Qur'an is believed to be the Word of God. For the last 14 centuries, it has been recited by all Muslims of all generations in its original, Arabic form as it was delivered and taught by the Prophet to the disciples who were the first generation of Islam.

In venerating the Holy Book, a Muslim does not touch its copy except after ablution, when he is spiritually clean. Muslims enjoy gathering to listen to recitations of the Qur'an by those endowed with beautiful voices. Recordings of popular "reciters," particularly from Egypt, are broadcast daily from all Muslim capitals and are often played in Muslim homes, even in America.

No sacred book has such a strong hold on its adherents as the Qur'an. In addition to the Qur'an, the recorded words and practices of the Prophet constitute a body of literature called Hadith, which supplements the Qur'an as a source of Islamic guidance.

### The Prophets

For man to lead the righteous life, he needed some basic guidance. God revealed His teachings through a series of noble men known as Prophets. This series of prophets began with Adam and ended with Mohammed. These righteous men, who were God's messengers to humanity, also included Noah, Abraham, Ishmael, Isaac, Jacob, Joseph, Moses, Aaron, David, Solomon, Zacharia, John, and Jesus. None of these men is seen by Muslims as divine. Only God is the divine being and He alone deserves worship.

Each prophet received a sacred book which contained God's message, such as The Torah of Moses, the Gospel of Jesus, and the Qur'an as revealed to Mohammed.

### The Five Pillars

There are five rituals which are to be observed by Muslims. These important ritual duties became popularly known in Western literature as the Five Pillars of Islam.

*Pillar One—Oral Declaration of Faith.* The first basic ritual is the oral declaration of the faith:

I bear witness that there is no god but Allah.
And I bear witness that Mohammed is the messenger of Allah.

It is believed that this statement implies the complete acceptance of the total creed of Islam, which consists of five elements:

Belief in God and his attributes.
Belief in the Angels who are spiritual beings and execute God's commands.

Belief in the Sacred Books.
Belief in the Prophets, the Messengers of God.
Belief in the Day of Judgment and Resurrection.

The declaration of this statement, usually pronounced in its Arabic original, is enough for conversion if the person also announces acceptance of its implications. It is repeatedly recited by Muslims as a measure of religious devotion. It is known by the term *shahadah.*

*Pillar Two—Observance of Duty to Pray.* The second Pillar of Islam is to observe the duty to pray five times daily, at dawn, at noon, in the afternoon, immediately after sunset, and at night. This major duty may be described as "formal prayers" because it assumes a special form, entailing certain body postures to be assumed by the worshiper. First, he stands erect, facing the Ka'ba, a house of worship in Mecca, reciting in humility the first chapter of the Qur'an. Then he bends forward; then rises; then kneels, prostrating himself; then sits up; and so on, all the while engaging in words of prayer and concentrating his thoughts on God.

A worshiper must be ritually clean. Prayers, therefore, must be preceded by ablution. This involves the washing of the outer limbs, or at times the full body, with pure water.

This mandatory prayer, which is incumbent on all adult Muslims, may be performed anywhere, and can be done individually or in a group. Yet, those who can, prefer to go to a *mosque,* the Muslim house of worship and prayers. In the mosque the congregation forms straight lines behind a leader, called *Imam.* Each prayer is preceded by a call to prayer. This call, heard five times from the tops of minarets in a Muslim town, is called *adhan.* Only the noon prayer on Fridays is to be in congregation; it is to be preceded by a sermon preached from a pulpit, called *minbar.* Women join the congregation in the mosque but form their own separate lines.

The mosque can be a simple structure or an elaborate building. Usually it has a niche carved in one of its four walls to denote the side of the Ka'ba close to the minbar. The mosque has become the focal point of the Muslim community.

*Pillar Three—Payment of Alms.* The next major article is the payment of *alms.* Two and one-half percent of the savings which a person has retained for one year will be paid in duty as alms. This duty also applies to certain other properties. The proceeds are used by the state to pay for services and to help the poor. In most of the contemporary Muslim countries, the payment of the duty, known as *zakat,* is left to the conscience of the believer. While some think that modern income tax has superseded this duty, others pay taxes to the state treasury and pay zakat directly to the poor.

*Pillar Four—Fasting.* The fourth ritual, called Ramadan, is fasting in the ninth month of the lunar calendar. Every adult Muslim who has no legitimate excuse for not doing so is to abstain from food, drinks, and sexual activity from shortly before dawn to sunset each day of this month. These prohibitions are lifted during the nights of the month, which are celebrated by a special prayer and Qur'anic recitation.

There is a festive mood during the month, which concludes with a day of celebration known as Post-Fasting Festival. It is the greatest Muslim holiday in the year, followed by the Festival of Sacrifice observed on the tenth day of the twelfth month of the lunar calendar. The latter marks the conclusion of the season of pilgrimage and is also in memory of Abraham.

Apart from these days, Muslims observe certain holidays of lesser importance, including the anniversary of the birth of the Prophet Mohammed.

*Pillar Five—Pilgrimage to Mecca.* Pilgrimage to Mecca during a special annual season is a duty of every adult Muslim who is physically and financially able to do it, though he is required to do this only once in his lifetime. Pilgrims, by the hundreds of thousands, assemble at Mecca in a very impressive ceremony. Kings and simple men are side by side, all similarly wearing modest white sheets or large towels, together performing some prescribed rite. This is done around and near the *Ka'ba,* the house of God built by Abraham and Ishmael, who were the grandfathers of all the succeeding Prophets, including Mohammed.

## Some Special Features of Islam

Although the basic meaning of the term *Islam* is purity, hence the purity of the concept of divine unity, it has also the connotation of "surrender" and "submission"; submission to the will of God and acceptance of whatever misfortune befalls the believer. The individual should seek to achieve objectives through hard work and sensible means. If successful, the believer should feel grateful to God; if not, he should not despair. This is not fatalism, but faith.

Islam may be described as a religion of centers. God is the center of realities. The Ka'ba is the center of worship. The mosque is the center for the community. And the Prophet Mohammed, who called for recognition of all the preceding missions and who cautioned against his being considered more than human, is the central model and ideal example of righteous conduct.

The divine teachings, laid down by God, are eternal and unchangeable. They are compatible with the needs of all times and all situations. Whether stated specifically or categorically, or in general terms such as the lawfulness of all that is useful and the prohibition of harmful things, they are not subject to human whims. Islam today is the same Islam as when it was born 14 centuries ago. There is no modern or ancient Islam, no Oriental or Western Islam. Reform movements aim at the return of the faith to its original purity and the removal of the ramifications of cultural traditions misunderstood in some areas to be part of the religion.

Islam is a religion of moderation, catering to spiritual and material needs. Neither should outweigh the other. While it is virtuous and righteous to be generous and charitable, arrogance and extravagance are condemned. A good Muslim observes the law of Islam, including the obligatory and supererogatory rituals, but a Muslim also endeavors to earn a living and to enjoy the lawful pleasures of life. Yet, some Muslims, from the third century of Islam onward, preferred to indulge in more rigorous religious practices. They fasted many days at times other than Ramadan, ate little at other times, spent most of the nighttime in prayers, and were nearly always reciting the words of prayers. With their thoughts in meditation, they sought greater spiritual purity and a closer relationship with God. Soon, they formed their own orders, known as *Sufiturug,* or "Muslim Mystical Guilds." Each of these was under the leadership of a *Sharhih,* whose disciples became known as *murids.* The development of this trend, which became known as *Sufism,* resulted from certain political and social upheavals within Islam, as well as some external influences, particularly from India. *Sufism* presupposes

Islam. Assuming its practices without the confession of that faith would be misguided mysticism.

The clarity and simplicity of the Muslim creed, the acceptance of which makes a person a Muslim, leave little room for interpretation. Yet there is some variety in legal interpretations where there is no specific guidance from the Qur'an. There was a break during the early part of Islam by some theological and legal schools founded by great thinkers and jurists. None of them pretended to hold the absolute truth in disputed areas, so the break is of no basic importance. The division of the *Sh'ia* is important. The Sh'ia advocated the right of the descendants of the Prophet's daughter to succeed the Prophet as rulers of the Muslim state. The root of this division was both political and religious, and the demarcation lines are being demolished.

In America, Islam is of special appeal to the black population for its egalitarian teachings and the sense of direction and identity it immediately gives to the convert. There are, however, some sharp divisions stemming from the urge to restore to blacks their human rights. Confusion springs from a mixture of Christian background with a shallow knowledge of Islamic theology. Beginning in 1934, a large group known as the "Black Muslims" formed under the leadership of Elijah Poole, who renamed himself Elijah Muhammed. He arrogated to himself the status of Prophethood and called for black supremacy. He also misinterpreted the Qur'anic statements in which reference was made to a promise of the Prophet Mohammed, who was to appear in America to raise the American blacks from the mud and make them into a mighty "Nation of Islam."

Other black American Muslims resented the "Nation of Islam" and formed their own groups under different leadership, calling themselves "Sunni Muslims." This term denotes adherence to the orthodox traditions of Islam. The tension occasionally led to bloodshed, as natural hatred, personal ambitions of leadership, uncontrolled misinterpretation, and personal arrogance became complicating factors.

With the death of Elijah Muhammed in February, 1975, and the assumption of the leadership of the movement by his son, Wallace D. Muhammed, the group began to reform—abandoning the father's claim to Prophethood, throwing away racial prejudices, conforming to the legitimate truths of Islam, and observing its traditional rituals. Even the "temples" are now called mosques, and the leaders of their divisions are no longer called "ministers" but Imams. The chairs and pews in the "temples" have been removed and replaced by prayer rugs. While these changes have been heartily welcomed by American Muslims of recent immigration, other black American Muslims, who sometimes call themselves "indigenous Muslims," are reluctant to accept the changes. Wallace D. Muhammed has won to his side a large portion of the core of the movement, but he is being met with some resistance, particularly from among the old supporters of his father.

# A GLOSSARY

**Adhan:** A call to prayer, announcing its time.

**Allah:** The Arabic term for God.

**Black Muslims:** Denotes a movement in America which called itself the "Nation of Islam" and now is called "The World of Islam in the West."

**Five Pillars:** A phrase used by Western writers, denoting the five basic rituals: the shahadah, the mandatory five prayers each day, payment of zakat, fasting during the month of Ramadan, and pilgrimage to Mecca at least once in one's lifetime.

**Imam:** A leader in congregational prayers.

**Islam:** The title of the religion, advocating an uncomprising concept of God's unity and surrender to the will of God.

**Ka'ba:** A House of God in Mecca faced by all Muslims in prayers and visited by millions annually, especially during the pilgrimage season.

**Mecca:** A town, now in Saudi Arabia, in which the Prophet Mohammed was born and in which he began to preach Islam when he was 40 years old.

**Medina:** A town about 280 miles north of Mecca to which the Prophet emigrated after an unsuccessful 13-year struggle with the pagans of Mecca, and in which he died and was buried in his mosque in 632 A.D.

**Mosque:** The Muslim house of worship.

**Mohammed:** The Prophet of Islam who was born at Mecca in 570 and died at Medina in 632 A.D.

**Qur'an:** (The Koran), the Holy Book of Islam, believed to be the word of God; it contains the essence of the teaching of Islam and its law.

**Shahadah:** The confession of the faith, saying: "There is no god but Allah; Mohammed is the Messenger of Allah."

**Shari'ah:** The canon law of Islam which treats all aspects of life.

**Zakat:** The religious tithe to be paid by a Muslim annually.

The following study questions will help organize your thoughts after you have read A Capsule View of Islam by Dr. Abdul-Rauf. Think through each question completely before checking your answers against the material in the Capsule View.

1. According to Islam, who or what is God?

2. In what ways is Islam a monotheistic religion, and compatible with the beliefs of Judaism and Christianity?

3. Muslims believe that man is created by God. But how do Muslims see man in relation to his fellow man?

4. In what ways does the Shari'ah law cover all human activities—social, economic, and religious?

5. How have Muslims reacted to European influences that led to behavior inconsistent with Islamic teaching?

6. What is the Qur'an to the Muslim?

7. In what way does a Muslim consider Moses, Solomon, and Jesus?

8. Briefly, name and describe the five pillars or rituals of Islamic faith.

9. In what way is purity the concept of divine unity for the Muslims?

10. What is there in Islam which supports the assertion that there is no modern or ancient Islam, no Oriental or Western Islam— that Islam today is the same Islam as when it was born 14 centuries ago?

11. In what ways is Islam a religion of moderation, catering both to spiritual and material needs?

12. Why is there little room for religious sects within Islam?

13. In what ways is the Black Muslim movement in America similar to, and different from, the basic tenets of Islam?


## AS YOU VIEW

Another perspective is provided by the television episode *Islam: There Is No God but God.* To organize your thoughts in advance, study the program description below. A review of the guiding questions in "Viewing with a Purpose" will help you to participate more actively in the viewing experience.

More than 400 million people profess Islam, and this number is said to be growing. In this television program we travel to Egypt to discuss the Islamic experience. Our journey takes us to an oasis village of Abu Howat, 100 miles from Cairo, for dawn prayers and to see a marriage contract being signed. At Cairo we visit the famous university and mosque of El Azhar. There we hear the Sheikh preach, and meet a devout married couple, both of them doctors, from whom we learn a great deal about the faith of Islam. The camera follows the couple to Saudi Arabia on their pilgrimage to Mecca but does not go to the sacred city, leaving them instead as they land at Jeddah.


## AS YOU READ

Based on your study of the material in this Student's Guide, in the program on Islam from the series "The Long Search," and from your readings in sources such as Huston Smith's *The Religions of Man,* you should be able to answer these questions as a self-assessment of your knowledge about Islam.

1.  What factors in the life of Mohammed would have contributed to his acceptance as the Prophet by Muslims?

2.  Even though claims of divinity are counter to basic Islamic theology, why do some Muslim groups regard Mohammed as a manifestation of divine essence?

3.  Why do Muslims prefer to read the Qur'an in the original Arabic language?

4.  It has been said that the Qur'an is neither a book of science nor a book of philosophy. How would you describe what it is?

5.  How is the Qur'an of Mohammed similar to The Torah of Moses?

6.  In what ways did Mohammed show his familiarity with, and respect for, the Bible as an inspired book?

7.  Is there evidence that Mohammed was influenced by the Bible in establishing the Muslim practice of circumcision and the prohibition against eating pork or drinking alcohol? Or were these parts of Islam theology based on other influences?

8.  What is the source of Islamic law?

9.  What is the most basic belief in Islamic theology?

10. Of what significance is Mecca in the hearts of Muslims?

11. How did Mohammed reform the religious and social life of his time?

12. Compare the attitude of the Muslim, the Hebrew, and the Christian toward other religions, especially nonmonotheistic religions. How does this differ from the attitude of a liberal, modern Hindu, such as a follower of the Ramakrishna movement?

## QUESTIONS FOR THOUGHT

The following questions raise concerns or points of interest related to Islam. Answer them on your own, using what you have learned about the Islamic faith.

1. Imagine that you and your entire community became Muslims. How would your life-style and that of other members of your community change? How would a strict adherence to Islamic law affect laws enacted by your local, state, and federal governments?

2. From what you now know about Islam, can you anticipate the types of problems which Black Muslims may have in an American community?

3. From a theoretical perspective, how does Islam deal with the women's movement? Is there any conflict between the theoretical perspective of male-female equality in Islam and the practical aspects of the Islamic life-style?

# Chapter 11
# WEST MEETS EAST

## A STUDY OF THE RELIGIONS OF THE EAST AND THE WEST IN CONTEMPORARY AMERICA

In contemporary America, the religious and cultural ideas of East and West have begun to mingle, as people brought up in a largely Christian and rational culture look to the East for inspiration in their daily lives.

There are new attitudes about how to regard the mind and how to care for the body. There is new emphasis on a saner and simpler life than most of America seems to present.

Yet there is also continuing confusion. It is often difficult for young Americans to discriminate among ideas which may have some genuine validity and those which are simply faddish or deceptive.

In order to make such judgments, it is necessary to understand what "West" and "East" represent, and to realize how they may offer either contradictory or complementary views. Furthermore, amid the enthusiasm which Americans bring to anything new, it is necessary to be aware of the dangers of self-deception and spiritual materialism. Only when there is a balance between the openness to receive new ideas and the critical intelligence which examines them closely can the meeting of East and West become a process of authentic communication and fertilization.

## A PREFACE TO YOUR STUDY

An outline of the major concepts related to a study of the meeting of religions of West and East in contemporary America begins your lesson. Use them to focus your study of this lesson. A basic source of material for your study of this religious phenomenon in America is provided by Dr. Joshua Zim. Dr. Zim is the Information Officer for the Nalanda Foundation, a nonprofit educational foundation which brings the inspiration of Buddhist teachings into secular American life.

The study questions will help assess your understanding of the material in this Student's Guide Chapter.

Another perspective on this topic will be revealed in the program "West Meets East," from the television series "The Long Search."

The Questions for Thought section at the end of this lesson leaves you with some issues and concerns which you will want to consider in making application of these concepts to your life and beliefs.

## IMPORTANT CONCEPTS

The major ideas in this lesson focus on three basic categories of concepts: the dualistic nature of Western reality; the nondualistic nature of Eastern reality; and the contemporary movements in America to blend these precepts of reality. Look for these concepts in organizing your thoughts as you read and view.

### Basic Assumption

"West" and "East" are terms which refer to models of reality.

### Western Reality

Western reality can be said to be dualistic.

The achievements of modern technological society can be attributed to the dualistic approach.

Dualism in the West can be viewed as having been expressed as a split between these factors:

1. "mind" and "body";
2. "knowledge" and "practice";
3. "life" and "meaning."

The split between mind and body can be described as the view that man exists outside the natural order.

The split between knowledge and practice can be seen as arising from the belief in an absolute and eternal truth.

The split between life and meaning can be viewed as the principle that man's existence is meaningful only as it reflects a higher power.


## Eastern Reality

Eastern reality is nondualistic.

The Eastern approach suggests that:

1. mind and matter are interdependent, as are heart and mind;
2. truth, which is relative, can be discovered personally through practice;
3. meaning is inherent in the fact that life is of itself, without need for reference to a superior principle.


## Contemporary Movements in America

Contemporary counterculture arose from the disillusionments of the 1960s.

California has always been a lodestar for new movements, and remains so with respect to the counterculture styles.

Some representative developments are: biofeedback; TM; est Training; and T'ai Chi Ch'uan. Each can be viewed along the continuum of duality-nonduality.

Gary Snyder is a well-known American poet whose life exemplifies the interplay of Western and Eastern concerns.

Basic problems which arise from the meeting of West and East, and from the spiritual search implicit in counterculture life-styles, are the tendencies toward self-deception and spiritual materialism.

# A CAPSULE VIEW
## OF THE COUNTERCULTURE LIFE-STYLES
## OF WEST AND EAST RELIGIONS

### Models of Reality

When we speak of East and West, we are really speaking of mind, states of mind, attitudes, models of reality. We operate with our own models of reality and test our perceptions, our experiences, our communications against these models all the time. Very often, we are not aware of the presence of these models in our lives or how they work to create our sense of "reality." For example, our perception tells us that railroad tracks meet at a point on the horizon; yet somehow we "know" that this is not the case. Our perception of the world is filtered through our concepts about it. Or take the case of looking down from an office building 100 stories above the ground and watching the "ants" scurrying about in the streets below. We know that, when we descend, the "ants" will have turned to people and grown to life-size. This shift from ants to people is not a process that is usually articulated in our daily lives. We don't ordinarily stop to examine our assumptions about what is real, because those assumptions are generally shared by the people around us. Our parents teach us a model of reality. Our society reinforces the model of reality and our language serves to maintain it. We operate on the basis of consensus. In fact "reality" is consensus.

Not only do we have this consensus which determines what we believe is "real" but we need it to function effectively, or so we believe. We require continuity from day to day. Imagine how confused our world would be if we were to ride down in our elevator and discover that the people walking the streets were just as tiny as they had appeared to be from the 100th floor. Imagine how difficult it would be to run a railroad if we could not remain confident that the tracks would not meet at a point on the horizon, or if we could only take this to be the case for today and not necessarily for tomorrow. Our model of reality provides us this sense of assurance.

So, our sense of reality is tremendously useful. We can talk to each other about what seems to be happening; we don't have to start from scratch each time. We have a sense of predictability and stability. The world is recognizable and we are able to exercise our influence over it, manipulate it, and in some ways, at least, control it. But relying entirely upon this ordinary reality can also be stultifying and even claustrophobic. Einstein, for instance, attributed his theory of reality to irritation with ordinary reality and ordinary descriptions of reality. He was puzzled by the commonplace "fact" that objects appear smaller at a distance and larger when close-at-hand, and he was unwilling to accept conventional explanations for this phenomenon.

## What Is "West"?

Does our sun revolve around Earth? We know that the sun rises in the east, travels across the sky, and sets in the west. We have abandoned the view that it is a fiery chariot rolling through the heavens, yet we have adopted another view which just as powerfully refutes our common sense. We hold that Earth revolves around our sun. This conceptual scheme is the product of science, of rationality; and generally speaking, when people attempt to describe the "Western mind," they call it "scientific."

The model of reality presented by the rational and scientific mind is said basically to rest upon measurability, upon quantification. The world is scientifically real when it is measurable; what is measurable can be analyzed. Reality, in the scientific or rational view, can be analyzed. But if we examine this process more clearly, we can see that an even more basic assumption underlies the model of the Western mind.

For us to be able to analyze reality, according to the Western view, there obviously must exist a distinction between ourselves and the phenomenon we are analyzing. There must be a split between the observer and the thing (object or event) being observed.

This division is at the heart of the Western model of reality, not only physical reality but psychological reality as well. This is the division between subject and object, between "this" and "that"; and in order for the world to be real or true, it is necessary for this separation to be equally real. Belief in this separation is called "dualism," and this belief characterizes Western reality. In science, despite recent developments in subatomic physics which make this distinction problematic, dualism is expressed in terms of the process of experimentation. The scientist is considered a neutral observer who acts upon and observes the phenomenal world which is separate from himself. In religion, dualism is expressed generally in terms of the fall of man, or of original sin. So we have the Christian view that man is a sinner, who is doomed to slavery and death and stands in need of salvation.

In order to understand the meaning which the East may have for the West, we need first to investigate this fundamental belief of dualism.


### Duality: "I" and "Other"

Psychologically speaking, we ordinarily believe that "I" exists and that "other" exists as two distinct and substantial entities. These seem to be solid facts. Things appear to be just that way. But if we apply the notion that this duality may be simply a *model* of reality, then we can allow ourselves to see how it might come into being, how it may be created.

Take our everyday lives, our patterns of thought and feelings. When we first encounter an object—whether it is a thing, or a person, or a situation—there is just the immediate perception, without conception or logic. We could say there is simply open ground. But immediately we seek to add something to our direct experience, we seek to name it or to categorize it in some way. Gradually our original perception comes to have a more definite sense of form, and our act of naming it also sets it apart. We may feel that the object is threatening to us, or seductive, or neutral. We think and act accordingly. If it is threatening, we may attempt to keep it from us; if it is seductive, we may seek to draw it toward us; and if it appears to be neutral, we may choose to ignore it. In any case, this process confirms the sense that there is an "I" to which this "other" relates. A kind of mutual conspiracy takes place. This process is instantaneous and occurs almost constantly. In this sense, the Western mind is continually creating and confirming duality.

But if, as we have seen, dualism is something that we create, then perhaps there is another model of reality which is not dualistic. Here the "East" may speak to the "West."


### What Is "East"?

The Western mind has produced the tremendous technological achievements of our culture, the affluence, and the material well-being which are unparalleled in the history of civilization. America in particular has achieved an extraordinarily sophisticated level of physical materialism. If something is wrong, we fix it. If we have pain, we take aspirin. If something is unpleasant, we can flush it away. In a shockingly clever and convincing fashion, our dualistic attitudes pervade our lives. Without even realizing it, we separate ourselves from the raw and rugged qualities of life, and then we are bewildered by our sense of dissatisfaction. There is affluence, yet at the same time gratuitous violence; there is constant entertainment, but we feel bored; there is idealism, but we mistrust ourselves. In the midst of our awesome wealth, we somehow feel impoverished.

The Eastern approach—Taoist, Buddhist, Hindu, Sufi, and so on—seeks to address this basic sense of division. Obviously, these widely differing traditions take different approaches to this question, but there are certain fundamental elements shared in common which are both challenging and provocative to Western culture. The "East" brings into question the entire dualistic approach to reality.

Generally speaking, dualistic attitudes in Western thought can be regarded as having manifested three major divisions: first, a split between "mind" and "body"; second, a split between "knowledge" and "practice"; and third, a split between "life" and "meaning."

*Mind/Body.* This division between mind and body (mind and matter) arises from the logic of empiricism which says that what is true is only that which can be verified through our five senses. The mind is a separate faculty which operates upon and translates the information provided by the senses. Mind does not influence matter, nor does matter influence mind. This is the basis for scientific experiment. Conventionally, if a scientist observes some natural phenomenon, his observation does not affect the nature of the phenomenon; he exists *outside* the natural order he is observing.

The Eastern philosophies have a wholly different emphasis, stressing the interdependence of all phenomena, whether material or mental. The Taoist speaks of *wu-wei,* or "nonaction" *within* the natural order; the Buddhist speaks of "dependent origination," or the view that events have multiple causes which are equally significant. Mental events are not different fundamentally from material events and they are inextricably bound together. Consider the following example.

You are standing on a scaffold and painting the side of a building. You reach for a can of paint and suddenly find yourself falling

225

off the rigging. If someone asks you what happened, you might just reply, "My foot slipped." But perhaps there is further explanation. We could say that you fell because you were not aware of what was happening. Here we have shifted from speaking about "matter" (my foot slipped) to "mind" (you were not aware). Of course, you might reply that your state of mind had nothing to do with the situation at all, and that the reason you fell was that your sneakers had worn-out and slippery soles. But again, we could ask why you chose to wear those particular sneakers. What were you thinking about, or not thinking about? Actually, the interplay of states of mind and material facts in such a case can be enormously complicated, involving the condition of the weather, your physical state, the noises and distractions of the surrounding environment, and on and on. The seemingly simple act of falling is really the effect of a convergence of multiple causes, both mental and material. From the Eastern viewpoint the mind/body split is merely a convenient distinction. It has no absolute truth.

Interestingly, recent developments in the realm of subatomic physics have led scientists to similar thoughts about the interrelationship of mind and matter. These insights were sparked by the discoveries of Werner Heisenberg, Nobel Prize winner and proponent of the "Uncertainty Principle." In investigating the activity of electrons, he concluded that electrons were, in effect, not so much "things" as "events." An event is an occurrence in space and time; as such, it does not exist in any absolute sense. Instead, it is merely a statistical probability. In attempting to locate this "electron event," Heisenberg discovered that you could not determine both its position and velocity at the same time. The measurement of one prevented the measurement of the other, and the very act of measuring, since you were dealing with statistical probability, subtly and unpredictably altered the "event" itself. This conclusion had astonishingly wide-ranging implications, because it is suggested that the observer was not separate from the object being observed. In effect, the conclusion was that the observer was not an observer at all, but a participant in the entire process.

This state of affairs challenges the conventional Western model of reality as something which exists "out there." Instead of being able to sit back and observe the natural order as separate from ourselves, we find that we are *within* that order from the very beginning. Our participation affects the course of the universe.

But we must be careful not to leap too quickly from the realm of the electron to worlds of a larger scale, or we may fall into superstition. It would be foolish, for example, to speculate on how our viewing the movement of the moon might be influencing that particular event. Nonetheless, a great Zen master once said, "When I look at the moon, I am the moon."

On the other hand, certain analogies for our everyday experience can be drawn from the Uncertainty Principle and from other findings which have been presented in a recent book by a California physicist, Fritjof Capra, whose work is aptly titled *The Tao of Physics*. Consider, for instance, the reporting of the results of a national election. The use of computers has made the projections of the outcome a part of the election process itself. Let us say that a candidate is declared the winner on the basis of votes cast in the eastern United States. How will voters in the west, where the polls are still open, be affected by these projections? Are people more, or less, likely to vote for a winner? Once again, the exact effect of this observation is unpredictable, but we can imagine a campaign designed to optimize such effects. In any case, the actuality of interrelationships raises all kinds of questions and possibilities.

We can view the split between mind and body in still another and more personal way. Here, mind could be spoken of as "intellect" and body as "feeling." Throughout Western history, these two elements have been seen as essentially contradictory; and generally, feeling has been considered to be inferior. Much of the inspiration which the Eastern approaches have brought to America has been in redressing this sense of imbalance and in calling to our attention the significance of the intuitiveness in our lives. The Zen Buddhist, for example, does not speak of "heart" or of "mind" but of "heart/-mind."

A danger in this, of course, is the possibility of creating antiintellectual cults of "feeling." Unfortunately, many young Americans have fallen into this trap, rejecting their intelligence and seeking simply the multiplication and satisfaction of "feelings"— feeling good, feeling high, feeling enlightened—in the name of Eastern spirituality. But this is a sad misunderstanding of the Eastern view.

*Knowledge/Practice.*   The second manifestation of dualism in the Western model, the split between knowledge and practice, arises from the belief in an absolute and eternal truth. It should be clear that this belief is the heart of any theistic religion, Eastern or Western. Any revealed religion, for example, Islam or Christianity, rests upon such a belief and is inspired by it. For the believer, however, certain problems may arise.

Dietrich Bonhoeffer, a Christian theologian who courageously resisted the Nazis in Germany and was killed by them, proposed that the true Christian must live "as though God did not exist." What could such a statement mean? Obviously, he did not propose a lack of faith. But he proposed that this state of mind was necessary for a Christian to be able to accept responsibility for his own life and for the lives of others. For the believer in an eternal truth, it can be reassuring to have something solid to hang onto, a fixed and comfortable way of looking at the world and his relationship to it. This also can have a deadening effect, however, removing from the believer the responsibility to actualize this truth in his own life.

For the nontheistic religions of the East, truth has a changing and relative character. It is not the word of God. It is not fixed for eternity. The Eastern approach suggests that the truth must be realized personally and individually; and through the centuries much emphasis has been placed on practicing the means which can facilitate this realization. Generally speaking, the Eastern approaches can be said to be meditative. While the meditative practices of the various schools and religions differ, they are all concerned with the workings of the mind and the emotions. The meditative traditions hold that by becoming aware of our own minds we can discover the truth for ourselves. This is referred to as "discipline" or "practice."

In recent years, such emphasis on personal practice has infused American culture. Many developments, from gestalt therapy to est (Erhard Seminars Training) to biofeedback training, have sprung from this insight. Indeed, many practicing Christians have found a practice, such as meditation, compatible with their beliefs and even enriching for their religious experience.

*Life/Meaning.*   The third and last expression of dualistic thinking which we are going to discuss is closely related to the second; for when there is a split between knowledge and practice, there follows that there is a split between life and meaning. In this duality, life just as it is—without reference to some eternal principle, whether God, Allah, Atman, whatever—has no meaning. From this point of view, man's existence has meaning or value only insofar as it reflects or links up with two superior and supreme principles. In Islam, for instance, we have the formulation that man is made in the image of God and is destined for life with God, but that he must be redeemed from sin in order to become one with God and share eternal life.

The view of the East diverges sharply from this attitude, both logically and psychologically. Since, in the Eastern approach, there is no eternal verity or principle which has an independent and substantial existence, there is nothing "out there" (or even "in there") to turn to for a reason for being. We are simply alive and that is a fact. We could say that, from the Eastern view, life has something of the character of a traffic court. If you are given a ticket and turn up at court, all that anyone wants to know are the facts. Explanations for *why* you are alive are not needed; it just happens to be so.

Many Westerners, when they first hear this attitude expressed, take it to be some form of pessimism or even nihilism, namely, that life has no meaning, so why bother? Or, taken further, this nihilistic approach may create the psychological attitude of fatalism. In this view, since nothing has any meaning and since events seem to operate in a kind of chain reaction over which we can exercise no control, we can perform *any* action; life is meaningless and yet somehow fore-ordained. This is a serious and tragic distortion of the attitude of the East.

Meaning, or value, inheres in the very fact of life itself. Because there is no *belief* in some fundamental sense of separation (such as sin) you can assume complete responsibility for your own life. Belief that human beings are capable of doing so is an absolutely basic tenet of the Eastern traditions. The Eastern ideal, whether it is enlightenment or living within the Tao, is not some condition which requires outside intervention in the form of salvation or grace. It is considered to be a potential which already exists, an intelligence which human beings possess, and which can be cultivated and awakened through "practice." This is not particularly a mysterious or mystical process; in fact, this basic intelligence is said to be continuously present in all the situations of life. Rather than being pessimistic or nihilistic, this attitude towards human potential is actually an expression of confidence in a basic dignity which does not require confirmation of any kind.

## The American Search, The Background of the Sixties

In order to understand the spiritual search of contemporary America, it is necessary first to survey the decade of the 1960s, a period of turmoil and ferment in American culture.

From the generation who came of age in the '60s, the world was especially suspect. Raised to believe in American ideals of justice and fair play, this generation felt acutely the disappointments of foreign policy, racism, and technocracy. Basically this was a phenomenon of the middle-class young, who formed their own community in and around college campuses and expressed their disillusionment by getting high on drugs, joining communes, or testing the authority of the police.

A particularly striking aspect of this youth culture was the linkage between political activity and the quest for visionary experience, sparked by the easy availability of psychedelic drugs. On the one side there were mystical longing, a fascination with the occult, an attraction to Eastern gurus, both authentic and charlatan, a frenetic pursuit of polymorphous sexuality and blissed-out experience; on the other side were community organizing, ecological awareness, the protests against the war in Vietnam.

During the decade of the '70s, there has been a remarkable shift in the way we perceive ourselves in the world. Somehow the preoccupations of the '60s have faded; political radicals have become earnest young lawyers; the draft has been repealed, and the troops have left Vietnam. While the use of marijuana has become something of a commonplace for the middle-class (so much so that its use is rapidly being decriminalized) other drugs have been supplanted by alcohol, formerly the symbol of the straight and up-tight world.

The feverish discontent of the '60s, the fury, violence, and irrationality of its disaffection could not be sustained without the surplus of money which allowed this youth culture the luxury of self-expression. When economic circumstances became tighter in the early '70s, and when the young inevitably grew older, the ardor of discontent cooled. Yet something remained, a sense of possibility which prompted a search for personal development, personal enlightenment of one kind or another.

**230**

## The Counterculture and California

The movement that arose in the 1960s eventually gave rise to an alternative society which has been loosely termed the "counterculture." The leading edge in this development is in California, which has a psychological character unique in American culture. California was settled by the lure for gold, by the attraction of sudden wealth and infinite possibility. Drawn from their familiar surroundings "back east," men came face to face with the Pacific Ocean. For the 19th Century, and for much of the 20th (until the exploration of space) it was the last frontier, as much spiritual as geographical.

California represented a new kind of freedom, mobility, affluence, and openness to the new direction of the Pacific. Chinese and Japanese immigrants brought an Oriental dimension to the culture of the west coast, and after World War II this influence had an even more profound impact. Just as military and defense spending brought vast economic resources to California, the Pacific cultures brought a psychological richness, and life on the west coast seemed to become an on-going experiment in living.

California today is swarming with alternative realities, some profound and some shallow Taoists, Pure Land Buddhists, Zen masters, New-Age Sikhs, bhakti yogis, Kabalists, gestalt therapists, transcendental meditators, est graduates, transactional analysts, followers of macrobiotic diets, high-fiber diets, megavitamin therapies, shiatsu, rolfing, practitioners of Tibetan Buddhism, Hindu tantra, the Fischer-Hoffman Process—every whim, every cult, every idea new or old seems to find some place in the mental landscape of California.

## Some Current Developments

It would be impossible to examine all the varied teachings and experiments which have mushroomed in the fertile ground of California and throughout America as the expression of the coming together of East and West. Nevertheless it is possible to look at a few representative developments and personalities, to catch something of the flavor of these contemporary spiritual and cultural phenomena. In considering these developments, we would do well to cultivate an attitude of openness and skepticism, attending to the possibility of separating the wheat from the chaff.

*Biofeedback.* This process is the electronically governed self-monitoring of biological systems, "involuntary" physiological activities ranging from blood pressure to intestinal contraction. It is specifically designed to bring these activities under conscious control in order to improve physical and mental health. The basic technique is quite simple; when the subject performs a particular physiological feat, such as relaxing a certain muscle, an electronic signal informs the subject of that success—and gradually, over a period of many trials, the subject learns to recognize that state (relaxation, for instance) and to produce it voluntarily without reinforcement.

This process is of special interest because it exemplifies the ways in which Western science is brought to bear upon phenomena associated with the Eastern tradition. Yogic practices and meditation have long been said to have beneficial effects on metabolism, heartbeat and other physiological processes; biofeedback research has corroborated these claims to some degree. Indeed, we could view biofeedback as a peculiarly Western approach to bridging the split between mind and body, establishing an intimacy of communication which expresses the nonduality of the East.

The most widely known type of biofeedback is EEG, which is concerned with brainwaves. Basically, four types of brainwaves have been discriminated: alpha, beta, theta, and delta. Alpha and beta waves occur alternately in the brain; alpha waves indicate a relaxed but alert state; beta are associated with concentration and normal thought; theta signal creative activity and are associated with the mind just before onset of sleep; and delta characterize the state of deep sleep.

Yogis and Zen monks have been monitored with EEG equipment and their practices have been associated with dominance of alpha activity, indicating a peaceful state without deliberate thought. Students have been trained to recognize their own alpha activity and to reproduce it at will, but only with moderate success. How this actually happens is a question, though there are signs that in order to "learn" this relaxed state some initial capacity for relaxation is necessary.

Other types of biofeedback are EMG, which monitors the electrical activity of muscles; EKG, which measures heartbeat; and GSR, which measures the electrical resistance of the skin. Biofeedback research is still quite young, but already there are potential applications in the treatment of headache, hypertension, epilepsy, and other disorders.

*Transcendental Meditation.* This technique is an extremely popular form of meditation which has four basic elements: a *mantram* (thought sound) which is used to disengage the mind from superficial mental activity; a quiet environment; a passive attitude towards one's mental activity; and the regular practice of the meditation at least 20 minutes per day.

In the early 1960s, transcendental meditation (TM) was associated with leading figures of pop culture such as the Beatles and Mia Farrow. Its founder, Maharishi Mahesh Yogi, became something of a cult figure in America. A large and well-organized international movement promotes these teachings. Considerable medical research has indicated that this particular form of meditation, which other meditative traditions view as a kind of mental gymnastic, can have various healthful effects.

Recently, *Time* magazine and other media reported that advanced TM meditators who act as trainers claimed that they were developing the powers of levitating and becoming invisible. They declined to supply evidence of these powers, however, announcing that they did not wish to create a circuslike atmosphere about their endeavors.

*est (Erhard Seminars Training).* This is a highly controversial program which was developed by Werner Erhard, a one-time salesman; it is a synthesis of a wide variety of disciplines, including yoga, Zen, and gestalt therapy, among others. It is a four-day "Standard Training" which is not therapy but which is said to allow trainees to become aware of their established beliefs, to generate a process which fosters the acceptance of direct experience, and to realize a transformation in experiencing others.

Because the training program is rigorous and often uncomfortable, it has the reputation of being militaristic. Nonetheless, the training has been performed by nearly 10 thousand people around the country, and many of the trainees feel quite positive about its effect in their lives. At the same time, however, there remains the question of the long-term usefulness of est, of whether its effects are only temporary or can actually be integrated into the everyday lives of the trainees. In terms of our earlier discussion of dualistic and nondualistic attitudes, this process seems to oscillate between the two, seeking integration while at the same time aggressively altering the (mental) environment.

**T'ai Chi Ch'uan.**   This is a system of exercise which is based on Taoist principles and is said to date from 1000 A.D. Circular movement and softness characterize the whole of T'ai Chi Ch'uan, which seeks to harmonize the active and passive elements of life.

While T'ai Chi Ch'uan is a body action, it is also the action of the mind, since the flow of forms is a logical one and the mind must apply this logic in order to cultivate continuity of motion. The forms are designed so that mind and body work with alternating intensity, so that there is time for both mental and physical rest. Tranquility is the aim of this process, but in this case tranquility is not a trancelike state. Instead, it is thought of as being the full expression of the powers of the human mind and body which are developed in equilibrium.

In a sense, T'ai Chi Ch'uan could be regarded as meditation in action, or active meditation. It approaches the mind/body split in a manner which differs significantly from most Western approaches, in that its emphasis is first on the body. In this view, when the body functions properly the mind will also function properly. Many of the experiments of counterculture life-style have taken this premise as the basis for their activities.

**Gary Snyder, poet.**   In many ways Gary Snyder epitomizes the spirit of the new-style seekers. Alan Watts wrote of Snyder, "His character requires a mixture of Oregon woodsman, seaman, Amerindian shaman, Oriental scholar, San Francisco hippie and swinging monk, who takes tough discipline with a light heart." Snyder first gained fame (and notoriety) as an associate of the Beats, and was the central character in Jack Kerouch's *Dharma Bums.* He was particularly responsible for the distinct taste of the East which flavored the whole Beat movement, yet his development as a poet took a distinctive course of its own. Snyder's early training was as an anthropologist, but interestingly he has moved from the role of observer to that of informant, a participant in the world, both poetic and politi-

both poetic and political. He has been working as a member of the California Arts Council in the administration of Governor Jerry Brown, seeking to create support for artists in a technological society in the same way that it is necessary to support any endangered species.

Snyder studied for nearly ten years as a student of a Zen master, and his poetry and life are infused with the spirit of Buddhist teachings. Here are Snyder's views on the subject of "practice":

". . . I wouldn't like to separate our mindfulness into two categories, one of which is your forty-minute daily ritual, which is 'practice,' and the other not practice. Practice simply is one intensification of what is natural and around us all of the time. Practice is to life as poetry is to spoken language. So as poetry is the practice of language, 'practice' is the practice of life. But from the enlightened standpoint, all language is poetry, all of life is practice. . . ."

". . . One of the first practices I learned is that when you're working with another person on a two-person crosscut saw, you never push, you only pull; my father taught me that when I was eight. . . . Another great teaching that I had came from some older men, all of whom were practitioners of a little-known esoteric indigenous Occidental school of mystical practice called mountaineering. . . . The real mysticism of mountaineering is the body/mind practice of moving on a vertical plane in a realm that is totally inhospitable to human beings. . . ."

". . . The whole world is practicing together; it is not rare or uncommon for people who are living their lives in the world, doing the things they must do, if they have not been degraded or oppressed, to be fully conscious of the dignity and pride of their life and work. . . . Buddhism, like Christianity, is responding to the alienation of a fragmented society."

". . . Part of our practice is not just sitting down and forming useful little groups within the society but . . . expanding our sense of what has happened to us all into a realization that natural societies are in themselves communities of practice."*

It should be apparent that Snyder's encounter with the approach of the East is neither faddish nor facile, but something which has become integral to his way of life.

## The Problem of Deception

The intermingling of West and East can be tremendously inspiring, but it can also be confusing, especially because it may be difficult to distinguish between teachings and teachers that are genuine and those that are false or misguided. In searching for spiritual direction, for a teacher, many Americans depend upon fame or an aura of wisdom as guidelines, but this actually is little more than the lure of the exotic. A real spiritual journey requires direct communication. Is it possible for you to talk with the teacher thoroughly and candidly? Does he know anything about you? For that matter, does he really know anything about himself? Can he actually cut through your self-deceptions? These seem to be among questions that need to be asked if the entire smorgasbord of growth movements, personal quests, and spiritual practices is not to be swallowed whole. For true significance, it is also necessary to view these practices, whether Eastern or Western or hybrid, in light of the issue of spiritual materialism.

## Spiritual Materialism

The problem of any spiritual discipline is the problem presented by the fact that we do not actually want to become or identify with the teachings. We may go through the motions, but we do not really want to sacrifice any part of our own security. Instead, we create a false spirituality which serves to insulate us from the impact of those teachings. This false spirituality—which may appear in any religious tradition—is expressed in the constant desire to avoid the basic simplicity of what we are by seeking some higher, more transcendental version of reality. This is spiritual materialism.

In maintaining this spiritual materialism, we seek to defend and better ourselves, but our egocentricity becomes an obstacle to surrender, the surrender of hopes and of fears which is necessary for direct communication with any authentic, spiritual tradition.

Therefore, in assessing a spiritual practice, it is essential that the student have the courage to ask the question, "Is this spiritually materialistic for me?" This question can serve to illuminate the seeming tangle of messages which are constantly springing forth from the counterculture mix of East and West.

## Summary

In the meeting of West and East, psychological attitudes of dualism and nondualism come into contact, and the result of this mix is actually quite unpredictable. Although the East has been an influence in America for some time, only recently have there been a widespread dissemination of its approach and the availability of teachers who can present it properly. It would be premature, therefore, to attempt to assess the impact of the East on the lives of Americans. We require the perspective of another ten years, or perhaps another hundred. It should prove a fascinating and perplexing development.

## STUDY QUESTIONS

The following study questions will help organize your thoughts after you have read A Capsule View of the Counterculture Life-Styles of West and East Religions, by Joshua Zim. Think through each question completely before checking your answers against the material in the Capsule View.

1. Dr. Zim asserts that "East" and "West" are really states of mind, attitudes, and models of reality. According to Zim, what models shape our perspective of reality?

2. Of what value to us is our own individual model of reality?

3. How is reality described by the rational or scientific view?

4. What is the major factor in the Western view of perceiving reality?

5. How does the Western model of reality embody the "I" to which some "other" relates?

6. Explain the dualistic attitude in Western thought that is manifest in a perceived split between "mind" and "body." How is this different from the perspective of Eastern philosophy?

7. Explain the dualistic attitude in Western thought that is manifest in a perceived split between "knowledge" and "practice." How is this different from the thinking in the nontheistic religions of the East?

8. Explain the dualistic attitude in Western thought that is manifest in the perceived split between "life" and "meaning." How does the East diverge from this attitude?

9. What was the world like to the generation which came of age in the 1960s? What changes have occurred in the perception of the 1970s?

10. Why has California traditionally and historically been the lodestone for countercultures?

11. Briefly describe biofeedback. What West-East differences has biofeedback attempted to bridge?

12. Name and describe the four basic elements of transcendental meditation.

13. What does est seek to do for the individual?

14. How would you describe the T'ai Chi Ch'uan? How does this method approach the mind/body split?

15. What does Dr. Zim mean when he talks of "spiritual materialism"?

## AS YOU VIEW

Another perspective is provided by the television episode *Alternative Life Styles in California: West Meets East*. To organize your thoughts in advance, study the program description below, and review the guiding questions in "Viewing with a Purpose" at the end of this Guide. You can then participate more actively in the viewing experience.

"The spiritual impulse of the time steps beyond the boundaries of religious tradition"; so wrote Theodore Roszak, protagonist for the counterculture and our guide to the new religious concerns of people living in the San Francisco Bay area. Here is a mingling of religious ideas and life-styles of East and West, where people brought up in a largely Christian cultural climate look East to Taoism and Hinduism for inspiration in daily living. We find a preoccupation with the search for a saner and healthier life, in which ecology is grounded in the sacred. The accent on health is fundamental. Investigating these life-style searches, we visit cooperatives, meet people who share jobs, and go to a biofeedback clinic. We go to a commune run by white Sikhs. Visiting the University of California at Berkeley, we meet research physicists who find that their latest adventures in subatomic physics led them full circle back to the Tao.

## QUESTIONS FOR THOUGHT

The following questions raise concerns of points of interest related to a study of the counterculture life-styles evident in the religions of California. Using what you have learned, answer them on your own.

1. What is your perception of reality? How did you first learn to perceive this reality? What factors in your life support your current perception of reality?

2. Think of some examples from your own life where you have displayed the split between "mind" and "body" typical of Western thought. Can you recall instances in which you reconciled this split? How have you dealt with the split between "knowledge" and "practice" and the split between "life" and "meaning"?

3. The Eastern perspective contradicts much of the "scientific" method which underlies Western thought. What might be some

of the implications of the mingling of Eastern and Western thought for the future of science?

4. In what ways has your personal experience or knowledge of the California counterculture affected your life?

5. What might be the typical American's life-style and consciousness in the year 2000, if the California fusion of East and West continues and spreads throughout the country?

# LOOSE ENDS

# An Epilogue

(The following is a personal commentary on "The Long Search" by Dr. Ninian Smart, editorial consultant for the BBC's film series of that title. Educated at Glasgow and Oxford, Dr. Smart has written books on the history of religions, the philosophy of religions, and modern Chinese ideology. He has taught at the Universities of Wales, London, and Birmingham, and has held appointments as visiting professor at Yale University, Hindu University in Benares, the University of Wisconsin, Princeton University, and the University of Otago, New Zealand. He is presently director of religious studies at the University of Lancaster and lecturer-professor at the University of California. For 1979-80 he has been nominated as Gifford Lecturer at the University of Edinburgh.)

As this exploration of the world's cultures and religions draws to a close, we can reflect upon the common themes running through them and the distinctive qualities of each tradition. Let me begin with the likenesses and then comment on each religion's unique nature and contributions.

But first a note on the fact that there are many loose ends in our own long search. Our exploration is only, I hope, at an end in a formal sense—surely the deeper issues must remain in our minds so that each one of us will continue to search and explore throughout our lives.

Secondly, there are loose ends because ultimately we are concerned with individual persons and groups. It is convenient to use such words as "religion" and "culture" and "a tradition," yet each religion in fact is lived out in a mass of different ways by human beings. People just cannot be fitted into stereotypes. So the world is richer than any analogies we may give of its history.

Thirdly, there are loose ends because we have had to be selective. Many movements in and on the fringes of the major religions have had to be left out. So have other aspects of these faiths, examined here, which we have not been able to look at in depth. Without a set of loose ends we may be a little arrogant—thinking we have neatly packaged the experiences of mankind and the complexities of man's living religions.

So, we do need to try to make sense of the variety of faiths which we have thus far explored. What are some of the common themes that cross many of the major religion boundaries?

First there is the recurrent theme of the prophet, mystic, or holy man who serves as a leader in the long search. We can think of men like the prophets of ancient Israel, Jesus, Paul, Mohammed, the rishis or seers of ancient India, modern saints like Ramakrishna, and great teachers like the Great Buddha, and Shankara. Such people serve, as it were, as a means of communication between the world beyond and this world.

Some are born prophetic in their own time and some are mystical. What I mean by this distinction is roughly as follows. Whereas Isaiah or Mohammed or other prophets report that they receive visions of a pre-Being who speaks to them as though he is outside them, the mystic tends to meditate in order to discover a vision within himself. Of course, these mystics may believe that God is "out there" and also within. This idea we find in the *Upanishads*. The poet Tennyson expressed it by saying that God is "closer than hand and breathing." Still, in general, one can make a distinction between the prophetic and the mystical approach to religion. Judaism, Christianity, and Islam have a predominately prophetic spirit, but in various ways, such as among the Sufis of Islam, the interior and mystical approach has also become an important thread in the fabric of the faith. Some people, like the author Aldous Huxley, and some religious leaders, especially among modern Hindus, have seen mystical religious themes running through all the great faiths. They point to such men and movements as Meister Eckhart, Christian monastic orders, the Jewish Kabbalists, the Sufis of Islam, Hindu Yogis, and so on.

But we can also point to a different theme, springing from the teachings of prophets in the past. That is the aspect of religion which focuses on a personal god, a type of religion which issues warmly in devotion, or as it is called in India, *Bhakti*. This devotion is seen in the Christian's love and worship of Christ, in the Muslim's devotion to Allah, in the personal relationship of the Jew to his God, in the theism of much of the Indian religions—above all the "Song of the Lord," *Bhagavad-Gita*.

Briefly, then, I would see three themes binding religions—the respect for the holy leader, the interior mystical quest, and the outer acceptance of and devotion to a personal god. Where mysticism predominates, the personality of the divine is not much stressed—and even the idea of a god to worship may practically disappear, as in the Buddhism of Ceylon. On the other hand, where the prophetic and conversional sign is central, God is usually seen as a personal being, though, of course, the worshiper should not think of God as a human being with knowledge, for God's nature goes beyond merely human ideas in infinite greatness. Such are the differing empathies of faith. The mystical approach is more quiet, and more interior; the devotional approach is more outward-looking and often dynamic.

There are other themes common in religions, especially in regard to ethics. Even if the shape of different moral systems may vary, nevertheless a substantial ethical concern is shared by the great religions. For example, the major religions condemn unnecessary killings, lying, and so forth.

Though there are common themes in religions, each faith shows ingenuity. The genius of Hinduism is to combine divergent practices and beliefs into one overall system, and this religion has pioneered tolerance in spiritual matters. Many modern Hindus see the different religions as so many paths to one goal. Buddhism's genius is found in its great exploration of the mystical and inward side of human life, and yet it does not neglect the concern and endurance of men in their ordinary life. The genius of Jainism is found in its single-minded nonviolence and its concern for living things. Sikhism teaches us that religious externals should not be a cause of bitterness and division, and that there is a middle way between the Muslim and the Hindu religions. The Parsees remind us that the great religion of Zoroaster, so vital in its influence on Judaism and Christianity, still can maintain its identity in the modern world.

Nearly all these religions believe in reincarnation—a framework in which the dramas of life are played out. Perhaps if there is one thing uniting the main faiths originating in India it is this belief, together with the accompanying idea that it is karma—namely, the pattern of our actions—which determines our future lives and therefore determines how we can then contemplate the future. The model of rebirth or reincarnation differs in spirit from the usual Western model found in the religions originating from the Middle East, in which one life is lived by man, having succeeded in God's judgment.

Buddhism developed beyond its Indian origins, in China, Ceylon, Japan, and elsewhere, encountering Confucius, Tao, and Japanese Shinto. The genius of Confucianism has been its justice for all and loyalty to the ancestral past. The mark of Taoism has been its belief in blending with nature and its disgust of artificiality. The genius of Shinto is its joy in the hauntingly delightful spirit of nature, a delight which reminds us of the religion of ancient Greece. But in China there is now a newer, more overwhelming faith, known as Mao's Marxism. This has reshaped China but has submerged its past.

Meanwhile, scattered throughout the world are many smaller societies, like the Torajas in Indonesia, the Indians of North America, many groups and small nations of Africa—all with their own religious quests, not always seen by us as part of the fabric of the great religions but important nevertheless. They often portray man as in close transaction with nature and with the ancestral past. Threatened by modern forces, they yet should command respect as varying experiments in living.

In the world of the Mediterranean and beyond, things are distinctively dominated by the Semitic faith—Judaism with its genius for the Bible and its love of the law as an expression of man's relationship with the one god; Christianity, the strange and powerful offspring of Judaism with its genius coming through its dynamic feeling for the actions of its historic founder, Jesus; and Islam with its new emphasis on creating a community regulated by God, blending the law-orientation of Judaism with the universal outreach of Christianity, a blend however given a new explosiveness by Mohammed's prophetic Arabian style.

Christianity proved to be the chief architect of European civilization. That civilization became the cradle of science and modern liberal democracy, together with revolutionary ideologies such as fascism and communism. Now these two unruly children affect reli-

244

gion in various ways—repressively, where Marxism rules, but encouraging dualism where liberal democracy is dominant; and where science is powerful it rules over dogma, but it means that we are now at a planetary turning point in the long search.

From all these many currents of man's spiritual and intellectual search, what can be concluded? I think something like the following, though each person can make up his own mind.

First, those who neglect faith and the symbols by which cultures have managed themselves are in error. The long search is as vital to man as is his science or his material advance. Second, no longer can any religious movement or faith tempt itself into isolation without paying a dreadful price. Men now know well that the world of faith is plural. This means, to put it in Christian terms, for example, that Christ is found in men's profounder probings, whether they be Hindu or Marxist or Toraja. Thirdly, no longer can religion turn its back on science and the magic of modern life. For good or ill, religion must come to terms with the new and perpetually amazing universe which science discloses to us.

In short, we are left with loose ends. We always are. And we have been in a world in which knowledge and mutual understanding are vital estimates of our own virtues. This, it seems, is the new phase of man's long search. To obey the pope, or accept the authority of the Bible, or treat another person as a guru may help in spiritual development, but now it is the individual who chooses the authority. For good or ill, one must choose. This makes the present period of the long search an amazing opportunity, and also a great responsibility.

## AS YOU VIEW

Another perspective on "The Long Search" is provided by the television episode *Reflections on the Long Search*. This is a look backward by Ronald Eyre, as host for the BBC series, after his many thousand of miles and many months of observing, probing, and questioning on behalf of not only his audiences but himself. The long search, he says, "doesn't have a tidy beginning, middle and end. You're on it the moment you start wondering where you were before you were born, where you'll go when you die, and what you're on earth for in the meantime."

# VIEWING WITH A PURPOSE

## GUIDING QUESTIONS FOR
## EACH VIDEO SEGMENT

### "HINDUISM: 330 MILLION GODS"

1. In this video segment the Hindu priest tells Ronald Eyre that there are 330 million gods in the Hindu religion. What does he mean? Compare this with the "diversity in unity" theme discussed in your readings.
2. We see many portrayals of gods and goddesses in this video segment. One festival is to the goddess of learning who is represented as a clay statue. What is the significance of this ceremony? How does it reflect the Hindu approach to religion as discussed in your readings? Eyre comes to the conclusion that the gods could be thought of as saints. Is this an appropriate analogy?
3. Coming from a western Christian background, Eyre finds many contrasts between his religion and Hinduism. What are some of these as shown in this video segment and as discussed in your readings? Why do your readings refer to Hinduism as "truly ecumenical?"
4. Identify the four stages of human development in Hinduism as presented in your readings. How does this aid our understanding of the nephew's remark that the sannyasi "used to be his uncle" (video segment)?
5. What is the function of caste in the Hindu religious system as presented in this video segment and in your readings? What is a Brahman? What is his place in the religious hierarchy?

## "BUDDHISM: FOOTPRINT OF THE BUDDHA—INDIA"

1. Ronald Eyre points out that it is sometimes said that Buddhism is not a religion. Is this a fair evaluation? According to your readings, how did Western scholars regard Buddhism when they first encountered it?
2. Buddhists do not hold that the Buddha was a god. What was his significance? What is the meaning of the word Buddha? How do the statues shown in this video segment illustrate the various stages through which the Buddha went toward this goal? What is the purpose of these statues?
3. According to your readings, one of the noble truths is that life is suffering. What is the attitude of the Buddhist toward this fact? Is he pessimistic? Optimistic? Resigned to his role in life? Can you illustrate this with evidence from this video segment?
4. A key word for Buddhism is "mindfulness." What does this mean as part of the Eightfold Path? In this video segment, how is it illustrated by the monk?
5. As shown in this video segment, an important Buddhist ritual is begging. What is the indirect objective of begging for the monk? Why do laymen willingly give? Why is the monk not looked down on, as beggars are in the West? How does the ritual fit in with Hinayana Buddhism?


## "TAOISM: A QUESTION OF BALANCE—CHINA"

1. According to your readings, Chinese religion must be studied in a societal context. Discuss this in connection with the worship of community gods as seen in this video segment. Do the community gods quarrel with the gods of other Chinese religions? What is the function of these village gods, their privileges and responsibilities to the people?
2. The cult of the ancestor is very important in the societal context. How does Confucianism operate here? How does a religion associated with scholarship meet the needs of the people? What purpose does the Spring Festival serve (video segment)?

3. Discuss the principles behind Taoism. What are the principles of balance? How do you see them at work in the actual lives portrayed in this video segment?
4. What is the function of the Taoist priest? In this video segment, how does the priest hired for the Chinese grandmother's funeral perform? What philosophy of death is apparent here? What is the purpose of the funeral ritual, its symbolism? How does it fit in with the principle of the Tao?
5. How do Chinese art and theatre illustrate Chinese religion? In this video segment, what do the gods on stage represent?

## "BUDDHISM: THE LAND OF THE DISAPPEARING BUDDHA—JAPAN"

1. Your readings discuss how Buddhism entered Japan from China. What in the Japanese culture made it hospitable to this influence? As illustrated in this video segment, how were typical Japanese arts such as calligraphy, swordfighting, and the tea ceremony adapted to the principles of Buddhism?
2. What type of Buddhism did the owner of the Zen Restaurant in Japan practice along with his employees? What is its emphasis? What is the purpose of the blow administered? What is the attitude of the girl toward it?
3. How is it possible to have a religion which emphasizes both self-reliance and complete dependence? Discuss this in connection with the point your readings make about Japan as a land of paradox. To whom does the Pure Land Sect appeal? To whom does Zen appeal? In this video segment, what do various devotees of each sect say about the appeal of their branch?
4. How does swordfighting illustrate the principles of Zen? What does the Zen archer mean when he says the target is himself? What is the point of the story in which the Buddha holds up a single flower without speaking?

5. As discussed in your readings, Buddhist sects place emphasis on different beliefs and rituals. Discuss these differences with regard to the Pure Land and Zen sects. Which is the closest to Christianity in its emphasis on a savior; on love and compassion? How do the statues of the Buddha in this video segment illustrate this?

## "JUDAISM: THE CHOSEN PEOPLE"

1. In his article titled "Who Are The Chosen People?", Rabbi Barry Tabachnikoff observes that Judaism has never been a monolith. Competition and diversity have always been hallmarks of Jewish history. In the Talmud, he further observes, one can find differing views on hundreds of issues. Contrast these observations with Norbert Brainin's personal view of music as shared with us in this video segment. Hint: Are the pieces played by the Amadeus Quartet open for interpretation; to discourse; to argument?
2. Discuss Elie Wiesel's observation in this video segment that one can be a Jew with God; one can be a Jew against God; but one cannot be a Jew indifferent to God. Compare this view with Rabbi Tabachnikoff's assertion that a Jew is someone who is involved with daily living.
3. In this video segment, Rabbi Peli asserts that the role of prayer is not making ourselves audible but, rather, making ourselves respondent. How is this similar to the observation that, in studying the Talmud, the purpose of learning is not learning, it is living.
4. Discuss the covenant or contract that the Jew has with God and how it strengthens Jewish feelings of self-identity and community membership.
5. In this video segment, Ronald Eyre discovers the definition of "Israel" to be "he who struggles with God and wins." How does this reflect the main concepts discussed in your readings?

## "CATHOLICISM: ROME, LEEDS AND THE DESERT"

1. The Roman Catholic Church is a visible expression of unity and faith. What is meant by the word "faith" as discussed in this video segment, and in your readings?
2. Discuss how The Little Brothers of Jesus reconcile their life style and meager material possessions with the Roman Catholic Church's great wealth as seen in the Vatican.
3. Why have The Little Brothers of Jesus chosen the desert as a place for worshiping God? Contrast the desert's symbolic importance with the basic tenets preached by Jesus, as discussed in your readings.
4. The American Abbot Primate of the Benedictine Order expresses the idea that prayer is an abstraction; it is a search. What is the nature of the search to which the Abbot refers?
5. Consider the phrase: "The Church as Christ wanted it to be." What did Jesus of Nazareth envision?


## "ORTHODOX CHRISTIANITY:
## THE ROMANIAN SOLUTION"

1. What role does the icon play in Eastern Orthodoxy? In this video segment, what is implied by the statement: "An icon is a window into heaven"?
2. Ronald Eyre observes that in Eastern Orthodoxy, "When you're saved, you're saved in a community; when you fall, you fall by yourself." Discuss this statement as it applies to Christianity as a whole.
3. Eyre comments after hearing the Jesus prayer ("Lord Jesus have mercy on me, a sinner") that it makes Jesus sound tyrannical. The monk, Justinian, replies: "When you pray, don't theologize." What does he mean? Is the Jesus prayer an act of faith?
4. "The greatest prayer is silent; it prays itself in the heart when the body sleeps." Contrast this Eastern Orthodoxy belief with

those of The Little Brothers of Jesus. Are they in accord with one another?

5. Eyre makes special mention of three remarks by Justinian. They are: (1) "You can know all about Jesus and still not know him." (2) "The Christians made a mistake when they turned Jesus into a religion." (3) "If we knew the truth of it, every day is Easter." Discuss one of these statements as it reflects Eastern Orthodoxy belief.

### "PROTESTANT SPIRIT, U.S.A."

1. The Hodge-Warfield definition of Biblical inspiration discussed in your readings is one of the foundation blocks of Fundamentalist belief as viewed in this video segment. How does the concept of blind inspiration affect contemporary evangelical teachings?

2. In this video segment, Protestantism is defined as "The gathering of Christian people, in a locale, in great simplicity, to hear the word of God and to meet each other." How does this description fit those sects presented and discussed in this video segment and in your readings?

3. "Doubt," Ronald Eyre comments, "is the companion of faith." Discuss this statement with regard to Christianity.

4. As practiced today, is the Protestant religion a religion of consent or a religion of dissent? Cite examples to support your view.

5. Eyre concludes this video segment by stating his personal view that "Protestantism is an impulse to keep things moving; and anyone who builds a shrine around an impulse . . . and courts it is deluding himself." With what does Eyre take issue? Can you cite examples from this video segment?

## "ISLAM: THERE IS NO GOD BUT GOD"

1. In Islamic religion there is no division between secular and spiritual domain, which are one and the same. Cite several examples in this video segment to support this assertion.
2. In your readings, Dr. Muhammad Abdul-Rauf states: "Islam may be described as a religion of centers." Discuss this statement as it relates to Islamic beliefs and practices. (Can you recall the architectual design of the mosque of El Azhar from this video segment?)
3. There are no ordained priests in the Islamic religion. Why?
4. After visiting an Islamic village Ronald Eyre informs us that "the religion of the village is the life of the village." How does this observation relate to the Islamic principles presented in your readings?
5. In this video segment we visit a modern hospital in Cairo. What Islamic teachings are observed in the hospital?

## "ALTERNATIVE LIFE STYLES IN CALIFORNIA: WEST MEETS EAST"

1. Ronald Eyre observes that in the religions of the counterculture there is a new awareness of "the importance of approximation; there is no absolute truth." Contrast this with Werner Heisenberg's "Uncertainty Principle," discussed in your readings.
2. Discuss Professor Needlman's statement "the positive side [of the new religions] is the search; the negative side is the findings."
3. Discuss how one's perception of reality would affect one's relationship to the environment. (Hint: How would a "mechanistic" view of the world differ from a "holistic" view?)

4. Eyre directs the question to Theodore Rozak: "Why are so many Westerners turning East?" What reasons would you cite?
5. In this video segment we see SAGE, a group consisting predominantly of older persons, seeking to find new paths. Their leader observes that when we fight dying, we are fighting living. What is she seeking to convey?

## "RELIGION IN INDONESIA: THE WAY OF THE ANCESTORS"

1. Our readings state that primal religions are ecologically oriented. Discuss how the Toraja integrate man and the natural world. What does Ronald Eyre mean when he speaks of the native home as the umbilicus or navel?
2. Your readings emphasize the importance of the oral tradition in primal religions. Discuss this tradition in the role of the Tominaa (the priest of life).
3. Your readings point out that the Christian faith has expanded at the expense of primal religions, which have been weakened by the technological advances of the 20th Century. What will we lose if such primal religions eventually disappear? What are the contrasts which Eyre sees between the Christian God and the gods of the Toraja?
4. Your readings state that the funeral is the most significant event in the life of the Toraja. How does their attitude toward death differ from that of the European? What does Eyre mean when he observes that a "carnival spirit" prevails? Discuss how life and death rituals complement each other.
5. Eyre describes the gods of the Toraja as a triangle configuration: God the Creator at the top; and the ancestor and Deata spirits at the base. What are their functions as discussed in your readings? What are the responsibilities of the village toward them?

## "AFRICAN RELIGIONS: ZULU ZION"

1. In our readings, we learn that the mission churches failed to meet the needs of blacks forced to live in impermanent townships, thus encouraging the rise of independent Christian churches. How do the Zionists address themselves to this sense of alienation, this need for place?

2. Your readings point out that the European's conception of the essentials of Christianity differs from that of the African. How does this video segment illustrate this? (How has Christianity been modified by traditional African beliefs and practices, especially in relation to the living dead?)

3. Your readings discuss the importance of the church of the Nazarites, founded by Isaiah Shembe in 1911. How does this video segment depict his success in bringing the Christian God to the Zulu nation? How do the Nazarites regard Shembe? How did he ensure that his church would continue?

4. What function do the ancestors and the living dead serve in Zulu Christianity? Discuss the actions of Ronald Eyre's guide, Peter, and contrast them with what you've read.

5. Cite examples from this video segment to illustrate the claim (from the readings) that Zulu Christianity is an example of the universality and particularity of Christianity.